Representing Lives

Also by Alison Donnell

THE ROUTLEDGE READER IN CARIBBEAN LITERATURE (*editor with Sarah Lawson*)

Also by Pauline Polkey

* WOMEN'S LIVES INTO PRINT: The Theory, Practice and Writing of Feminist Auto/biography

* *From the same publishers*

Representing Lives

Women and Auto/biography

Edited by

Alison Donnell
Senior Lecturer in Postcolonial Literatures
Nottingham Trent University

and

Pauline Polkey
Formerly Senior Lecturer in Women's Writing and Feminist Theory
Nottingham Trent University

First published in Great Britain 2000 by
MACMILLAN PRESS LTD
Houndmills, Basingstoke, Hampshire RG21 6XS and London
Companies and representatives throughout the world

A catalogue record for this book is available from the British Library.

ISBN 0–333–75076–4

 First published in the United States of America 2000 by
ST. MARTIN'S PRESS, INC.,
Scholarly and Reference Division,
175 Fifth Avenue, New York, N.Y. 10010

ISBN 0–312–22667–5

Library of Congress Cataloging-in-Publication Data
Representing lives : women and auto/biography edited by Alison Donnell and
Pauline Polkey.
p.   cm.
Papers presented at the conference Representing lives: women and auto/biography
on July 23–25 1997 at Nottingham Trent University.
Includes bibliographical references and index.
ISBN 0–312–22667–5 (cloth)
1. English prose literature—Women authors—History and criticism—Congresses.
2. Autobiography—Women authors—Congresses. 3. American literature—Women
authors—History and criticism—Congresses. 4. Women—Biography—History
and criticism—Congresses. 5. Women and literature—Congresses. 6. Self in
literature—Congresses. I. Donnell, Alison, 1966– II. Polkey, Pauline, 1958–

PR756.W65 R46   2000
820.9'492072—dc21
                                                    99–055929

This book is printed on paper suitable for recycling and made from fully managed and sustained
forest sources.

10   9   8   7   6   5   4   3   2   1
09   08   07   06   05   04   03   02   01   00

Printed and bound in Great Britain by Antony Rowe Ltd, Chippenham, Wiltshire

Alison Donnell and Pauline Polkey dedicate this book to their mothers – Audrey Donnell and Elizabeth Ellis

Contents

List of Figures

Acknowledgements

We would like to thank the many people who assisted and supported the 'Representing Lives' conference, in particular Carmen Glover, Professor Roger Bromley, Professor Dick Ellis and Professor John Tomlinson; our Dean, Professor Stephen Chan, for his address at the exhibition opening, and our Head of Department, Professor Sandra Harris for her address at the conference opening. A special thanks goes to our colleague and friend, Patrick Williams, who agreed to be unofficial photographer, as well as to Pat McLernon who patiently videoed the proceedings. We are very grateful to the curator of the accompanying exhibition, Pauline Lucas, to Stella Couloutbanis of the Bonington Gallery and to Professor Robert Ayers for co-funding of the exhibition, as well as to the artists, Hilary Cartmell, Lubaina Himid, Sonia Lawson and Denise Weston, for such inspirational work. Many thanks to the conference's key speakers – June Purvis, Marion Shaw, Liz Stanley, Maud Sulter and Julia Swindells – and to Jackie Kay for her remarkable poetry reading and workshop. We would like to thank each of the contributors for their patience in dealing with our queries, suggestions and reminders, and for their commitment to a project that has been on-going for over two years. Thanks are also due to Pam Lilley and Karen Mitchell who assisted us in the final putting together of this book.

Alison Donnell wishes to thank her family for all their support, especially Jeremy and Max for waving to her at the study window during the two summers taken up by the conference and the book. Pauline Polkey pays tribute to her family, friends and feline companions for their endurance and encouragement throughout the past two years, and offers a *very* special thank you to her son, Tom.

The Publishers and editors wish to thank the following for permission to reproduce material in this volume:

C. Corman, for permission to reproduce extracts from Lorine Niedecker's letters, in Lorna Jowett, 'Lorine Niedecker: Auto/biography and Poetry', chapter 5.

Pennine Pens, for permission to reproduce extracts from Jill Liddington, *Presenting the Past: Anne Lister of Halifax*; Smith Settle, for permission to reproduce extracts from Helen Whitbread, *No Priest But Love*; and West Yorkshire Archive Service, Calderdale, for permission to reproduce extracts from Anne Lister's papers held in their archive; all in Anira Rowanchild, '"My Mind on Paper": Anne Lister and the Construction of Lesbian Identity', chapter 16.

Faber and Faber Ltd and HarperCollins for permission to reproduce extracts from 'Dialogue over a Ouija Board' and *Three Women*, by Sylvia Plath, in *Collected Poems*, ed. Ted Hughes (1981), in Nicola Shaugnessy, 'One Two, Three: Sylvia Plath's Verse Dramas', chapter 20.

Roger L. Conover, for permission to reproduce extracts from Mina Loy, *Anglo-Mongrels and the Rose* and 1925 from the *Loy Collection*, Beinecke Rare Book and Manuscript Library, Yale, © the Estate of Mina Loy, in Alex Goody, 'Auto/biography/Auto-mythology: Mina Loy's *Anglo-Mongrels and the Rose*', chapter 23.

The South African Library, Cape Town, South Africa, for permission to reproduce Figure 1, photograph portrait of Olive Schreiner.

Postscript

During the summer of 1999, Pauline Polkey discovered she had ovarian cancer. She would like to take this opportunity to thank her family, friends and colleagues for their enduring support, without which the struggle to survive would have been so much more terrible, if not impossible.

Eternal thanks to my good friend Alison Donnell for – literally – saving my life by insisting that I go to see a doctor (in the nick of time). Thank you to all my family, especially Elizabeth Ellis (who came to see me every day in hospital for four weeks at great cost to her own health), John Ellis, Sian Stammers, Tom Ellis, Mary Ellis, Ron Thompson, Queenie Thorne, Joyce McKie, the furry Queen Lizzie, Princess Willow, Countess Babushka and Prince Seamus, and last, but by no means least, my son Tom: my very reason for living.

David Barnes has sent his love across the seas – via letters, e-mails and phone calls – and I am indebted to his endless, unconditional, unfailing friendship. Larry Brown has offered the stimulation of speedy intellectual debate and affection, and I can only thank fate for bringing us back together as friends after an absence of six rather desperate years. Christine Smith has offered her support and friendship in deeply touching ways, and her immense creativity has been a profound resource during some very bleak times. Thank you to Sonia Lawson for a wonderful letter that made me re-evaluate my attitude to life's slings and arrows.

Thank you to the following students-cum-friends for their understanding and patience, and for believing that I will come through this ordeal: Jeremy Fry for his immense gentleness and humanity, intellectual perception and insight, countless stimulating conversations, for introducing me to Dostoevsky, and for bringing me the gift of music; Matthew Smith for his quirky and incorrigible humour, and wonderful, tremendous originality of mind; Karen Mitchell has shared a great many laughs and tears with me, and is always a source of irrepressible hope, feisty humour and damned determination; Jane Weir has made me gifts of stones and grasses, tapestries and relics from past lives, and make me feel so very glad to be alive for having known her.

Though I have the gift of prophecy, and understand all mysteries and all knowledge, and though I have enough Faith to move the mightiest mountains, if I have not Love, I am nothing. Love is patient. Love is kind. It bears all things, it hopes all things. . . . And now shall abide Faith, Hope and Love. But the greatest of these three is Love. (Corinthians)

A Tribute
By Elizabeth Ellis,
Pauline's mother

Pauline was born in Liverpool, before midnight, on Sunday, 6 July 1958; she died at home in Nottingham, with all her family, at 11.15 am on Thursday, 2 December 1999. I saw her lovely face and eyes moments after I had given birth to her and held her in my arms as she died, aged 41 years and a few months. We grieve that she is not with us to talk, love and share, but we also grieve for Pauline's loss of life.

Pauline spoke so much on behalf of others, often those who did not have the words to articulate their injustices or hopes. In her opposition to racist and anti-Semitic thinking and the privileges that some people receive and the denial of equality, she translated her words into actions, and met theory with practice. She was opposed to oppressive regimes, and supported those wrongly imprisoned and those described as marginal people. We often said that people are not on the margins on a clean piece of paper, and it was through her writing that Pauline found a way to make a difference, and to make others see things differently.

In all aspects of her work Pauline was professional, organised and determined. And she could clean a house and cook a meal and take equal pleasure and pride in these. She was a careful and loving mother and a true friend to her son, Tom. Pauline was a fine daughter, a good sister, but a good friend most of all, and for as long as we breathe she will never be forgotten.

Heraclitus

They told me, Heraclitus, they told me you were dead,
They brought me bitter news to hear and bitter tears to shed.
I wept as I remembered how often you and I
Had tired the sun with talking and sent him down the sky.

And now that thou art lying, my old Carian guest,
A handful of grey ashes, long, long ago to rest,
Still are thy pleasant voices, thy nightingales, awake;
For death he taketh all away, but them he cannot take.

William Johnson Cory

Notes on the Contributors

T. G. Ashplant teaches cultural history at Liverpool John Moores University. He has published on working-class autobiography, and is currently researching the lives and writings of working-class and lower-middle-class women involved in the socialist and suffrage movements.

Elaine Aston is senior lecturer in theatre studies at Loughborough University. Her major publications include: *Sarah Bernhardt: A French Actress on the English Stage* (1989); *An Introduction to Feminism and Theatre* (1995); and *Caryl Churchill* (1997). She is co-author of *Theatre as Sign-System* (1991) and co-editor of collected plays by women for Sheffield Academic Press and Harwood Academic Publishers. Her new study is *Feminist Theatre Practice* (1999).

Erzsébet Barát lectures in Linguistics and Gender Studies, Attila József University, Szeged, Hungary; she is also a part-time PhD student at the Department of Linguistics, Lancaster University. Her research interests include the theorization of identity construction in oral autobiographies, and the discursive construction of gendered and sexualized subjects in contemporary Hungarian society from within a postmodernist materialist feminist perspective

Nicola Brice studied for her BA in German Studies (1995) and her MA in Modern Languages Research (1996) at Lancaster University. She is currently working on her doctoral thesis entitled 'Political Dimensions of Mother–Child writing in German Novels of the 1970s and 1980s' at Birkbeck College, University of London. Her research interests include post-1945 Parent–Child Literature, and the works of Lily Braun.

Tonya Blowers lectures in English Studies at Oxford Brookes University. She has recently completed her doctoral thesis at the Centre for the Study of Women and Gender, University of Warwick, where she ran an interdisciplinary workshop on autobiography and organized a conference 'Autobiographies: Strategies for Survival'. Her thesis, 'Locating the Self', is a study of autobiography as theory and practice and uses the writings of New Zealander Janet Frame as a case-study.

Alison Donnell is senior lecturer in postcolonial literatures at Nottingham Trent University. She is co-editor of *The Routledge Reader in Caribbean Literature* (1996) and has published articles and book chapters on Caribbean women's writing and on postcolonial and feminist theory. She is joint editor of *Interventions: International Journal of Postcolonial Studies*.

R. J. Ellis is Professor of English and American Literature at The Nottingham Trent University. In 1998 he edited a modern edition of *Our Nig* (Nottingham: Trent Editions) and has recently completed a study of Jack Kerouac, *Jack Kerouac, Novelist*.

Alison Fell is a research student in the Department of French Studies at the University of Birmingham. She is currently working towards her doctoral thesis on representations of maternity and the mother–daughter relationship in twentieth-century French women's auto-biographical writing. Her corpus includes the work of Simone de Beauvoir, Violette Leduc, Marie Cardinal and Annie Ernaux.

Deborah Gaitskell grew up in Cape Town and obtained her PhD at the School of Oriental and African Studies, London University, where she lectured in history for four years after a long (but enjoyable) stint in adult education teaching. A Senior Research Fellow at the Institute of Commonwealth Studies, where she runs a seminar on Gender in Empire and Commonwealth, she is presently teaching South African history at Goldsmiths' College and writing a book on women missionaries.

Vanessa Gill-Brown lectures in Design Studies at Nottingham Trent University. Her first degree was in textile design, followed by an MA in Cultural Studies at the University of Leeds where she developed interests in feminism, popular culture and postmodernism. She writes cultural criticism and stories for children, and is currently working towards a PhD in fashion and identity in the urban context.

Vesna Goldsworthy lectures in English literature and drama at Birkbeck College, University of London, and the London Centre of

St Lawrence University, New York. Her book *Inventing Ruritania: the Imperialism of the Imagination* (1998) discusses Rebecca West in its examination of women's writing about the Balkans.

Alex Goody completed her PhD on Mina Loy's poetry at the University of Leeds, conducting part of her research at the Beinecke Library, Yale. She writes on Mina Loy and other women modernists (Djuna Barnes, H. D. and Gertrude Stein) and is currently working on the sexual politics of the early twentieth-century New York avant-garde.

Helena Grice has recently completed a doctorate on the work of a group of Asian American women writers. She has published several articles on the same subject, in *Melus, Hitting Critical Mass: A Journal of Asian American Criticism, Recollecting Early Asian America, An Asian American Studies Reader* and *Asian American Ceremonies: Continuity, Rupture or Invention?* (forthcoming). She is co-editor, with Tim Woods, of *I'm Telling You Stories: Jeanette Winterson and the Politics of Reading* (1998). She currently teaches at the University of Wales, Aberystwyth.

Nike Imoru is a lecturer in drama at the University of Hull. Her research covers race and gender in theatre and performance. She combines her academic work with her work as an actor, choreographer and dramaturg in the UK, America and Africa.

Lorna Jowett is a lecturer in American studies at Nene University College, Northampton, where she teaches a range of literary and cultural topics. Women's writing, feminism, twentieth-century American poetry, science fiction (in film, TV and literature), and representations of the vampire (in film and literature) are some of her research interests. Current projects include work on late corporate capitalism in science fiction, and a paper on gender in utopian science fiction.

Helen Nicholson is based at the University of Manchester Department of Drama where she is completing a PhD on the life and works of Georgina Weldon. Her main research interests are women on the nineteenth-century stage, and the relationship between theatre and psychiatry. She has published articles in *Theatre Annual* and *Occasional Papers on Women and Theatre*.

Alison Oddey is a Senior Lecturer in drama and theatre studies at the University of Kent. She teaches courses on the theory and practice of contemporary performance and devised theatre. She has published *Devising Theatre* (1994), and has recently completed *Performing Women: Stand-ups, Strumpets and Itinerants*, (1999). She is currently writing *Different Directions: Women Directors in the Twentieth-Century Theatre* with Nicola Shaughnessy.

Pauline Polkey is senior lecturer in women's writing and feminist theory at Nottingham Trent University. Her research focuses on politically active women's autobiographies (1880–1920), and she is currently preparing *Passionate Landscapes of Selfhood: Women, Politics and Auto-biography* for publication. She recently published *Women's Lives into Print: the Theory, Practice and Writing of Feminist Auto/biography* (1999).

June Purvis is Professor of Women's and Gender History at the University of Portsmouth. She is the author of *Hard Lessons, The Lives and Education of Working-Class Women in Nineteenth-Century England* (1989) and *A History of Women's Education in England* (1991). She has published widely, the two most recent edited collections being *Researching Women's Lives from a Feminist Perspective* (1994, with Mary Maynard) and *The Women's Suffrage Movement, New Feminist Perspectives* (1998, with Maroula Joannou). She is the founding and managing editor of the journal *Women's History Review* as well as the editor for a *Women's History Series* with UCL Press.

Anira Rowanchild is a postgraduate student in the Literature Department of the Open University. She has published articles on nineteenth-century women writers, including Emily Brontë and Elizabeth Barrett Browning (*The English Review*, Spring 1997 and Spring 1998), and on twentieth-century lesbian fiction in 'Ideology and Narrative Structure in the Novels of Maureen Duffy and Caiea March' in *Beyond Sex and Romance?* (1988).

Christiane Schönfeld lectures at the University of Wales, Lampeter, where she teaches courses in German cinema, women writers and nineteenth- and twentieth-century German literature. She is the author of *Dialectik und Utopie: Die prostituierte im deutschen Expressionismus* (1996), has written articles on expressionism, early German film and Emmy Hennings, and has edited a book on *The Prostitute in German Literature*.

Nicola Shaughnessy lecturers in drama and theatre studies at the University of Kent. She teaches gender and theatre, theatre history, performance theory, autobiography and American drama. She has published on Gertrude Stein, feminist theatre, the director/teacher and dramatic auto/biography. She is completing a monograph on Gertrude Stein and is also working with Alison Oddey on *Different Directions: Women Directors in the Twentieth Century Theatre.*

Anna Snaith moved to England from Canada in 1992 to complete a PhD on Virginia Woolf at University College London, where she taught for four years. She is now Lecturer in English at Anglia Polytechnic University. She has published articles on Virginia Woolf and Katherine Mansfield and is currently completing *Virginia Woolf: Public and Private Negotiations.*

Liz Stanley is Professor of Sociology and Director of Women's Studies at the University of Manchester. A lesbian by luck, living in the North of England by choice, her abiding interests are in ideas, food, books, music and the other 'earthly pleasures' so seductively invoked by Colette. Having just finished a book on Olive Schreiner's social theory, she's just started writing about her own.

Julia Swindells is Director of English Studies at Homerton College, Cambridge. Her publications in relation to autobiography include *Victorian Writing and Working Women, The Other Side of Silence*, and, as editor, *The Uses of Autobiography*. She is currently working on the relations between autobiography, theatre and politics in Britain in the later Georgian period.

Lynnette Turner lectures in English at Oxford Brookes University. She has published articles on gender and ethnography, on Mary Kingsley, and on nineteenth- and twentieth-century anthropological discourse. She is currently completing an anthology of travel and ethnographic writings *Travel Writing Race.*

Introduction

All the essays included in this volume were presented at the 'Representing Lives: Women and Auto/biography' conference which took place on 23–25 July 1997 at Nottingham Trent University. Our particular intention in hosting this conference was to generate a forum for interdisciplinary work around the issues of female subjectivity, the relationships between representation and lived experiences, and the politics of being a woman who seeks to represent herself and/or others. The conference not only staged panels with academics working in a variety of disciplines – from literary, historical, cultural and women's studies through to art, drama, politics and social sciences – but also incorporated other events less routinely recognized as being connected to the scholarly work conducted in the university.

The accompanying exhibition of women artists (30 June–26 July 1997, Bonington Gallery) curated by Pauline Lucas, provided the focus for the conference opening. The talks given by each of the artists – Hilary Cartmel, Lubaina Himid, Sonia Lawson and Denise Weston – as well as the plenary address and auto/videography by Maud Sulter, facilitated connections between the representations on view and the life-narratives which informed them. From Hilary Cartmel's 'Juggling Women', through Sonia Lawson's strong female figures and Denise Weston's emblems of vulnerable girlhood, to Lubaina Himid's representations of women architects: all the works suggested the ways in which acts of identification are constituted through gendered and cultural imaginations, as well as personal experience. The workshop and poetry reading by Jackie Kay, one of Britain's most prominent women poets, whose own works have consistently addressed the auto/biographical subject in searching and insightful ways, enabled some of us to explore the processes of crafting a life story, as well as to enjoy the product of that craft in her reading.

It was our aim to provide delegates with alternative modes of representation to those commonly worked within (either as practitioners or as critics, or as both). Although everyone came to the event aware that 'being a woman' had no stable meaning and was crucially dependent on historical, cultural and geographical positioning, we were given different modes of representation through which to trace these differences. It was our hope that the conference, with its range of representational frameworks, would enable us both to extend and develop a critical awareness of the way in which auto/biography is always determined by the act of *representation*, as well as by the act of *being*. In this way, we wanted the conference to allow disciplinary or generic status to be considered as another position which makes a difference to women's auto/ biographical representations. As the essays in this collection reflect, gender identity does function as a conscious starting point for delineating self-identity for many women artists, performers, writers and academics. Indeed, with a strong generic tradition, women's auto/biography is perhaps less a field of enquiry under dispute than a field on the move, inhabiting new intellectual spaces as feminist scholarship and ideas concerning situated knowledge begin to intersect more meaningfully with other theoretical frameworks, including colonial discourse theory, queer theory and performance theory. Many of the essays map out the particular directions and consequences of this movement; but by necessity, much of the variety and texture of the conference event has been flattened out to produce a collection of academic essays. Nevertheless, we not only hope that the essays themselves will reflect the diversity of critical debate currently taking place amongst academics, writers and artists, but that the photographs (see Aston, Gill-Brown, Oddey and Stanley, this volume) and the image on the front cover (reproduced from Sonia Lawson's 'Inner Self') will also suggest to the reader dimensions of the wider collective event which generated this volume.

*   *   *

The past two decades have witnessed a profound intellectual shift in terms of feminist analysis of women's autobiographical and biographical writings (see Personal Narratives Group, 1989; Stanley, 1992; Marcus, 1994; Swindells, 1995), and the diversity and verve of that critical engagement are manifest within this volume. Discussions offered herein range from the ontological examination of gendered subjectivity and sexual, social, cultural and ethnic identities, through the political dimension of historical experience and geographical location, to the vicissitudes and aesthetics of autobiography's hybrid genre. By offering this divergent mix of topics, our aim is both to stimulate and challenge the reader's response;

and, in so doing, to facilitate yet further critical exchange about women's auto/biographical discourse.

Our use of the term 'Representation' in the book's title signifies, on one level, an explication of feminism's project to intervene critically within recuperative and re-evaluative research. But on a more expository level, our aim is threefold: first, to interrogate the methods, uses and assumptions which inform feminism's 'representational' project; second, to formulate arguments and opinions to effect a shift in perception about women's lived experience; and third, to elucidate, clarify, exhibit and/or symbolize the subject's auto/biographical 'I'. Thus, whilst we recognize the fallibility of 'representing' a life for what it was/is 'really' like, there is a shared commitment to explore what Virginia Woolf defines, in the epigraph to this book, as the 'magic tank' of women's lives and works.

One of the principal points that have been contested within feminist analysis of women's personal narratives concerns the deployment of key terms: auto/biography, (auto)biography, autography, auto-biothanatography, octobiography (see Marcus, 1994: 12, 1995; Stanley 1992). Our use of the slashed term 'auto/biography' draws on Liz Stanley's insistence that 'accounts of other lives influence how we see and understand our own and that our understandings of our own lives will impact on how we interpret other lives' (Stanley, 1994: i; see also Polkey, 1999). Whilst we acknowledge the distinction between autobiography and biography, our utilization of 'auto/biography' proffers a theoretically informed approach, which not only embraces a hybrid version of generic categorization but also recognizes the intersubjective, reflexive potency of self-inscription. Moreover, as the plenitude of auto/biographical material discussed in this volume reveals – ranging from letters, journals, memoirs, travel writing, ethnography, biography, fiction, poetry, theatrical performance – the auto/biographical I/eye enjoys a remarkable narratological landscape. In grouping the chapters into six main parts– 'Placing the Subject', 'Revising Genres', 'Staging the Self', '(Auto)biographical Representations', 'Recovering Lives – Revising History' and 'Matrilineality' – broad-based commonalities emerge both within and across those group divisions to reveal some of the new intellectual spaces of feminist scholarship.

*   *   *

Liz Stanley's contribution to this volume, entitled 'Is There Life in the Contact Zone? Auto/biographical Practices and the Field of Representation in Writing Past Lives', is situated as a keynote address and powerfully draws attention to the fundamental questions about feminist auto/biography that each of the other contributors seeks to address. Moreover, her careful and engaging critical history of the representation of Olive Schreiner stages the academic, intellectual, epistemological and philosophical issues at stake in documenting 'then' from 'now', 'there' from 'here' and 'other' from 'self'. With an insistent focus on the I/eye of the writer/scholar, Stanley argues that this I/eye is implicated – whether visibly or not – in each act of representation; and becomes an active agent – marked by place, time and a politics of reading – which demands proper recognition and consideration within the contact zone of past/present and writing/materiality where meanings are made and may be prematurely settled. Indeed, Stanley's efforts are directed against the consolidation (or canonization) of intellectual orthodoxies and towards inciting more critical self-questioning on the part of the contemporary feminist auto/biographer.

Part I Placing the Subject

In order to question the 'politics of autobiography's uses', Julia Swindells focuses on Margaret Thatcher's memoirs, offering a reading of a text which both deploys a distinctly Churchillian 'British' discourse of the self in order to make claims to 'speak for' history, and a dialectic synthesis wherein the 'Right' triumphs over the 'forces of disorder'. Whilst Thatcher's representation of herself as a singularly heroic, combative and self-righteous figure is a fitting testimony to the 1980s, Swindells does not suggest that we can now look back with relief or complacence to Thatcher's use of the autobiographical 'I' as symptomatic of an exceptional, 'megalomanic' woman who is no longer Britain's political leader. Rather, she draws her discussion to its conclusion with a wider and more provocative question about self-inscription and authority: 'But does the autobiographical I in general rely on a similar process of accumulating to itself power and authority?'

In some ways, this question is usefully, if only in one instance, answered by Helena Grice's chapter on Theresa Kyung Cha's work, *Dictee*. Unlike Swindells's work, which seeks to disclose the way in which Thatcher wrote her own story as that of the establishment, perhaps even that of the nation, at a particular moment in history,

Grice examines the profound democratic awareness of *Dictee* and the very inclusive and self-conscious narrative that unfolds from the fact that this auto/biographer knows that her story cannot be told in isolation from those of others. As in Swindells's chapter, the relationship between individual identity and state identity is extensively explored, but for Cha national history is revealed as both complex and collective, as personal narrative is interspersed with official documents. Indeed, as Grice shows, Cha's work foregrounds exactly the kinds of disciplinary and political pressures exerted upon representations of female subjectivity that Thatcher's memoirs, and those of Mary Kingsley, as discussed by Lynnette Turner (this volume, chapter 3), seek to suppress.

Turner examines how, as a nineteenth-century professional woman, Kingsley sought to position herself within the discursive boundaries of conventional femininity in order to achieve professional recognition and status. In this way her position was similar to that of Elizabeth Garrett Anderson and Mary Somerville, whom Swindells discusses (this volume, chapter 1). However, as Turner analyses in great detail in relation to the work of Kingsley, for the female 'ethnographer' the inscription of feminine roles and language was a careful and strategic device through which to construct an authenticating self in line with the demands of her particular profession. The process of seeking to produce in writing a self which has successfully negotiated the demands of national, gendered and personal identity is common to all three chapters. But whereas Grice is concerned to demonstrate that Cha makes the points of rupture and dissensus the very subject of her writing, both Swindells and Turner locate these fissures in the writings of women who seek to construct stable subjectivities to serve their professional ends within male rhetorical traditions.

Part II   Revising Genres

The essays already discussed demonstrate the way in which autobiographical writings are often situated at the crossroads of the generic matrix, and Part II is particularly concerned with the ways in which generic categories operate in terms of establishing a politics of writing and reception. R. J. Ellis's detailed reading of Harriet Wilson's *Our Nig* scrutinizes the narrative strategies of this text in order to argue that its position on the boundary between novel and autobiography has less to do with the competing claims of scholars situated within these fields, than with Wilson's careful textualization of a self that cannot unproblematically either show or declare itself. This deliberately speculative auto/biography of Wilson/Frado enables the writer/protagonist to mediate an identity around dominant generic boundaries, an act of textual manoeuvring which Ellis argues is crucially involved with her politics of identity as an African American woman writing about slavery in nineteenth-century America 'under freedom's complex servitude'.

Like Ellis, Lorna Jowett explores the generic boundaries of women's autobiographical representation, and uses Lorine Niedecker's life and works to support her thesis that 'poetry can be read as autobiography'. Offering a carefully researched and contextualized reading of Niedecker's poetry, this chapter reveals the fastidious intellectual energy that went into her autobiographical creations, sometimes 'sit[ting] for two months on six line / of poetry'. Clearly, Niedecker was intent upon experimentation and innovation in her writing, encasing her life 'between the lines' of poetry's compact form and taking pleasure from the poetic configuration. Also seeking in poetic craft a space to converse with a silent, isolated female self, for Niedecker identity and subjectivity intersected within a hybrid modality, creating a new space for autobiography's generic landscape.

Whereas in the case of *Our Nig* and other women's writing scholars have often been keen to establish the autobiographical links and thereby trace the 'personal' element within women's work, Vesna Goldsworthy discusses how Rebecca West's autobiography, *Black Lamb and Grey Falcon*, has never received due critical attention. Tracing its history, Goldsworthy suggests that although it is acclaimed even today as a definitive piece of travel literature, this modernist account of a journey through the Balkans can be read as much as a testimony to the subjectivity of a writer, as an account of a region and its peoples. Ironically, it is the highly charged politics concerning this region in recent years which has further strengthened the critical propensity to read this text as a sourcebook, bestowing on it the status of objectivity which the personal voice of this modernist narrative seeks to eclipse both through its subjective tone and the particular political context of its own time.

One of the few women writers who have not been marginalized within modernist literary history is Virginia Woolf. However, while most male modernists explored the ethics of impersonality, as Anna Snaith's chapter discusses, Woolf's writings, like those of several of her female contemporaries, remain an interesting subject for debates concerning auto/biography as a genre. Like West, Woolf's modernist style meant that she was acutely conscious of generic boundaries and the problems such frames could impose. Indeed, despite her commitment to the act of writing women's lives, both obscure and ordinary, into literature and history, Woolf never wrote easily identifiable autobiographical writings, seemingly unable to work with the stable 'I' that autobiography can suggest. With this in mind, rather than reading Woolf as being torn between the demands of fact and fiction, Snaith argues that Woolf's writings work across the seams of these two forms to good effect, generating a mode of writing through which both the politics of being a woman and the politics of representation can be observed to be mutually informing and enriching.

Tonya Blowers's chapter provides a useful survey of the theoretical debates concerning the crossover between history, fiction and autobiography, in order to offer a reading of Janet Frame's autobiographical writing. By enacting Lejeune's textual contract, Blowers argues that Frame is also able to escape the rigid positioning of an individual 'I' on the page and to offer the reader access to acts of both history and representation, and thereby foreground the questions concerning the representation of women's lives.

Part III Staging the Self

Elaine Aston's chapter offers an account of teaching feminist theatre practice, and is particularly focused on a devised performance entitled *Self-ish*, through which students were encouraged both to consider and to enact self-representation within the context of their growing awareness of wider feminist debates about personal and political identities. The fact that this performance, based on individual life-stories and utilizing personal objects (such as shoes and handbags), was devised, meant that the women students were able to claim the ways in which they were represented, playing roles and staging gendered histories that were both their own and shared. In this way, *Self-ish* became a model of locating the auto/biographical 'I' within new theatrical and theoretical contexts, thereby offering the possibility of reinventing the self – with sharpened critical awareness.

Nike Imoru's chapter, although centred on ideas concerning the politics of identity in the classroom, is very much concerned with a crisis of identification and differentiation precipitated by the awareness of herself as a black tutor/actor taking on the role of unwitting spectacle before white students/spectators. For Imoru, her role as performer became at once more self-conscious and more crafted. Thinking back through others with whom she identifies, she was able to draw on the tradition of dissembling and reassembling the self, and in this chapter she describes the process of bringing this awareness of self-fashioning into the present, the personal, the classroom.

In part a devised performance re-rendered on the page, and in part a narrative of that performance, Alison Oddey's chapter takes up, both performatively and intellectually, the new identity of a female academic in the age of computerized communication. In so doing, she equally explores and dismantles her exhaustive roll call of identities – mother, lover, performer, academic – and her management of those responsibilities in 1990s Britain. As Oddey composes a reflective narrative of 'Show and Tell', a narrative disclosing the personal experiences which informed the public display helps to locate the 'drives' and ideas which create the performing, auto/biographical 'I'.

Part IV (Auto)Biographical Representation

This part is concerned with (auto)biographical representations of women's lives, looking at the reflexive exchange between biographer and autobiographical material/subject. Vanessa Gill-Brown's lively chapter on the intersecting stories of her mother, herself and 'Tupperware' addresses the ways in which the 1950s version of femininity was powerfully influenced by Hollywood cinema and postwar consumer culture. However, as Gill-Brown argues, domestic space has historically been the primary theatre for women's identities; and although being a 'Tupperware Lady' enabled her mother to play the Hollywood icon within the home, the (auto)biography reveals some of the complex reasons why she took up the job. Far from being a glamorous jaunt, it was a strategy for postnatal survival: 'Well, it was after I had you, you know, I went all silly and wouldn't go out.' In telling her mother's story, Gill-Brown (auto)biographically reassesses her own gendered identity, conscious that she plays a very different social role from that of her mother. This forthright tribute reveals Gill-Brown's retrospective, albeit equivocal, appreciation of the way in which her mother's work ensured her daughters success: 'She was too successful with us. . . . There's glib rejection on the one hand but – and here's the thorn in our side – guilt and longing on the other.'

Erzsébet Barát's discussion of Hungarian women's biographies focuses on the way in which the mode of representing the self – here, via oral transmission – has an impact on both the narrator and the narrated, acknowledging that 'We make sense of the world and ourselves in it from the stories we tell.' Barát also raises the question of how can we take into account the oral and bodily dimensions of self-inscription within an academic world that so consistently relies on scribal forms. Her (auto)biographical project is recuperative in purpose and sets out to locate the historical vicissitudes and contexts that shaped her biographical subjects' lives; in turn, she also considers the impact on her own life. In summing up her research findings, Barát indicates that the women she interviewed all privileged gender as the most crucial determinant of their social identity (despite significant differences in terms of generational and class identities) and that gendering still functions as an explanatory narrative in women's self-representation.

Deborah Gaitskell's chapter comprises five biographical vignettes of women missionaries – Julia Gilpin, Dora Earthy, Frances Chilton, Dorothy Maud and Hannah Stanton – who worked in South Africa in the early twentieth century. Gaitskell not only explores the ontological significance of religion and politics in formulating a gendered identity, but also evaluates the way in which the five women traverse the boundaries of class and racial difference to forge a 'politics of the personal'. Like Barát's, the discussion is (auto)biographically framed, in so far as Gaitskell recognizes the way in which her own Christian belief reflexively sustains her 'academic curiosity' about her subjects' lives and the way in which she situates their lives as a 'mirror' to her own.

In her discussion of Emmy Hennings's autobiographies, Christiane Schönfeld evaluates the disjuncture between Hennings's personal narrative and the biographical narratives that have been produced about her. In problematizing the biographical tendency to position Hennings's life as linear, unified and 'true', Schönfeld deconstructs such epistemological certainties to reveal a life that is disparate, multi-faceted and illusory. Indeed, as Hennings herself admits when discussing her autobiography: 'Although what I expressed seemed in parts quite entertaining, it was not truthful, not honest enough . . . I tended to embellish, skate around or exclude'. Like many other women discussed in this collection, what we perceive is a life embroiled in flux and strife which Hennings explains via a teleological paradigm, viewing 'every event [as] merely another step towards the present form of self'.

Part V   Recovering Lives – Revising History

The practice of 'recovery' and 'revision' is well established within feminist scholarship; and it is readily acknowledged that autobiography – with its generic slippage and hybridity – abets feminism's recuperative practice. Each of the contributors to this part is intent upon (re)presenting the historical significance of women's experience as recounted in auto/biographical discourse – from the extraordinary to the ordinary, the public to the private, the defiled to the deified – recognizing that the point, surely, is 'to walk with the dead and yet see them with our eyes, from our vantage point' (Forster, 1995: 309).

Anira Rowanchild's discussion of Anne Lister's holograph journals – which record 34 years of Lister's life and include over four million words – are testimony to a life that refused to comply to the gendered norms operating in British society during the late eighteenth and early nineteenth centuries. The journals are written in code (painstakingly decoded by Helena Whitbread (1988)) to conceal not only Lister's lesbian proclivities – which are explicitly and indubitably recorded – but also those of her friends, lovers and allies. However, whilst we may partake in a celebration of Lister's unyielding refusal to comply with societal norms, we should also take note of the fates of her childhood lover, Eliza Raine, and her partner, Anne Walker: they were both committed to asylums.

Helen Nicholson's chapter concentrates on the multifaceted life of Georgina Weldon (1838–1914), as recorded in her 28 leather-bound journals. Like Lister, Weldon flouted the conventions of her day; but unlike Eliza Raine and Anne Walker, she successfully evaded (her husband's) conspiracy to have her committed to an asylum. Throughout her discussion, Nicholson resists the urge to synthesize her subject's life history unproblematically, choosing a more complex ontological approach which leads her to explain that 'at the end of the process of uncovering the endless autobiographical conceits, I have come to the conclusion that there was no single self to discover'. Resistance and obduracy thus become the central tenets of a life that was not so much a singular, transparent life, but a complex, often opaque, layering of lives.

Whereas Nicholson and Rowanchild are concerned with women whose lives have – until very recently – been lost to history, June Purvis's chapter focuses on one of British history's most (in)famous female icons: Emmeline Pankhurst. However, Purvis is not so much intent upon recovery, as on rebuttal and revision, claiming that feminist scholarship has significantly misconstrued Pankhurst's political contribution to women's history. With fastidious historical detail and a robust evaluation of the 1907 WSPU split, Purvis challenges liberal- and socialist-feminism's representations of Pankhurst's reputation as autocrat, betrayer of the women's movement and failed mother, in favour of a radical-feminist perspective that reclaims her as a 'champion of womanhood'.

Bringing this part to its conclusion, Timothy Ashplant's chapter concentrates on two of Pankhurst's lesser-known contemporaries, Ruth Slate and Eva Slawson, whose diaries and letters – transcribed some 60 years after they were written (see Thompson, 1988) – reveal, in intimate and fascinating detail, the minutiae of day-to-day existence set within the wider historical backdrop of women's suffrage, trade union politics, the pacifist movement, the First World War, *inter alia*. Ashplant both flags up the complex points of convergence between education, religion and class, and demonstrates that the educational pursuit was significantly more consequential in shaping these women's lives. Not only does this discussion reveal Slate and Slawson's remarkable personal struggle to attain life-long learning, but also the wider historical impact of women's nineteenth- and early twentieth-century campaign for education, which made that experience irrefutably possible.

Part VI   Matrilineality

This concluding part focuses on both the significance of the mother within women's auto/biographical discourse and the linguistic and creative efficacies produced by mother–daughter/parent–child relations. Construing the female body as a site of gendered subjectivity and self-inscription, attention is given to the various ways in which matrilineality is inscribed within women's personal narratives as a profoundly troubled expression of the female imaginary.

Nicola Shaughnessy's chapter on Sylvia Plath examines the problems of locating the 'autobiographical voice' in Plath's two verse-dramas. Whilst Plath recognized the way in which many of her poems emanated from personal experiences, she also warned that poetry 'shouldn't be a kind of shut-box and mirror-looking, narcissistic experience'. Critically attending to this awareness concerning the personal voice within Plath's works, Shaughnessy explores the complex configurations between autobiography, poetry and drama that are played out in 'Dialogue over a Ouija Board' and *Three Women*. Not only do these works provide a 'private theatre' for Plath's troubled relationship with Ted Hughes, and an outlet for her existential crisis after she learns of her pregnancy, but they also connect her own experiences as a woman, a wife and a mother to the pressures exerted upon these forms of feminine identification by the demands of the social and cultural politics of her time within which she struggled to live and to write.

Whereas Shaughnessy takes up the issue of a *mother's* troubled identity, Alison Fell's chapter on Simone de Beauvoir's *Memoirs of a Dutiful Daughter* and *A Very Easy Death* deals with a *daughter's* painful subject-position in relation to her mother. But whilst Beauvoir's representation is characterized by claustrophobic possessiveness, jealous rivalry and repeated conflict, Fell maintains that the relationship was both more complex and more 'blurred' than has hitherto been recognised. In part, the relationship is fractured by a disjuncture between the mother's internalization of nineteenth-century matriarchal codes of meaning (through which identity is mediated), and Beauvoir's personal, political and philosophical resistance to those codes. Paradoxically, it is only on the point of recounting her mother's deteriorating illness and near-death – when Beauvoir is uncontrollably provoked by grief's intensity – that she is able to reassess their fractured relationship.

Moving from the troubled relations between mother and daughter, parent and child, Nicola Brice examines Lily Braun's celebration of that relation within the 'blurred boundaries' of Braun's autobiographical and fictional works: 'Maternal love is the strongest feeling in the world, stronger than sexual passion, stronger than hunger,' claims Braun. However, there is little in the way of romantic sentimentality about Braun's fictional representation of the mother; rather, she provides a politically informed, socialist-feminist analysis of the ideology of separate spheres wherein women's productive and reproductive roles are symbiotically positioned within the sexual politics of capitalism's *modus agendi*. Nevertheless, in exploring the connections between Braun's autobiographical and fictional writings, Brice argues that paradoxes are evident (as shown in Braun's craving for a son rather than a daughter and her 'silencing' of the female voice) and concludes that even this radical representative of women's rights is constrained by the conventions of her day.

Alex Goody's chapter on Mina Loy's modernist poem, *Anglo-Mongrel and the Rose*, brings this volume to its conclusion. Defining her auto/mythological approach to the poem, Goody explains: 'In using myth, personal experience and history, *Anglo-Mongrels* functions as a form of analysis at multiple levels, producing both a psychic analysis of self and artistic consciousness and socio-cultural analysis of the ideological conditions of personal realization and artistic expression.' Thus, the grand narratives of historical circumstance (First World War, Bolshevism and Jewish dislocation) alongside the personal narrative of the daughter's autobiographical I/eye transmogrify within the 'complex web' of identity and self-inscription. Ova – the poem's female protagonist – not only suggests 'a nascent feminine selfhood', but also recalls the name of Loy's daughter who died on her first birthday. Autobiography's hybridity thus stretches beyond the auto/mythological to auto/biographical and (auto)biographical dimensions. Goody argues that *Anglo-Mongrel* depicts Ova's abject expulsion from the maternal/semiotic realm and portrays the linguistic manifestations of that experience and, furthermore, suggests that Loy uses women's auto/biography as a means through which to revise Freud's dominant explanatory narrative of feminine identity.

*   *   *

The discussions on offer in this volume testify to the immense activity both within and outside of the academy in terms of feminist auto/biographical theory and practice, reading and inscription. We trust that it will facilitate yet further discussion and debate on auto/biographical representation.

Alison Donnell and Pauline Polkey, 1999

References and Further Reading

Anderson, L. *Women and Autobiography in the Twentieth Century: Remembered Futures* (Hemel Hempstead: Prentice Hall/Harvester Wheatsheaf, 1997)

Corbett, M. J. *Representing Femininity: Middle-Class Subjectivity in Victorian and Edwardian Women's Autobiographies* (Oxford: Oxford University Press, 1992)

Forster, M. *Hidden Lives: A Family Memoir* (London & New York: Viking – Penguin, 1995)

Humm, M. *Border Traffic: Strategies of Contemporary Women Writers* (Manchester: Manchester University Press, 1991)

Marcus, L. *Auto/biographical Discourses: Theory, Criticism, Practice* (Manchester: Manchester University Press, 1994)

Personal Narratives Group (eds) *Interpreting Women's Lives: Feminist Theory and Personal Narratives* (Bloomington & Indianapolis: Indiana University Press, 1989)

Polkey, P. (ed.) *Women's Lives into Print: The Theory, Practice and Writing of Feminist Auto/biography* (Basingstoke: Macmillan, 1999)

Simons, J. *Diaries and Journals of Literary Women from Fanny Burney to Virginia Woolf* (Basingstoke: Macmillan, 1990)

Stanley, L. *The Auto/biographical I: The Theory and Practice of Feminist Auto/biography* (Manchester: Manchester University Press, 1992)

———'Introduction', *Lives and Works*, 3: 1–2 (1994) i–ii

Swindells, J. (ed.) *The Uses of Autobiography* (London: Taylor & Francis, 1995)

Thompson, T. (ed.) *Dear Girl: The Diaries and Letters of Two Working Women, 1899–1917* (London: The Women's Press, 1987)

Woolf, V. 'I am Christina Rossetti', *Virginia Woolf: Women and Writing* (London: The Women's Press, [1930] 1979)

Here is the past and all its inhabitants miraculously sealed as in a magic tank; all we have to do is to look and to listen and to listen and to look and soon the little figures – for they are rather under life size – will begin to move and to speak, and as they move we shall arrange them in all sorts of patterns of which they were ignorant, for they thought when they were alive that they could go where they liked; and as they speak we shall read into their sayings all kinds of meanings which never struck them, for they believed when they were alive that they said straight off whatever came into their heads. But when you are in biography all is different.

Virginia Woolf, 'I am Christina Rossetti' (1930)

Keynote Address

Is There Life in the Contact Zone?[1] Auto/Biographical Practices and the Field of Representation in Writing Past Lives

Liz Stanley

Some Introductory Matters

In this chapter[2] I discuss some of the key representational issues that necessarily impinge upon auto/biography as upon all other fields of intellectual inquiry. I do so by invoking a particular 'case', that of the feminist writer and theorist Olive Schreiner (1855–1920),[3] and by working in a particular way, through the lens of 'feminist auto/biography', broadly conceived.[4] My purpose is to illuminate pertinent issues surrounding the representation of lives in general. These issues always take particular forms, in relation to particular lives, contexts, times and places; but, like life itself, this does *not* mean that there are not 'things in common', while it *does* mean that my implicit argument (I shall make it no more explicit than this) is that the 'whole' cannot be grasped apart from particular instances. That is, the general cannot be apprehended directly, for it is composed of its variant particulars. I deal with these issues in, but particularly through, the 'shape' they take in relation 'representing the life of Olive Schreiner', pointing up the implications for the representation of lives more widely, the feminist representation of lives especially.

Book chapters, like journal articles, seminars, conferences, meetings and lectures, are all part of the academic occasions that Nancy Miller (1991) has discussed in a feminist context as occasions that are performances. These are also performative: they accomplish things other than themselves. For Miller, the 'other' things are in fact contained *in* the performances as well as *without*, as autobiographical

3

occasions, occasions in a life that constitute that life. These academic feminist occasions are biographical too, for they are occasions in other lives and for other people, not just for the writer, the teacher, the seminar leader, the administrator, herself. They resonate with other lives, for they require, or rather they intend, *an audience*. They are in fact occasions on which people engage reciprocally in auto/biographical practices, and in doing so they unsettle the assumed but shaky boundaries between self and other, public and private, ideas and materiality, work and non-work.

Consequently, such occasions prompt a recourse to feminist auto/biography as an appropriate analytic frame for thinking about them. And by 'feminist auto/biography' I mean an epistemologically-oriented concern with the intellectual and other ramifications of the shifting boundaries between self and other, present and past, writing and reading, fact and fiction, within the oral, visual and written texts that are 'biographies' and 'autobiographies' in both their formal and usually textual or visual variants as well as in their everyday incarnations.[5] Feminist auto/biography displaces the referential and foundational claims of writers and researchers, unsettles notions of 'science', problematizes the 'expert' claims of research, and questions the power issues most researchers silence or disclaim. And, of course, it does this in relation to 'claims about lives', lives in the past as much as the present, then as well as now.

Thus my starting point is composed of a number of assumptions which have implications for the argument I go on to make. Stated baldly, these are as follows: the general cannot be fully apprehended apart from through the particular, for an important aspect of its defining attributes concerns the interconnections between particularities. 'Autobiography' and 'biography' may be separate genres of writing, but 'in life' (and also in the vast majority of these kinds of texts) lives are interconnected. Academic occasions are certainly autobiographical occasions, but they are also biographical ones; and this interconnectedness is to be discerned in relation to the 'products' of academia (including books and, of course, book chapters) as well as to its 'processes' (researching, teaching in lectures and seminars, conference presentations). My discussion is not just about feminist auto/biography; it is itself an example of auto/biographical practices.

Issues surrounding representation must be taken seriously and, indeed, as fundamental in an analytic sense. These issues do not arise through mistakes which better methodology or better objectivity or better anything else can remove from academic work any more than from life itself – these are problematics, not problems, and we necessarily work and live within the field of representation, starting with language itself. Along the way in discussing these matters, I address representational issues in terms of claims-making, in which knowledge is assumed, claimed, counter-claimed: is precisely represented and contested.

Touching up the Past: The Contact Zone, Representation and Metaphor

I begin with, rather than in, figurative more than literal space. Mary Louise Pratt has interestingly discussed and used the notion of the 'contact zone' in relation to travel writing and ideas about transculturation, and she notes that:

> 'Contact zone' in my discussion is often synonymous with 'colonial frontier'. But while the latter term is grounded within a European expansionist project . . . 'contact zone' is an attempt to invoke the spatial and temporal copresences of subjects previously separated by geographic and historical disjunctures, and whose trajectories now intersect. I aim to foreground the interactive, improvizational dimensions of colonial encounters. (1992: 6–7)

Pratt makes interesting use of three concepts in circulation 'elsewhere', intellectually speaking: the contact zone, transculturation and autoethnography. Her idea of the 'contact zone', in particular, has immediate interest for me, given that the focus of my discussion is 'the field of representation' surrounding Olive Schreiner, born on the frontier in what was, in 1855, the then frontier of the Cape Colony in what later, post-1910, became part of South Africa. Moreover, as well as writing novels and allegories, Schreiner also wrote about the mixtures of colonial and indigenous people in southern Africa and the changing nexus of relationships between them, in the particular imperial and colonial 'moment' that took place between Cecil Rhodes's first ministry in 1890 and the Act of Union between these states in 1910 (see, for instance, Schreiner, 1896, 1899, 1908, 1923, 1926). Schreiner's 'South African' writing is not strictly speaking of the travel writing genre, unlike the travel books on South Africa from the mid-eighteenth century that Pratt discusses in one of her chapters. However, it did form one component in the way metropolitan publics engaged with imperial expansionist projects, in Schreiner's case through a critique; and certainly it promoted transculturation, a term Pratt uses to examine ways in which modes of representation were used in a two-way process, from metropolis to colony, and also from colony to metropolis.

However, the issues surrounding representation take particular shape when we now, in the present, look back at then, the past. In addition, it seems to me that Pratt unnecessarily limits the analytic utility of the idea of the contact zone by specifying it around 'colonial encounters' as such. The 'contact' I am concerned with in relation to Olive Schreiner is *both* that which took place within the historical 'moment' of the colonial past, *and* that of the claims made now about this 'moment', who composed it, what they were like, where they were and why, what happened, why, and what it all meant. Moreover, the former cannot be apprehended without the latter: the latter is 'all about' apprehension, and uses a variety of representational means for accomplishing this, including photographs, letters, diaries, government documents, taped conversations, notes of archive visits or interviews, and so forth. None of these is 'the past itself'; all are accounts, representations, which offer a variety of different kinds of claims about 'what it, she or he did and was like'.

'The past' is not a time and place that 'exist' (like Auckland in New Zealand; or Grahamstown in South Africa; or Austin, Texas, in the USA) – it does not go on its own sweet way whether I visit it or not. Its time is over and done with and it exists, now, only in and through representational means. Its 'then' no longer has existence except through 'now' and those moments of apprehension which are concerned with it. These representational means are rather like a set of Russian dolls: one 'sits inside' the other, sits inside another, then these another, and so on, until we approximate to that small kernel, the thing itself, the 'moment' being invoked, described, redescribed, analysed, explained, concluded through the 'voices' and positions within this field of claims and counter-claims. And 'the thing itself' now exists only in some representational form or another.

The consequence is that, in thinking about these matters in relation to past lives, like Michel de Certeau (1988), I am at least as concerned with 'the writing of history', and biography and autobiography, and with claims-making about 'past times' and 'past lives' more generally, as I am with 'the past itself'.[6] Consequently, I am interested in the sometimes consonant – and sometimes not – relationship between my struggles to know and those of other people

Figure 1 Passport photograph of Olive Schreiner, un-retouched (1920) [INIL 3187]. Reproduced by permission of the South African Library, Cape Town, South Africa

interested in the same, or a related, person, life, moment of the past. Another way of expressing this is to emphasize that 'writing itself' is not outside the field of representation or outside the complexities of auto/biographical acts. Thus, for instance, this chapter is a part of the phenomenon it inquires into; it is an auto/biographical act; and it is composed by, as well as being concerned with, a representational occasion. It is also a small part of 'writing itself', and it exemplifies the issues and problematics it raises and addresses.

I can perhaps show, as well as write about, what I mean here in relation to a passport photograph of Olive Schreiner, taken immediately before she sailed back to South Africa from London in mid-1920, that accompanies this chapter (see Figure 1). It was found in Schreiner's possessions after her death by her estranged husband, Samuel 'Cron' Cronwright-Schreiner, who sent a copy of it to one of her closest friends, Betty Molteno, writing that:

> I knew how you'd value the photo of Olive . . . I managed to unearth . . . taken on the 6th August (she sailed on the 13th). I then had it touched up. . . . It is Olive old, weary &, so to say, dying, with her back to the wall. One misses the violent force & the radiant energy & vitality which characterized her in her glorious power & which she showed at times even to the last; but I am so glad to have it. (SCCS to Betty Molteno, 12 February 1921, UCT)

This photograph is in fact a copy of the original, the one that had *not* been 'touched up'. There is an implication in Cronwright-Schreiner's accompanying comments that this photograph of Olive Schreiner, the one which is not 'not touched up', is the real one in the sense of showing her as she really was in August 1920; but also that there was another even more real Olive Schreiner antecedent to it, the one her friends would want to remember 'as her', and thus the 'touching up' to reinscribe this Olive Schreiner back into the mimetic Olive Schreiner. What can be concluded about this is that what *is* 'touched up' and what has *not* been 'touched up' are both representations as much as – although in different ways from – each other.

I find this idea of 'Olive Schreiner, touched and not touched up' useful as a metaphor for thinking about representation, in the sense of providing a means for focusing on the complexities of 'the contact zone'. Here in this particular contact zone there exists: Olive

Schreiner, caught representationally in that *momento mori* which is a photograph; an antecedent Olive Schreiner; after Schreiner's actual death, Cronwright-Schreiner, and through him a photographer, 'touching up' for some purposes and audiences, but keeping the 'not touched up' for others; an audience of people who had known Schreiner, who looked upon the 'touched up' photograph and 'saw through' it to aspects of the woman represented therein and a variety of moments of her life and theirs which had intersected; archivists and others professionally involved in acquiring, conserving, classifying and making available both the photograph and also outline information about it in catalogues and other 'finding aids'; I, Liz Stanley, who saw the photograph, had thoughts about it and then subsequently produced different kinds of public presentations about this; the various audiences for these presentations, many of whom may have pre-existing knowledges about Schreiner scholarship, but many of whom may not; and now this specific audience, of those readers of this present piece of work, the chapter you are reading and the photograph you can look at.

I have invoked 'Olive Schreiner, touched and not touched up' as a metaphor for the field of representation (itself a metaphor, of course) and the issues that arise concerning it. The metaphors we use to represent how we think, how we write, how we theorize – nomad, traveller, parachutist, performer, actor, exile and so on – are important and we should be alive to uses of them, not least because embedded within them are overlaying knowledge-claims which position authors and readers, knowing subjects and the objects of their knowing, in ways which may or may not be intended but which are always consequential. The central assumption of, for instance, biography immediately raises issues and questions of epistemology, for it is, fundamentally, one of 'I the knower, Olive Schreiner/X or Y the known'. In addition, the surrounding metaphors and tropes also condition what kind of 'knowing' relationship this is – certain, provisional, partial, complete, supreme, shared, and so on.

We should learn to think *through* metaphor, not think *by* metaphor (Grimshaw, 1997). This means not just developing a reflexive awareness of the consequences that our metaphors for thinking and theorizing have. It also requires displacing the analytical position of a metaphor *as*, and not just *at*, the apex of a set of knowledge-claims we make. The aphorism 'we should think through metaphors, not think by them' becomes a tool, a procedural means of promoting, rather than concluding, inquiry. That is, I could simply stop, now that I have invoked the 'touched and not touched up' photographs. But what does it *mean*, what are the *consequences*, of positioning the 'contact zone', not as the literal borderland of colonial frontiers, but instead as a figurative space in which things are done and time is undone?

In relation to the untouched up photograph of Olive Schreiner, I sketched out the literal interlocking elements of the field of representation involved in thinking about just this one single piece of archive evidence and commented that these fit together 'like a set of Russian dolls'. This is both an apt and a misleading way to characterize the relationship between these, and forms a kind of metaphor that assumes, presumes, through the words or terms of its formulation. Thus, the last doll is presumptively the biggest, that which has privilege over and thus in this sense encapsulates the others, and this conveys very well the epistemological, as well as temporal, privileging built into the relationships operant within this 'field'. However, it also both assumes and presumes that there is a 'tiniest doll' which is the kernel the others enfold, which sits at the centre, which acts as that which all else makes claims about, which is 'it', the moment itself on which all those others are predicated.

To think in this way is to treat time as a line, a line between then and now, and in biographical or historical research a line which goes back again as well, from now to then. Here history, the past, in the form of some point, time, event, person, within it, becomes the 'it' that the researcher progressively works back to, seeks and finds. However, if we take seriously, in an analytic sense, debates concerning representation, this comforting model, metaphor or trope must be given up (these are different terms, of course, and which is most appropriate will depend on how an analysis is shaped up). There are two ways of thinking about this which, in their very different ways, I find helpful here.

R. G. Collingwood (1927 and 1948), as well as being a philosopher, carried out archaeological research concerned with Romano-Britain. In his discussions of the philosophical issues involved in such work, he points out that the historian typically works with 'traces' of the past, all of which are material traces in the sense of being, whether ideas or artefacts, materially and impingently here in the present. Collingwood, both famously and infamously, works from these traces to an interpretational issue which is concerned with how and the extent to which historians can think their way into the mind or *Zeitgeist* of the time, place and people they are concerned with.

The only aspect of Collingwood's argument here I want to pick up on is his insistence that all such traces are necessarily, in some way or other, apprehensible in present-day terms; they must be, or we would not even 'know' them in historical terms at all. We can and could struggle to know the past in its own terms, but for Collingwood we can accomplish this only by reference to the fact that the kind of historicism that Philip Abrams (1982) poked fun at as 'resurrectionalism' is by definition an impossibility, given that our means of apprehension have to be those of now, of precisely looking back, not of being there or going there. Succinctly, then, Collingwood's 'take' on this is that we select, organize, think, conclude, *now*; this is what is epistemologically prime, even though scrupulousness requires as much modification of the pervasive presentism of our thinking as possible.

In a different and more labyrinthine discussion, the deconstructionist philosopher Jacques Derrida (1989), in writing about his memories of his dead friend, the critic Paul de Man, proposes that the name of a dead person and the (former) person become one in the mind of the rememberer. The name then acts as a kind of hallucination, because we think through the name to a palimpsest of the dead person, a person who now 'never answers', as Derrida puts it. We can no longer separate the name and the memory, because memory is all there is. And whilst Derrida is particularly concerned with how to understand personal memory, his argument also covers social memory, including that located within ideas and artefacts, the kind of things that Collingwood refers to as 'traces'; thus Derrida notes that 'Despite all his suspicions of historicism or historical rhetorics blind to their own rhetoricity, Paul de Man contended with *the irreducibility of a certain history*' (1989: 52–3; my emphasis). What we have and work with is historicism and historical rhetoric (historiography), including, indeed especially, that which lays claim to facticity; but, in the last resort, there is the irreducible fact that someone *was* or something *happened* in past times. And of course, Derrida's ideas here cover all situations in which 'the other is not there'. It is not only death that has the effect or result he thinks and writes about, but other kinds of separations and removals as well.

For Derrida, autobiography acts as a defacement, an effacing of the 'I'. This works by autobiography constructing a version of 'I', one that consists only of name and memory. Biography, I conclude, is to be seen as doubly an effacement of 'I': it is a rhetoric founded on logical argument and temporizing, a rhetoric apparently blind to its rhetoricity because it excises the 'I' of the writer/ biographer; and also it constructs the 'I' of its subject around their name and memory (that is, typically, through social memory, traces, although sometimes also expositions of slices of the personal memories of those who knew the name's subject).

These two discussions differently point out that the excised 'I' of historiography, biography and autobiography depends on a complicity between, on the one hand, a writer/researcher actively at work, and, on the other, the artefacts or traces or memories actively being worked upon. The tie that binds is that 'moment' of investigation, interpretation, explanation and exposition that takes external, material, visible forms which we know as 'a lecture', a seminar', 'a book', 'a chapter', and so on. There are two aspects of this I want to comment on. One concerns the mechanics and programmatics involved in the writing of history/biography/auto-biography; and the other concerns time and life in the contact zone in relation to claims of facticity.

The Acts and Occasions of Writing

'Writing' is an apparently simple term, one we all know the meaning of. But writing is also a philosopher's stone which transmutes from one form into another, from talk to text, past to present, facts to fictions, life to art. It is in fact a translation device, one through which what is translated becomes irreducibly different from what has been translated. The act of writing – writing this, writing that – actually encapsulates many occasions of writing, some the writer's own, some those of other people writing the 'that' that the 'writing this' invokes, trades upon. Historiography, biography and autobiography transmute or translate time in particular: these all deal in times more than in persons or places or events, for persons and places and events are located in time, and time is of the essence. Each of these genres is predicated upon the assumption or belief that there is a fundamental difference between present and past, while earlier forms of 'telling the tale' do not (necessarily) make this assumption: in an oral tradition, the tale or story is an event within the present, and what is told once may be different told twice. But writing invokes the sign of authority; it authorizes, gives solidity, fixity; it produces a text, something apparently inert and 'there', a thing rather than an occasion. However, in spite of this, it is indeed occasioned, a product that is rhetorically produced, a work of artifice, artfulness, art.

All this is obvious enough when applied to writing fictions. But writing facts is usually treated as different in kind. Facts, the assumption is, have independent existence and are external to the text, the writing and the writer; the facts are discovered, not invented. Leaving on one side the interesting questions that arise around claims to facticity, I want to focus on what this notion of 'the facts' means in relation to historiography, biography and autobiography. Cronwright-Schreiner (1924), in his *The Life of Olive Schreiner*, argues that Schreiner's insistence in the early 1900s that she had a heart problem was the product of her imagination; she consulted first this doctor and that; the good and respected ones told her she had no heart disease; only charlatans told her she did; and this 'fact' is located in connection with others, some occurring in the 1890s or earlier, others occurring later, confirming this trait in her character. His claims about 'the facts' of her heart rest upon these earlier and later descriptions of exaggerations; and these, in turn, on his privileged claims to know this woman who had been his wife. 'The facts' work successively: they are composed by things that are successions in time. However, there are some interesting things going on here. One is the excised matter of the inclusions and exclusions of facts, that there is selection around an argument: the facts serve the rhetorical purposes to which they are put. The other is the epistemological rupture which is necessary to make the facts 'speak': 1. A set of things is described successively in time. 2. A conclusion is drawn about their meaning.

The epistemological rupture lies in what is actually a gulf, a chasm, lying between these two things. The rupture is healed, the sides of the chasm drawn together and made to appear as though one, by the presumption that things that are described as successive in time are causally linked, that the one does indeed follow the other and the posterior explains that which is antecedent. However, what is elided is that causality is not being deduced in this proposition by discovering the facts and the meaning inherent in the conclusion of these. Rather, the causality comes first, is antecedent to the facts; it is the arrival at causality which determines what will be selected as '*the* facts', and what will not because 'merely facts', facts that are unconnected and thus irrelevant. Time, then, is indeed of the essence, for it is by doing things with time that historical, biographical and autobiographical arguments and conclusions are made.

Time is important, epistemologically speaking, in another sense as well. Writing flattens time. It removes time from 'its time' into the time of the writing, which almost immediately becomes a kind of perpetual present locked in the perpetual and peculiar kind of past that are books, articles, book chapters – like so many flies caught in amber, but caught there on different days, weeks, years. As a consequence, there is an interesting conundrum at the heart of these kinds of writing: in the very act of re/creating the truth of the past they betray it, because another of the essences of time is that time passes; it is not a state but a process: and it is memory that makes the process masquerade as a state.

There is another elision here, one that also has consequence for 'the facts'. The production of historiography, biography and auto-biography occurs in place and space as well as in time and doing things with time. 'The writer' is apparently alone but is actually immersed within sets of actual as well as figurative relations. As de Certeau comments:

> It is therefore ruled by constraints, bound to privileges, and rooted in a particular situation. It is in terms of this place that its methods are established, its topography of interests can be specified, its dossiers and interrogation of documents are organized. (1988: 58)

The activities of 'this place', of particular epistemic communities, result in only some things, some facts, being seen possible; they produce what de Certeau calls the 'ideological range', the limits of what can be thought, and more mundanely what will be admitted 'as (true) fact'. I now want to move on to look at one such 'particular situation', that of Schreiner scholarship, for doing so suggests that matters are perhaps not quite so simple as de Certeau proposes, or, rather, that it is, but that it is also contested, and constitutes a discourse in the Foucauldian sense of the term.

Life in the Contact Zone: Canonical and Contrary Facts

At this point, with time and contestation, I want to return to the notion of the contact zone, and to use it again as a tool for think-ing. While Pratt is particularly concerned with the contact zone as an arena involving spatial and temporal *co-presences*, she is also concerned with 'bringing together', analytically speaking, people previously separated by geographic and historical disjunctures. That is, in the latter instance, people separated by time. The travel writing she is concerned with itself travels, temporally as well as spatially, although the temporal move involved is not one foregrounded in her discussion. However, while this writing may time-travel (her opening example is of a 1613 document addressed from Incan Peru to the Spanish king, which 'turned up' in a Danish archive in 1908), it is its place within a particular historical 'moment' that she is concerned with, as 'social spaces where disparate cultures meet, clash and grapple with each other, often in highly asymmetrical relations of domination and subordination' (1992: 4).

This puts an unnecessary limitation on the analytic uses to which Pratt's idea of the contact zone can be put, specifically so in relation to the question of time. It is the asymmetrical meeting of disparate cultures *across time* I want to focus on, to stretch her metaphor temporally. If we connote the encounters in part inscribed in travel writing around the idea of a colonial frontier, an imperial borderland, it is interesting to contemplate that the same terms might have utility in relation to another frontier, the temporal frontier between past and present. Pratt explains one dimension of the contact zone thus:

> A 'contact' perspective emphasizes how subjects are constituted in and by their relations to each other. It treats the relations among colonizers and colonized, or travelers and 'travelees', not in terms of separateness or apartheid, but in terms of copresence, interaction, interlocking understandings and practices, often within radically asymmetrical relations of power. (Pratt, 1992: 7)

This is an interesting and sensible way of requiring the researcher to reflect upon, indeed to *see*, the complexities of that transcultural 'moment' of travelling and writing: these are asymmetrical relations, but the peoples concerned are not separate but co-presences, and their relations are interactive. The 'moment' Pratt is concerned with is conceived fairly broadly and in a sense involves 'historical disjunctures' (thus she looks at travel writing of the mid-eighteenth century on southern Africa, from the Caribbean from 1780 to 1840, from Spanish America from 1800 to 1840, and, in her least satisfactory chapter, from the Victorians in central Africa in the 1860s on to postcolonial travel writing of the 1960s–1980s). However, there is something important missing, temporally speaking, from her analytic account, which relates to her periodization of time.

This 'missing something' can be pointed to, in its outline at least, by reference to de Certeau's focus on the figurative space of researching and writing. There is no context of contemporary reading and thinking and interpreting and concluding in Pratt's discussion. There is no indication of the ways in which the figures in *this* landscape – the landscape of the study (or kitchen table), the lecture room, the conference setting, the publishers and their readers – relate to each other nor what their relations are to the 'historical' figures herein. Mary Louise Pratt as the locus of researching, writing, concluding, publishing, reading is a thoroughly excised 'I'. Hers is certainly a sharp, interesting, engaged, critical 'voice' in, or rather around and about, the text. However, the text itself is presented as an exercise in temporal and spatial travelling: it invokes the chosen set of historical 'moments', which are linked analytically by the conceptual frame of contact zone, transculturation and autoethnography; but these 'moments' are apparently of *then*, the mid-eighteenth century in Africa, the Caribbean between 1780 and 1840, and so on, and there is very little of the *now* of the context of the production, distribution and consumption of these interlinked accounts. In a sense, of course, why should there be, for isn't Pratt's purpose a rather different one, after all? But this question misses the point, which is that such matters can only be excised and elided, never removed; the text produced by such moves is a palimpsest, a ghostly echo, a shadowy product of the greater moment of its production, a 'moment' which collects into it these other 'historical moments', wrenched from their time 'then' into this time 'now'.

Like it or not, tell it or not, historiography, biography and autobiography are indeed writing and do indeed do things with time. These things should not be excised and elided because writing and time are the means by which 'texts talk', by which they are made to reveal precisely what Pratt is interested in. And this is the interactive, improvizational dimensions of colonial encounters, those that are not only ethnographic (a knowing, writing 'I' whose analytic gaze is cast on those times, places and peoples by outsiders) but also autoethnographic (a knowing, writing 'I' whose analytic gaze is cast on those other writings, as well as the times, places and peoples themselves, by insiders) as well. The 'something missing', then, is the figure of a woman in this landscape; a woman in relations with others within it, not a woman alone; and some of these others are of 'then' but others are of 'now'. There are two aspects of this

I want to explore particularly. One concerns the conjunction of writing/travel, and the other contestation in the contact zone.

Olive Schreiner's collection of essays *Thoughts on South Africa* was published posthumously in 1923, and can be seen as a piece of travel writing, albeit one that points to the shifting boundaries of the genre, as well as those other frontiers of the colonial past. A number of its composing essays were originally written for publication in magazines and journals, while Schreiner wrote others for the book, which she first intended to publish in 1896, and then in 1901, while thereafter she abandoned publication plans. Its opening essay commences with a panoramic sweep across southern Africa, looking at its land, its climate and its peoples and their histories; and it identifies its defining fundamental 'problem' as occurring because it is

> peopled everywhere by a mixture of races overlaying and under- lying each other in confused layers; but these mixtures of peoples are re-divided into states whose boundaries, except in the case of a few of the necessarily ephemeral native states, have no re- lation to the racial divisions of the people beneath them and therefore have in them, at the core, nothing of the true nature of national divisions.[7] (Schreiner 1913: 49)

The other essays look historically and politically at some of these peoples, starting with its Boer or Afrikaner pastoral farming popu- lations, and with the intention of including as many chapters on its English and its various black inhabitants as well. This intention was one foreshortened at two 'historical disjunctures' which I will say a little more about later, while here I focus on the status of Schreiner's text. I take it for granted that it is a piece of travel writing, and want to reflect on what kind of travel writing it is.

Schreiner was born into the English colonial population of what was then the Cape Colony; she was 'of the metropolis' and her 'I' cast analytically on this landscape and its peoples is in this sense a European one, and it classifies and considers and seeks to know, not just to record. Her text can therefore comfortably be seen as 'ethnographic' in Pratt's sense. However, Schreiner did not see her- self as English (a term she associated with the imperial presence of Britain, which she thoroughly critiqued elsewhere in her writings), and instead described herself as either African or English South African, classificatory terms she used to emphasize her own (and many other people's) ontological in-betweenness, doing so in particular in her 1899 anti-war polemic *An English South African's View of the Situation*. In many ways the essays in *Thoughts on South Africa* are autoethnographic in Pratt's sense, for she uses the apparatus of outsider writing to represent indigenous cultures by reinscribing the complexities of their ontological situatedness that the ethnographic (and its fictional variants, such as those of Rider Haggard, an earlier focus of sharp criticism from Schreiner) had removed; and for Schreiner these are the complexities inflected in her depiction of 'the problem' of South Africa.[8]

Schreiner's twice interrupted text points up the epistemological dimensions of her autoethnographic project, and its role as a counter to the scientific and imperial dimensions of the ethnographic project. That is, its aim was *knowing*, not knowledge; her concern was the production of a knowing subject, who was the writer, and not an object known, which was what was written. Its two 'interruptions' were occasioned by points in time at which 'events' happening externally made it apparent that the knowingness being worked out in these interconnected pieces of writing was incomplete, mistaken or overtaken by political developments. Schreiner's *Thoughts on South Africa*, then, points up the fact that these ontological frontiers or boundaries are more complex than Pratt's ultimately binary account (then/now) proposes, and that the ontological and the epistemological cannot be easily prised apart therein. It is an awkward text in another interesting sense too.

Pointedly, *Thoughts on South Africa* ruptures any easy binary distinction between 'then' and 'now', for it is a book not easily placed in time (if indeed books ever are). It is a book that, literally, could not be read at the time of its writing by anyone other than its author, for it was never published 'then'. Certainly the book had readers when it was eventually published in 1923, but, as the archival record shows, not many: it sold very few copies; and it has probably had as many readers over the past two decades of burgeoning Schreiner scholarship as in the intervening period. Consequently, it is a text which 'appears' and 'speaks' in present-day reading of the Schreiner corpus, especially that which has taken place approximately since 1980 (the date at which Ruth First and Ann Scott's proto-feminist biography of ideas, *Olive Schreiner*, was published). And what casting an eye upon events in this contact zone makes clear is the existence of the claims and counter-claims, the privileging of some ways of thinking and understanding but not others, that de Certeau is concerned with wrenching into historical sight. That is, it reveals the specification of topographies of interests, methodologies, dossiers, that occurs within a particular epistemic community. What this specification does, amongst other things, is to condition and shape readings of the documents of the past. However, herein there is no single sovereign epistemic community that rules absolutely, that conditions and frames and disposes in any absolute sense. There is precisely contestation. In relation to Schreiner's *Thoughts on South Africa*, some of this contestation, the competing claims to know, surrounding this and her other South African writings can be easily shown:

> It is the product of an exacting thinker, a polemical writing which more cogently, and graphically, expresses the character of South Africa and its people than any book before or since. (Beeton, 1974: 53)

> Schreiner's important and much-praised book, *Thoughts on South Africa*. (Lewsen, 1983: 215)

> Its contents might indicate why it has been so unattractive to a modern readership ... on the face of it, the essays are a panegyric to the Boer ... little wonder, then, that ... [it] has been a difficult text for those critics who have praised Schreiner for outspoken condemnation of the injustice of sexual, racial and class oppression. (Burdett, 1994: 225)

> Schreiner advocated a federation rather than unification for South Africa, and in doing so she anticipated precisely a dialogue going on in 1994 at the moment of the elections in South Africa. (Horton, 1995: 77)

The particular conjunction of writing/travel that is Schreiner's *Thoughts on South Africa*, then, points up some of the issues about time involved here. In particular, it points up temporal uncontainability, the fact that time cannot be so easily tamed and fixed within neat dates as Pratt's discussion implies, for once we un-excise the 'I' of the researcher/writer, time spills over periodization in untidy, awkward and interesting ways. We witness the return of the repressed, unchained from a neat periodization that excludes the knowing present of 'now' and the claims that it makes about 'then'.

Turning now to look at contestation in the contact zone more closely, my focus is 'the emergent Schreiner canon', the things that are said to be known about this woman; I represent these elements of the canon by single quotations from pieces of feminist work in the temporal order of their publication, using these to stand for many more such statements which could have also have been provided (and see here Stanley, 1999). 'The facts' are these:

Olive's power . . . her extraordinary intensity . . . her serious, direct, merciless intelligence . . . the blaze of eye and explosive energy . . . the ringing vibrant tones when Olive was aroused . . . by physical mannerisms, by strange emotional manifestations, and by unexpected limitations of the intellect in fields where its superb quality is not operative: as though there were an intense concentration on certain qualities and not on others, or partly at the cost of others, the incalculable power and illumination of the one throwing into more glaring contrast the comparative inequalities and limitations of the others. (Cronwright-Schreiner, 1924: 22–34)

Olive Schreiner was neither a born letter-writer nor did she choose to make herself become one. She wrote carelessly, egotistically, of her health, her sufferings, of her beliefs and desire. . . . This carelessness, while it has its charm, imposes some strain on the reader. If [s]he is not to drop the book. (*The Letters of Olive Schreiner* edited by Cronwright Schreiner) [S]he must seek some point of view which imposes unity. (Woolf, 1979: 180)

Friedmann . . . is obviously right to describe Olive as neurotic. . . . We are . . . applying a Freudian theory of the mind and its constructs to that part of our source material which concerns Olive's inner world and the course of her life. . . . Significantly, Olive's asthma developed in late adolescence after an emotional involvement. . . . Olive became a sick girl, and then a sick woman. (First and Scott, 1980: 22–3, 335–6)

In the South African context . . . the woman issue withers with the issue of the voteless, powerless state of South African blacks, regardless of sex. It was as bizarre then . . . as now . . . to regard a campaign for women's rights – black or white – as relevant to the South African situation. (Gordimer, [1987] 1980: 225)

Schreiner's racial primitivism ... is a way to avoid confronting gender as a cultural construct. The belief in archetypal maternity and its blurring of history into a set of transtemporal values obviates the need for political change in the present while justifying the rule and reproduction of 'virile' white men and women ... Darwin's ideas, based on warfare and domination, are not antipathetic but inextricably linked to Schreiner's belief in timeless maternal values. (Barash, 1986: 339)

The central problems of this often incoherent work [*The Story of An African Farm*] arise from its author's inability to find a plot commensurate with her own and her heroine's desires ... even while Schreiner argues for female freedom, she cannot seem to represent such freedom effectively in the life of her heroine. Not only do Lyndall's [a central character's] pleas for women's independence appear after many chapters devoted to seemingly unrelated issues but also, like several other characters, Lyndall almost inexplicably disappears and reappears from the world of the farm throughout the novel. (Gilbert and Gubar, 1989: 52–3)

[Of] her three novels, *Undine, The Story of An African Farm* and *From Man to Man* ... Schreiner was still revising *From Man to Man* some 40 years after she began it ... [but] the great bulk ... of her three novels was completed ... at the age of 26 ... Schreiner's own life was racked by conflicts ... Duty to self or others? Woman or author? The personal or the impersonal? This last conflict ... destroyed her as a creative writer ... Schreiner used ... [*From Man to Man*] as the repository of the major part of a lifetime's thoughts on women, and on herself, so much so that to have finished it would have been like suicide.... It is, we might say ... a year-by-year confessional in fictional form. (Parkin-Gounelas, 1991: 83–106)

[Schreiner's unfinished Wollstonecraft Introduction] consists almost entirely of a sketchy and crude evolutionary narrative which relies upon the racist figuring of African womanhood to speak an unmediated 'truth'.... If, as I have claimed, Schreiner's attempt to write [it] ... can be read as a submerged history of the writing of *Woman and Labour*, then it is clear that that text ... is certainly limited in a way that Schreiner could not acknowledge, by the terms of the evolutionary science which she employed. (Burdett, 1992: 111–13)

It is *Woman and Labour* which has generally been singled out for attack in relation to Schreiner's racial supremacism. Her evolutionary idea of humans . . . is painfully clear in this much-lauded feminist tract. . . . [Her] deployment of eugenic theory in the name of feminism is of course particularly troubling in the late twentieth century when notions of racial strength and purity immediately bring to mind the shadow of the Third Reich. . . . If Schreiner's anti-imperialist stance is clearly enough articulated . . . her position apropos of racism is much less clear cut. Her implied criticism of Tant 'Sannie's [a character in *The Story of An African Farm*] crude racism is undeniable. . . . [But] nor can Schreiner's representation of Tant' Sannie be exonerated from the charge of racism. . . . In this instance Schreiner's eugenicist thinking is cruelly racist towards 'the Boer woman' whom elsewhere she had defended. (Ledger, 1996: 74–81)

These quotations encapsulate the interlinked components of an emergent canon of facts about Olive Schreiner and her writing, facts inscribed by a succession of scholarly writing. What they add up to is a portrait of a woman, one in which the facts run along the following lines: Schreiner was a tempestuous genius in some respects, a child in others; her mind, like her letters, was egoistically focused on the trivia of her own life; she was also a neurotic whose damaged mind/emotions produced her own illnesses, first asthma and then heart disease; her prime concern was with gender issues, and, as gender is irrelevant to race, to be concerned with gender in a racist state like South Africa is to be a (proto-) racist; Schreiner was a Social Darwinist and racial primitivist; she was a bad novelist because she couldn't write a realist text; her novels should be read autobiographically and the 'failure' of these is emblematic of the failure of her life, for her inability to escape the confines of her egoistical self led to her failure as a novelist as well as a person; her eugenicism led her to be racist towards white as well as black people; and 'if, as the scholar claims', all these things are true claims the status of 'then it is so'.

However, these are *presumptively* canonical facts and they constitute 'a discourse' in the Foucauldian sense, as a successive set of claims-making located in a process which remains contested. That is, knowledge about Olive Schreiner does not exist in any absolute way, and these are emergent facts, claims-*making*, rather than claims-*made* and finished and settled for once and for all. Although relations within the contact zone may be asymmetrical, still there *are* contrary voices writing, speaking, finding, living, contrary facts. And so I now want to contrast these facts with some contrary facts which provoke and unsettle the truth-claims of the emergent orthodoxy. I turn attention to 'then', introducing these awkwardly contrary facts 'of the time' (which come from letters and other documents archived in South Africa) to stand alongside the presumptively canonical ones of 'now'.

The selections which follow address a number of the elements of the canonical claims-making:[9] that Schreiner's published letters can be taken as representative of what all her writing, and so she herself, was like; that her heart complaint was the product of neurotic exaggeration; that she did not support black civil rights; that issues of gender are separate from those of 'race'; and that because she wrote negatively about characters from oppressed 'racial' groups, she was racist:

> Today burnt all of Olive's Manuscripts, papers, &c, &c (including remainder of her journals). Those remaining are only a few . . . [and] are unimportant & [immaterial?]. . . . The last great holocaust was at Rosebank House, when I was with Alfred in 1921, before I went to England . . . Her letters to me were destroyed as I read them. (Cronwright Schreiner's diary, 22 November 1924, NELM 30.1.c ms. 1)

> Mrs Scott [a niece] kindly sent me this morning a sight of Dr Murray's [autopsy] report . . . I enclose you a rather poorly typed duplicate. . . . The 'coronary arteries' which were found so much 'occluded' are the only arteries which supply the substance of the heart with blood. Being for many years in the state they were found in, the heart has for all that time been starved of the blood necessary to enable its [filters?] to [be] nourished, so that they could contract, and so drive the blood through the body. This is the cause for all her life long sufferings – & eventually her death. (John Brown to CS, 16 December 1920, NELM 30.35.h)

> I am strongly opposed to the redistribution bill. I am a one adult one vote man [*sic*]. I believe that every adult inhabiting a land, irrespective of race, sex, wealth or [poverty?] should have the vote . . . I hold this view with exceeding conviction, & can give

reason for the faith that is in me. (Olive Schreiner to Will Schreiner, 12 June 1898, UCT)

Dear, to me the question of Woman emancipation in all ways seems just one of the root questions. Of course men must fight for it if they are freedom loving & human, just as women must fight for men. The whole question seems to me not one of sex but of common human duty & right. The insult seems to me to be, to take any notice of the sex of an individual in things which have nothing to do with the reproductive function or sex. (Olive Schreiner to Betty Molteno, 20 April 1907, UCT)

The woman's question is so truly just a part of the great democratic movement, & cannot be rightly looked at or understood in any other way. (Olive Schreiner to Will Schreiner, 12 August 1913, UCT)

Tante Sannie is a Dutch woman, Bonaparte Blenkins [another character in *The Story of An African Farm*] is an Irishman. Fancy my Home Rule friends crying out that I am false to the cause that I have traduced the Irishman!! It would be a sad day when each . . . character not ideally perfect was regarded as an attack upon the nation whose nationality it shared! (Olive Schreiner to Will Schreiner, February 1896(?), UCT)

These contrary facts do not 'add up' to the same sum as the canonical ones; they sit awkwardly, slantwise. But there is more to them than this, which relates to the 'I' which I have been trying not to excise from this text; that is, the 'I' of the writer.

What is apparent in this slantwise relationship of the canonical and the contrary is a process of claims-making which relies on an originatory point, occurring in 1924 or thereabouts; and this is contested and challenged by facts which cut across, contest, challenge, these claims. What is less apparent is that neither the canonical nor the contrary are 'natural facts', as it were. Both result from artifice, from those processes of selection in and out, arrangement, disposition, conclusion, which are as much foundational as the foundational facts of 'the things which irreducibly happened'. That is, the rhetoricity surrounding and representing these, and the irreducible things that happened themselves, are not now separable, if indeed they ever were.

There is something else here too. And this is that the 'then and now' effect that I have produced is precisely an *effect*. There is and there can be no 'then' in this piece of work, and this apparency of time is revealed by returning the excised 'I' to the text: 'I' now do this; these were not like this in their own time because not organized in this way and for such purposes. And the 'these' here who were not like this of course refers as much to the canonical claims-making as to the contrary voices I have set against this. I have selected and chosen, I have produced, I have written.

I have thereby demonstrated another of my points, the openness of the temporally uncontained contact zone to contestation. The writing 'I' is of course a part of the field of representation, not apart from it and merely commenting on it. It might be claimed, on behalf of some or all of the 'voices' I have included in my lineage of canonical claims-making, that I have been unfair by my ruthless excisions and selections, that I have excised the contrary positions *within* what they have written which dispute my argument and the use to which I have put their words here. I cheerfully assent to this charge, for this is precisely my point. In the material I have presented, I characterized some Schreiner scholars constructing 'the facts' in a way that shows their facts riding roughshod over contrary facts about Olive Schreiner. And part of my method has been to remove from sight the fact that there are other notable Schreiner scholars, for instance Joyce Avrech Berkman (1979, 1989) or Cherry Clayton (1983, 1997), who do not assent to some or all of these would-be canonical facts, who work with rather different ones. The result is that I thereby turned the interpretational tables, by putting the canonical them (and 'they' are of course in a more general sense all of us, myself included, who 'represent lives') in the position that they, we, put Schreiner and other 'past lives' in.

Having Your Representational Cake and Eating it Too

In this chapter I have been concerned with a number of general issues regarding how we think about, understand, research and write about lives in the past. Indeed, these are some of the most fundamental issues regarding inquiry and knowledge of *all* kinds, about inquiry in general, not only about past lives in particular. There is a foundational importance to taking seriously, in an analytic sense, the argument that we apprehend through representation and that there is no 'outside' the field of representation, for this is not something we can abandon, as an optional extra, but is precisely fundamental. However, 'representation' by itself provides an interesting but limited way of thinking about the consequences of these matters, for it keeps the inquiry in the realm of abstract discussion. And so 'thinking about representation' does not appear as an end in itself in what I have discussed, but is rather used as a stepping off point for thinking through metaphors and tropes, as a tool for inquiry and not a conclusion to it.

In this spirit, I have 'thought through' a number of metaphors or frames for thinking about past lives: a photographic representation 'touched up' or not, historiography/biography/autobiography as a Tardis or a time machine, thinking back from 'now' to 'then' being like a set of Russian dolls one inside another, and the central metaphor I have used, that of Pratt's 'contact zone'. The contact zone, I have proposed, is a tool to use, a means to think through, a frame for pursuing what can be done with it, and also what cannot. There are two caveats that occurred to me about the limitations Pratt imposes on the utility of the concept as a consequence of the uses to which I put it: its unnecessary temporal limitations, and its consequent excision of the writing 'I'.

Given my pursuit of lives in the past and how we apprehend and write about them, I have been interested in thinking through my re-working of the notion of the contact zone with time and 'I' inside, to historiography, biography and autobiography. Writing, I have proposed, acts as a kind of translation device that transmutes from one form into another, and it is a device that involves the elision of the argumentative chasm or gulf at its heart. Some of the aspects of writing histories and lives that particularly interest me are those which cohere around the rhetoricity of historiography, the excised or elided 'I' in the text, and the way time is 'flattened'.

'Putting time back in' by insisting upon the 'moment' of now, and thus of researching and writing and reading, as well as the 'historical moment' of then, when the events happened and the people lived, also has the paradoxical effect of removing it. This is because re-working the notion of the contact zone as a time zone including 'now' as well as 'then' points up the inevitable privileging of 'now', the point from which we apprehend. Insisting upon the role of writing as authorizing occasions the return of the excised 'I', the author; and it also places this figure in a landscape with other figures. That is, it makes it apparent that there is an epistemic community at work here, within which there are prevailing ideas about the topics, the methods, the ideas, the facts, the documents, and through which domain ideas become dominant discourses. However, like other discourses, those of scholarly epistemic communities are not absolute; rather, they involve centres and peripheries, contestations and change over time. And I have shown some aspects of this at work in relation to Olive Schreiner and the claims-making that has taken, and is taking, place around 'her'.

But what of 'actual lives' within what I have argued? Am I proposing that there is only writing and that lives of the past are not recoverable at best, mere fabrications of the researcher and of writing at worst? Am I arguing that there is no life in the contact zone? I have a number of responses here.

In insisting upon the importance of knowing and thinking about past lives, it remains important not to turn away from fundamental intellectual issues, to assign these to a different and antithetical form of academic feminism. If a feminist engagement with past lives is worth the candle, then the damned thing must burn; that is, it must consider, explore, take seriously, ideas which raise fundamental problematics in knowing, and it must not fudge the issues involved by retreating into descriptive notions of 'recovery'.

A key component in feminist inquiry is a commitment to accountable feminism, to a feminist position that is intellectually as much as politically accountable. The term I have invoked elsewhere to indicate this is 'intellectual biography' as a means of making accountable by inscribing the processes of researching and thinking within (rather than beneath the surface of) research accounts. It is important not to produce feminist knowledge in the same 'take it or leave it' form that other academic positions do. As part of this, it is important that we promote active readers who can engage with the claims-making of the things that are written; and to do this it is crucial to explore the processes, mechanics and effects of writing, as well as reading, about past lives.

The things I have been discussing here help in revealing the apparatus of power in the contact zone. Terms like 'canon', 'discourse', 'intellectual biography', 'claims-making', 'accountable feminism', are not twee little words. As an analytic set of tools for 'thinking through', they have the potential to make life uncomfortable for many people, feminist scholars among them. That is, these analytic ideas point up the fact that we too are implicated, that power does not stop; and they also suggest that there is something extremely intractable at work here, for giving up the assumed knowledge claims involved means confronting the possible demolition of (feminist or any other) academia as a source of epistemic privilege.

However, I am determined to have my representational cake and eat it too, for I do indeed want it all. There is a certain irreducibility to the past, for there were things that happened, howsoever rhetorically inscribed, surrounded and apprehended these may be. I am at least as interested in 'what happened' as other people, and indeed much of my scholarly life has been in pursuit of thinking about and thinking through the lives of Hannah Cullwick, Arthur Munby, Emily Wilding Davidson and comrades, and Olive Schreiner. However, I have never thought this was easy, nor have I ever thought that academic feminism should be a means of legitimating claims to epistemic privilege. Even so, I determinedly retain the right to see some facts as preferable to other facts; but the question, the awkward, contentious, contested, fascinating question, is, which ones are these?

The bald answer to my title's question, 'Is there life in the contact zone?' is, then, both no and yes. No, there isn't, in the resurrectionalist sense of 'recovering the past'; yes, there is, in the sense that there were things that happened and people who lived. But the answer isn't terribly interesting – it is the question, and the issues it raises, that incites, provokes, interests.

Notes

1 I am extremely grateful to the Faculty of Arts at the University of Auckland, New Zealand, who awarded me a Senior Research Fellowship during 1998, during which time this chapter and a good deal more was written. My Fellowship was held in Women's Studies, and I am grateful in particular to Hana Mat' au, Maureen Malloy and Heather Worth for making my time there enjoyable as well as productive. I am also very grateful to Mary Madden for some interesting and useful comments on a draft. I wish to acknowledge the National English Literary Museum (NELM) in Grahamstown and the J.W. Jagger Library at the University of Cape Town (UCT) for helpful assistance and permissions to publish from their Schreiner collections. I am particularly grateful to Ann Torlesse at NELM and Lesley Hart at UCT.
2 The origins of this chapter lie in a plenary address, 'Holding out an Olive branch: Representational issues in the feminist interpretation of lives in relation to canonical and contrary facts about Olive Schreiner', which I gave to the conference on 'Representing Lives: Women & Auto/ Biography', Nottingham Trent University, 1997. My thanks to Pauline Polkey and Alison Donnell for inviting me to do this, and also for their invitation to contribute to this collection.
3 See First and Scott (1980), Berkman (1989), Clayton (1997) and Stanley

(1999) for successive and contrasting approaches to understanding the life, work and context of Olive Schreiner.

4 My theoretical ideas about 'auto/biography' are drawn together in Stanley (1992) as well as having been discussed in a number of articles published both before and after this. For a more detailed discussion in relation to Olive Schreiner, see Stanley (1999).

5 For one discussion of everyday autobiography, see Smith and Watson (1996); for a contrasting approach, see Stanley (1998).

6 I couple (or rather triple) historiography, biography and autobiography herein because they are the prime genres of writing concerned with the past.

7 And this, she notes in 'The South African Nation', published as a 'note' to *Thoughts* by Cronwright-Schreiner (332–4) is unlike any other British colony, for if the English left New Zealand or Australia then over two-thirds of their population would vanish; but in South Africa, even the Cape Colony, they constitute only around a twentieth of the population and their entire absence would be hardly missed because of the socially, educationally and occupationally increasingly differentiated Afrikaner population.

8 Some readers may object here that Schreiner, as white and of English extraction, was an outsider in 'race' terms in South Africa. This is part of her point, that all the composing peoples of South Africa were outsiders to the others. Howsoever readers may want to dispute her ideas about the peoples involved and the ensuing relations between them, it cannot be denied that she is centrally aware of the problem and the issues involved.

9 But not all of them, for reasons of space.

References

Abrams, P. *Historical Sociology* (Shepton Mallet: Open Books, 1982)

Barash, C. 'Virile Womanhood: Olive Schreiner's Fantasies of a Master Race', *Women's Studies International Forum*, 9 (1986) 333–40

Beeton, R. *Olive Schreiner, A Short Guide to Her Writings* (Cape Town: Howard Timmins, 1974)

—— *Facets of Olive Schreiner: A Manuscript Sourcebook* (Johannesburg: Donker, 1987)

Berkman, J. A. *Olive Schreiner: Feminism on the Frontier* (St Albans, Vt: Eden Press, 1979)

—— *The Healing Imagination of Olive Schreiner: Beyond South African Colonialism* (Oxford: Plantin Publishers, 1989)

Burdett, C. 'Thrown Together: Olive Schreiner, Writing and Politics' in Kate Campbell (ed.) *Critical Feminism: Argument in the Discipline* (Milton Keynes: Open University Press, 1992) 107–21

—— 'A Difficult Vindication: Olive Schreiner's Wollstonecraft Introduction', *History Workshop Journal* 37 (1994a) 177–87

Certeau, M. de *The Writing of History* (New York: Columbia University Press, [1975] 1988)

Clayton, C. (ed.) *Olive Schreiner* (Johannesburg: McGraw-Hill, 1983)

—— *Olive Schreiner*, Twayne's World Authors Series (New York: Twayne Publishers, 1997)

Collingwood, R. W. *An Autobiography* (Oxford: Clarendon Press, 1927)

—— *The Idea of History* (Oxford: Clarendon Press, 1948)

Cronwright-Schreiner, S. 'Cron' *The Life of Olive Schreiner* (London: Fisher Unwin, 1924)

Derrida, J. 'The art of *Mémoires*' in his *Mémoires for Paul de Man* (New York: Columbia University Press, [1986] 1989) 47–88

First, R. and Scott, A. *Olive Schreiner* (London: André Deutch, 1983)

Gilbert, S. and Gubar, S. *No Man's Land: The Place of the Woman Writer in the Twentieth Century, Vol. 2: Sexchanges* (New Haven, Conn.: Yale University Press, 1989)

Gordimer, N. 'The Prison-house of Colonialism: Review of First and Scott's *Olive Schreiner*' in C. Barash (ed.) *An Olive Schreiner Reader* (London: Pandora Press, [1980] 1987) (reprinted from the *Times Literary Supplement*, 15 August 1980, 221–7)

Grimshaw, J. 'Philosophy and the Feminist Imagination'. Transformations, Feminist Theory Conference, University of Lancaster, UK (1997)

Horton, S. *Difficult Women, Artful Lives: Olive Schreiner and Isak Dinesen, In and Out of Africa* (Baltimore, Md: Johns Hopkins University Press, 1995)

Ledger, S. (ed.) *The New Woman: Fiction and Feminism at the Fin de Siècle* (Manchester: Manchester University Press, 1996)

Lewsen, P. 'Olive Schreiner's Political Theories and Pamphlets', in C. Clayton (ed.) *Olive Schreiner* (Johannesburg: McGraw-Hill, 1983) 212–20

Miller, N. *Getting Personal: Feminist Occasions and Other Autobiographical Acts* (New York: Routledge, 1991)

Parkin-Gounelas, R. *Fictions of the Female Self: Charlotte Brontë, Olive Schreiner, Katherine Mansfield* (London: Macmillan, 1991)

Pratt, M. L. *Imperial Eyes: Travel Writing and Transculturation* (London: Routledge, 1992)

Schreiner, O. *The Political Situation* (London: Unwin, 1896)

—— *An English South African's View of the Situation. Words in Season* (London: Hodder & Stoughton, 1899)

—— *Closer Union* (London: Fifield, 1908)

—— *Thoughts on South Africa* (London: Unwin, 1923)

—— *From Man to Man; Or, Perhaps Only . . .* (London: Unwin, 1926)

Smith, S. and Watson, J. (eds) *Getting a Life: Everyday Uses of Autobiography* (Minneapolis: University of Minnesota Press, 1996)

Stanley, L. *The Auto/Biographical I: The Theory and Practice of Feminist Auto/Biography* (Manchester: Manchester University Press, 1992)

—— 'Auto/biographical Practices and Self-surveillances: On Organizational Encounters and Audit Selves', Surveillance: An International Conference, Liverpool John Moores University, UK (1998)

—— *Imperialism, Labour and the 'New Woman'* (London: Sage Publications, 1999, in press)

Woolf, V. 'Olive Schreiner' in V. Woolf, *Women and Writing*, M. Barrett intro. (London: The Women's Press, [1925] 1979)

Part I
Placing the Subject

1

First Person Suspect, or, the Enemy Within . . .

Julia Swindells

This chapter, not accidentally drafted two months after the first Labour government in 18 years had come to power, is not so much a recantation – although there are elements of that – as an attempt to review some of the assumptions which I have brought to bear on the study of autobiography over a period of about 20 years. In the process, though, I aim at more than an autobiographical account, in the sense that I do not believe that I have been alone in making some of these assumptions. The period of which I speak, from the emergence of what we have come to call the second wave of the women's movement until the present, has given a particular character to autobiography, and to its uses and its study. This movement has not been confined to Britain, but because my approach is one that also sets out to engage with British national politics, I hope I may be forgiven for engaging exclusively with writings emerging from this context. What I may not be forgiven for, though, is that my approach also deviates from the past, in that most of my work on autobiography has focused directly on the writings and oral testimonies of working-class women and others speaking from a position of oppression. However, despite the change of focus for this account, I shall hope to persuade you that the politics of oppression and the means of resisting it remain my primary concern. To be more specific, I shall turn away for the purposes of this exercise, from the other side of silence, from hidden writings and voices, and turn to a much more noisy sphere, that of the autobiographical writings of some distinguished individuals. I do so in an attempt, not to give more exposure to those already in the public eye, although of course I run that risk, but to illuminate some questions about the politics of autobiographical use not so readily available from a scrutiny of oppressed people's representations of self.

One of my major assumptions has been that there is a certain exclusivity and gender specificity with which prominent men have asserted their claim to speak for history via autobiography. An obvious twentieth-century example has been the way in which Winston Churchill's memoirs of the Second World War (1948) have now come to stand for, albeit perhaps only from the British perspective, the authoritative version of how that history happened. Feminist historians have redressed the balance with an insistence on the inclusion of documenting women's contribution to that set of experiences, but the agenda has been rather specifically that of augmenting the account, perhaps at most implying that the male-authored account is incomplete. There has been little direct criticism, though, of the Churchill account itself, either to contest its historical accuracy, or more importantly for my purposes here, to challenge his use of autobiography to assert and further the prominence of himself in that history.

I have argued elsewhere that it was Victorian Britain that consolidated various strong relationships between men and professional power (Swindells, 1985). The kind of authority which Churchill could claim in the twentieth century derives not only from the mere fact of his having been a British wartime prime minister, but from a powerful legacy authenticating the representation of male selfhood. John Ruskin has by no means made the claims of a Winston Churchill, but his autobiography, *Praeterita*, is notable for the confidence with which it establishes a version of this confident male selfhood of which I speak. Ruskin could be acclaimed for having produced the model autobiography of the nineteenth-century critical commentator and analyst. The persona is that of the professional writer whose selfhood is confirmed and consolidated by his readership.[1] It appears ironic and certainly poignant that the autobiography was written at the very moment of greatest mental turmoil and incoherence in Ruskin's life. Biographers comment on the 'violent and bitter' character of most of his later writings, and on the apparent mental instability, in the form of rages and 'brain fever', which beset his later years (Ruskin, 1885–9). However, the autobiography to which he wrote the initial preface in 1885 took even its author by surprise in its qualities of ease and amusement, and in its ability to reach beyond the measure of 'an old man's recreation in gathering visionary flowers in fields of youth' (Ruskin, 1885: Preface). It appears

that, at the very moment of greatest personal uncertainty and confusion, Ruskin puts autobiography to the service of asserting and
promoting professional identity. In an uncertain world, the one
thing he can be certain of is his readership, which will be constituted out of 'my friends' and 'those of the public who have been
pleased by my books' (Ruskin, 1885: Preface). The dynamic and
coherence of the autobiographical narrative come from the writer's
relationship with his public, constituting the autobiographical persona in ways which significantly bypass and perhaps even compensate
for the growing incoherence of what is commonly understood as
personal life. The capacity for autobiography to authenticate a male
self in the public sphere overrides and overtakes the disturbances
of the personal. It is this kind of legacy on which Churchill and
others draw in the twentieth century, as the tradition is one in
which, whatever the personal vicissitudes of the author, the public
and professional world will supply coherence, and will do so across
the male kinship of that world, from writers to politicians.

A related assumption to the one that men could use autobiography in this particular way has been that women could not do so.
One might assume that a contemporary of John Ruskin's, living in
England, of a similar class background, might have access to autobiography, both in relation to how they might perceive an authorial
use of the mode and a readership for autobiographical writing, in
similar terms to those of Ruskin. Although this is a very cursory
glimpse at their writings, I have therefore chosen to make reference to two Victorian women, Elizabeth Garrett Anderson, the doctor,
and Mary Somerville, the scientist, born a generation earlier, who
might in some senses be seen as occupying an analogous space to
that of John Ruskin. Both write, like Ruskin, to engage specifically
with the relationship between the professional and the personal
life. Both write, like Ruskin, out of a sense that that activity can
provide a means of surviving difficulties. In each case, though, there
is no formal autobiography, but interventions from devoted daughters
seeking to affirm the lives of mothers who undertook the struggle
for political power and professional recognition for women.[2] Louisa
Garrett Anderson, the daughter, comments directly on the importance to her mother of writing as part of the means of 'survival' of
medical training, but the activity takes place at personal and intimate levels in the form of letters, mostly written to women friends.
It is arguable that Elizabeth Garrett Anderson and Mary Somerville
did not write formal autobiographies because their focus was elsewhere

than on the documentation of personal success. Certainly, there is evidence from those who correspond with them, and from their daughters, that driving ambitions in relation to their professional pursuits derived more from a passion for fighting in the cause of women's political and professional rights, than the pursuit of personal glory (see Anderson, 1939: 106–7). This, in itself, raises significant questions about the autobiographical act. It is also possible, though, that the mode would not have been available to them in the way that it was to Ruskin, in that professional identity could not compensate for the personal life in the same way. Rather, to the contrary, it was the precariousness of relationship to their respective professions which threatened to destroy personal life rather than cover for it. Elizabeth Garrett Anderson writes to Emily Davies, 'Do you ever feel wearied with your own want of power?', as if to offer one of a number of indicators that the relationship between personal and professional life is a source of fatigue and friction, not able to supply coherence, let alone authentication (68–9).

These nineteenth-century differences between the genders in the production of autobiographical discourse can be categorized in terms of minorities and of margins. Women were, of course, exceptions in terms of professional power and influence, and their lack of access to autobiography as an authenticating form can be explained in socio-political terms peculiar, perhaps, to the nineteenth century. These forms of rationale are not so easily available in the late twentieth century, when women have greater access to professional power and assured roles in the public sphere. For this reason, and prompted by the valediction to Conservatism enacted in the 1997 general election, I decided to read Margaret Thatcher's *The Downing Street Years* (1993), taking a look in one direction at what the contrasts might be with women writing a century earlier, such as Elizabeth Garrett Anderson and Mary Somerville, and in another direction at the male model from John Ruskin to Winston Churchill. At first glance, Thatcher's autobiography would appear to share many features associated with Churchill's memoirs. Here is a prime minister who can speak, through her own life-experience, of an entire decade and longer, of British political history. Like Churchill, she has a set of enemies to demonize, reserving her greatest intransigence for 'the enemy within', Arthur Scargill and the National Union of Mineworkers. Hers is a Manichean world in which the first person of autobiography is sustained in a crusade against her adversaries, who are deployed as the antagonists of the autobiographical plot.

(This is not exclusively class war in that the miners are not the only enemy. Other targets are the British Broadcasting Corporation and indeed the state itself.)

Chapter 13 of *The Downing Street Years* documents the miners' strike of 1984–5. In a prelude, Thatcher establishes that she 'had never had any doubt' about the background to the strike. It was politically motivated by Marxists, for whom 'the institutions of democracy' were no more than 'tiresome obstacles' (1993: 339). On the very first page of the chapter, Thatcher inscribes herself as the heroine of the piece, defending the institutions of democracy against their enemies, Marxists and miners. And this is not the only occasion on which she uses the word 'doubt' to declare that she has none; hers is a position free of anything other than the utmost certainty about her own identification with democracy and the strategies necessary to defend it. Indeed, there is a rather curious lack of reflection about her inscription of the autobiographical I, as if she simply believes herself to personify democracy, representing herself as apparently disinterested, constituting herself not as an individual absorbed in self, but as an iconic or symbolic figure, the Iron Lady, Britannia. The more this conflation is made, though, the more the representation of miners eludes any kind of rational explanation for her. Mining is construed as an industry where 'reason simply did not apply', and by the 1970s, it has 'come to symbolize everything that was wrong with Britain' (340). Arthur Scargill, president of the NUM, is a 'Marxist', a 'militant', whose purposes are 'openly political' and 'ulterior', and who is 'preparing to lead his troops into battle' (343). The more that Scargill is demonized, the more Thatcher assumes her ability to eradicate both the mining industry and its union, in the name of democracy, and the more she adopts the stance of a military rather than a political leader. The criticism that Scargill has a political purpose, whilst it is meant to defame him, actually illuminates the ulterior purpose of her own endeavour to engage not in a political struggle or strategy, but in a military one. She intends to wage war.

When the strike begins on 12 March 1984, she declares that it marks the end of 'rationality and decency' (345). Her ratification of her own persona and role accretes to the point where she believes herself to be the personal target of the enemy who represents the destruction of all significant values. She has no doubt that she *is* reason and decency. Militaristic images accumulate as other parties enter the 'battle'. When the management of the National Coal Board appears to waver in its coercive tactics, she insists a 'responsible government' has to intervene. She justifies the same strategy with the police, who must have 'the complete moral and practical support of the government' (348). These are bodies which had the means to maintain their autonomy, and their doing so is central to the operation of a democratic state; but the controlling 'I' of Thatcher extends to the management of all forces of perceived disorder, in this Manichean world, where all must take sides. Whilst acknowledging the sanctity of the judicial system ('the independence of the judiciary is a matter of constitutional principle' (348)), she even has to resist an impulse to interfere here, so that more of 'the men of violence', not the IRA, but the striking miners, can be brought to justice. As the strike gathers force, the Manichean world intensifies to the point where she believes that 'there was a preternatural alliance between these different forces of disorder' (354).

The only moment of apparent faltering of the forward movement of the juggernaut occurs when Harold Macmillan goes public in his support of miners and their communities.[3] Suddenly, there is the possibility of a different stance from militarism within the Conservative Party, marked by compassion and understanding. The strategy which she decides to adopt in the wake of support for Macmillan, though, is as calculated as previously in terms of military tactics against the enemy. She sets out to drive a wedge between striking miners and working miners, whose wives she invites to her home to offer tea, sympathy and – some might say – crocodile tears.

This discussion is not intended as anything resembling a comprehensive account of Thatcher's self-representation, a process which has been carried out more systematically by others. Additionally, my perspective shifted during the course of my reading, from the expectation that the narrative and first person would embody some distinctive and revealing characteristics of the woman as governmental and national leader, to the growing certainty that the country had been in the hands of a fanatic, unable to distinguish between military and political decisions, and intensely conflating the country's interests with her own, to the point of utter denial of any discrimination. Initially, I had been somewhat deceived by that apparent disinterestedness in the autobiographical text, deriving from the iconic status which Thatcher confers upon herself, and in which there is very little explicit representation or promotion of the personal life. The book opens with one or two touches about life with Dennis – 'What a man. What a husband. What a friend' (23) – and the need for new wallpaper at Number 10; but otherwise, what we generally take to be the personal is largely absent. However, as I read on, I began to see that this apparent lack of absorption in self, alongside the absence of explicit reference to self-interest or acknowledgement of individual drive or competition, was part of the success of the strategy. All interests were subsumed in that of the leader of the cause, and the authentication of that leadership.

As the narrative develops, the autobiographical 'I' accumulates to itself suggestions of megalomania and paranoia, as in the suggestion that 'preternatural' forces are conspiring against the autobiographical subject. 'The enemy within', a phrase which Thatcher somewhat unconvincingly attempts to distance herself from, later, in its literal application to the miners, begins to be a significant way of describing Thatcher herself, the autobiographical subject, engaging in warfare at every level, in the name of the country's interests. A return to the issue of the autobiographer's gender draws us to consider Margaret Thatcher as a woman modelling herself on such male leaders as Churchill, utilizing his ability to speak for the nation via a displacement of self into the vocabulary of combat, competition and triumphalism. The distinction, though, is that Thatcher writes of peacetime, rather than of war. The woman prime minister thus pathologizes the male model of leadership, transforming the projection of self as hero into a version of the autobiographical subject dependent, for its coherence, upon discovering enemies everywhere.

In the long term, I doubt if Thatcher's autobiographical writings will come to stand for an epoch (the 1980s) in the way in which Churchill's have for the war years. It is no secret and no shame that she was helped by a team of researchers in putting the text together, and the book reads as if one or more of them may have acted in some capacity as 'ghost' writer. Certainly, her own highly characteristic speech, however far it was modified over time by the Saatchi and Saatchi treatment, is not particularly apparent in the first-person voice. Unlike Churchill, the distinctiveness and distinguishing character of a personal, political rhetoric has been rendered anodyne. Nevertheless, it is on his model that she draws, with the supposed success of the nation standing as alibi for the coherence of the self. Earlier women – Elizabeth Garrett Anderson and Mary Somerville – could not have mapped themselves on to that mode of writing, not only because they were not in a position to simulate or emulate male leadership, but also because that elision of the personal into the public would not have been acceptable in Victorian women. Questions about the hidden agenda of the personal would have prohibited such an evacuation.

If we could discuss *The Downing Street Years* as utterly peculiar to an excessively dangerous woman, or even as a neutral account of Conservatism, or the 1980s, or any other specific category, we might consign Thatcher's autobiographical writings to the dustbin of history, glad that we have now got shot of her and not too concerned at what kind of betrayal of women she represented. The case, though, can be taken beyond Thatcher to other political leaders, the powers they aggregate to themselves, and the ways in which they use memoirs to justify, endorse, consolidate and further their world-view, making use of the capacity of the autobiographical text to generalize from the self to the entire moral and political panoply. Less obviously, the case can also be taken in the direction of ourselves, including in the direction of feminism and the women's movement.

The final stage of my discussion, at once the most tentative and the most potentially controversial, relates to the question of how far autobiography in general, even that which has been written and read in the context of the women's movement, is inescapably caught up in something like the Thatcher mode, in which the engagement of the first person is necessarily suspect, inseparable from the promotion of self in terms which make aggrandising claims about the individual and beyond the individual to the social structure, or pathological in relation to a model which derives from male leadership and authority, demonizing others as the enemy. On occasions, it is as if experiencing as a woman is not only held to be an authentication in itself, but also manages that authenticity by rendering all other positions from the one held by the protagonist as potentially demonic.[4] Thatcher seems to me one who, par excellence, establishes identity as power, to be used for the purposes of her own empowerment. But does the autobiographical I, in general, rely on a similar process of accumulating to itself a power and authority, in the name of a supposedly charismatic individualism, that no single person should claim in a democratic society?[5] Moreover, did the influence of 18 years of Conservatism in Britain result in the gradual hardening of the case, so that the articulation of the first person has become indistinguishable from the exercise of self-interest, alongside a tendency to find the self at war with the other(s)?

In short, is autobiography in Britain, for the moment at least, too hopelessly compromised (not *least* by 18 years of Conservatism) to service the politics of oppression? Should the activity of considering autobiography as a means of celebrating women's lives be subjected to more rigorous scrutiny than it has been until now? We might now turn to other, more public genres in the world of creativity, such as theatre and other performance arts, such as film and television, in our search for less self-absorbed versions of the female self? Such a move would not mean, though, that there is not a substantial amount of critical work to do on writings like those of Margaret Thatcher, which use autobiography as a means of abusing the institutions of democracy whilst operating in their name, and persuade the reader to collude in that gross deception.[6] Most importantly, if we are to prevent from happening again anything like that régime, we should certainly be alert to that projection of self which sustains its own supposedly charismatic individualism on the basis of a Manichean universe which demonizes its own version of the enemy within, particularly where that projection imposes upon us woman against women.

Notes

1   Ruskin (1988) first published in 28 parts between 1885 and 1889. My claim for the autobiography rests predominantly on volume I of the three-volume work, which forms the major part of it. Ruskin does not attempt to maintain the fluency of his prose in the subsequent volumes. In volume III, it is as if he eschews coherent prose altogether (his command over which contemporaries, including Oscar Wilde, had commented with much approval) in favour of note form, anecdote and, towards the conclusion, a transition into biography of those who had brought warmth into his life. It is as if the autobiographer as writer is laying himself to rest. Columbus (1979) goes further in arguing that *Praeterita* does not demonstrate 'the art of autobiography' so much as, 'thanatography, the re-expression of repressions of original and static death'. Also Peterson (1986) for a comprehensive and compelling account of Ruskin's hermeneutic method and the relationship of *Praeterita* to spiritual autobiography.
2   Anderson (1939), Somerville (1873).
3   All that Thatcher explicitly says about the Macmillan speech, apart from the fact that it criticized the government's handling of the strike, is that it was 'characteristically elegant', and that it was given at the Carlton Club (1993: 370). Immediately following this reference, though, comes a specific association of the NUM leadership with the terrorists who had planted the bomb at the Brighton Grand Hotel during the Conservative Party Conference, killing and maiming some members of the government.
4   A recent example in Cambridge is of how Germaine Greer has relied on

her prominence as a feminist to make a public attack on a woman physicist, vituperatively attacking the latter's right to be at Newnham College, which still has an exclusively female fellowship, on the sole grounds that the applicant was born a man. The logic of Greer's position is that only she who is born a woman can claim the rights and benefits that should accrue to that gender. However, my point is not primarily that Greer ignores 20 years of debate about the cultural construction of gender, although that is glaring, but that she foregrounds biological womanhood both as an authentication of her own critical position and in demonizing another human being.

5   When we come to write a curriculum vitae, we necessarily engage with a Thatcherite strategy, aggrandising our own role in history, deliberately, if only by implication, at the expense of other people. Do we, in the process of writing autobiographically in *whatever* context, promote ourselves, inadvertently or consciously, at the expense of other women, at the expense of members of oppressed groups, in the name of the supposedly radical female first person?

6   I am grateful to David Whitley, English Department, Homerton College, for a reading of this chapter, and his summary of its intended message, that of, 'maintaining vigilance against the rhetorical and autobiographically sanctioned manoeuvres of the dark, still recent, Thatcherite past'.

References

Anderson, L. G. *Elizabeth Garrett Anderson, 1936–1917* (London: Faber, 1939)

Churchill, W. *The Second World War*, 6 vols (London: Cassell, 1948)

Columbus, C. K. (1979) 'Ruskin's *Praeterita* as Thanatography', in G. P. Landow (ed.) *Approaches to Victorian Autobiography* (Ohio: Ohio University Press, 1979)

Ruskin, J. *Praeterita, The Autobiography of John Ruskin*, K. Clark intro. (Oxford: Oxford University Press, [1885–9] 1988)

Peterson, L. H. *Victorian Autobiography, The Tradition of Self-interpretation* (New Haven and London: Yale University Press, 1986)

Somerville, M. *Memoirs of Mary Somerville: Personal Recollections, From Early Life to Old Age, with Selections From her Correspondence by her Daughter, Martha Somerville* (London: Murray, 1873)

Swindells, J. *Victorian Writing and the Working Woman: The Other Side of Silence* (Cambridge: Polity Press, 1985)

—— (ed.) *The Uses of Autobiography* (London: Taylor & Francis, 1995)

Thatcher, M. *The Downing Street Years* (London: HarperCollins, 1993)

2
Korean American National Identity in Theresa Hak Kyung Cha's *Dictee*

Helena Grice

Theresa Hak Kyung Cha was born in Korea in 1951, and emigrated with her family to the United States in 1962, where she lived first in Hawaii, then San Francisco. She was educated at the University of San Francisco, then at the University of California at Berkeley, where she studied performance and film theory. After graduating, Cha embarked upon a varied and experimental career as a film-maker and artist, and her work won several prestigious awards, including a Beard's Fund award in 1982. Her auto/biographical text *Dictee* was first published by Tanam Press in 1982, just before she was tragically killed in New York City, on 5 November of that year. Critical recognition of *Dictee* has thus largely occurred posthumously, with a range of articles discussing the text appearing with increasing frequency from 1983 onwards. This critical attention has most recently culminated in the publication in 1994 of a collection of essays on *Dictee*, entitled *Writing Self, Writing Nation*.

Many of the responses to *Dictee* which have appeared in recent years have focused upon its postmodernist tendencies, most notably its fragmented nature, suspicion of the mimetic capabilities of language and its challenge to the authority of certain discourses.[1] However, as Elaine Kim has insisted, *Dictee* must be read first and foremost as a Korean (American) text, in which Cha elaborates upon a gendered and hybrid – but, yes, also fragmented and uncertain – national identity which she claims as her own. It is true that *Dictee* may offer the reader the promise of many of the narrative strategies and textual features that have been identified with postmodernism in recent years. The same is true of many other Asian American

43

texts: one may think of Maxine Hong Kingston's *The Woman Warrior* (1976) and *China Men* (1981) as other apposite examples. However, as with Kingston's works, Cha's text utilizes a range of writerly strategies that have come to be associated with postmodernism as part of her primary project of creating a Korean (American) national identity which is gendered. As I will argue, Cha attempts to tell her personal and national stories through female voices which are fractured and at times evasive, in contrast to the male 'authorized' narrative voices with which they are juxtaposed in the text.

Dictee contains nine sections: each named after one of the Greek muses. Of these, three of the earlier sections deal explicitly with issues of Korean and Korean American national identity and history from a gendered perspective, and these will form the basis of my discussion. 'Clio/History' deals with the Japanese invasion of Korea and the student uprising against that regime in 1919; 'Calliope/ Epic Poetry' with the experience of deracination, both during the period of Japanese occupation and Cha's own experience of immigration to America; and 'Melpomene/Tragedy' deals with Korean division into the North and the South in 1949 by the United States and the then USSR, and the subsequent war between the two newly created countries. Before the first section opens, one of the epigraphs of the text introduces the themes of alienated identity and division, themes which are developed throughout the text. This epigraph lists the many ways in which identity may be classified officially:

> From A Far
> What nationality
> or what kindred and relation
> what blood relation
> what blood ties of blood
> what ancestry
> what race generation
> what house clan tribe stock strain
> what lineage extraction
> what breed sect gender domination caste. (1995: 20)

These identity classifications proliferate and multiply through the epigraph, moving from national differences, to those of genealogy and biology. The shoring up of these differences stresses the myriad potential divisions between people and thus serves to set the tone of division and schism that dominates the text.

The first section, 'Clio/History', immediately sets Cha's agenda, by opening with female history: a picture and brief biography of Yu Guan Soon, a Korean female nationalist revolutionary. Elaine Kim has written that Yu Guan Soon's role in the nationalist movement in Korea was de-emphasized in national histories. By opening with her picture and biography, Cha places Soon in a position of central importance in her version (1994: 16). Cha's self-proclaimed aim in this section, as its title suggests, is the re-examination and re-evaluation of national history: 'to examine whether the parts are false real according to History's revision' (1995: 28). Cha continually emphasizes her nationalist sentiments. She writes: 'There is no people without a nation, no people without ancestry. There are no nations no matter how small their land, who have their independence. But our country, even with 5,000 years of history, has lost it to the Japanese' (28). This statement leads into a quotation from a history text's version of Japanese colonization, which is then juxtaposed with the far more personal story of Yu Guan Soon's involvement. It is the personal tale of a 'heroine in history', Cha tells us, directing us how to read her story (30).

Rather than measure the events according to the nation's time, in telling Yu Guan Soon's story events are measured in relation to Yu Guan Soon's own life. Thus, Yu Guan Soon's own life and experience are placed on a par with the national story. 'History' is treated as a burden by Cha, the 'old wound' from which both nation and individual are struggling to recover (30). This intensely personal exploration of Cha's relationship with her history is contrasted strongly with its location alongside the quoted petition from Koreans in Hawaii to President Roosevelt requesting intervention in Korea, which follows. This repeatedly enacted shift from personal to national, from subjective to objective, argues for the inextricability of personal and collective experience and identity. In this section, as well as dealing with the Japanese invasion, Cha addresses both the student uprising of 1 March 1919 and Yu Guan Soon's role in this. So Cha not only relates the historical story of repression, but always also includes the resistance to that story.

'Calliope/Epic Poetry' shifts the attention from one female Korean to another, in this case Cha's mother's experience during the Japanese invasion and occupation. It relates the story of Cha's mother, Hyung Soon Huo, through utilizing her own journal material to construct the story of Hyung's flight from Korea to Manchuria, where she became a teacher (45). Although reliant upon Hyung's journals,

Cha relates this section through the construction of a second-person address to her mother. This is another way of affording the woman control over her own story: she is both source and addressee of her own tale. This continues the dual emphasis upon the experience of deracination and the burden of remembering, as the references to 'Refugees. Immigrants. Exiles' in Hyung's 'ever-present memory' show (45). Cha continually stresses the 'either/or' logic of conflict and of identity at this moment: the mother can be either Chinese or Korean, but not both: 'You are not Chinese. You are Korean' she notes, as later, the choice becomes even more specific, between North or South Korean identity (45). In fact, Cha suggests that identity is always defined in oppositional ways and is subject to a binary logic: one is what one is not, a logic that continually stresses difference.

When Cha told Yu Guan Soon's story, the tale kept narrative pace with the national story. Here, too, Cha demonstrates how Hyung's life patterns the developments in Korean history. For example, she tells us that her mother became a teacher in Manchuria when 'Japan had already occupied Korea' (48). This serves to stress the causality of history upon the individual: all of these women's lives are controlled by their national as well as personal histories.

Cha then shifts her perspective to the United States. She tells us that she still looks back to Korea psychologically: 'I write. I write you. Daily,' she says, addressing both mother and nation (56). From this perspective, she turns to her own deracination, providing an explicit parallel with her mother's political exile. Cha recites the American naturalization oath, thus shifting from the process of colonization and its damaging effects upon personal and national identity to the process of naturalization, the conferment of citizenship and the national identity that this is supposed to provide:

> I have the documents. Documents, proof, evidence, photograph, signature. One day you raise the right hand and you are American. . . . Pass port. The United States of America. Somewhere someone has taken my identity and replaced it with their photograph. The other one. Their signature their seals. Their own image. (56)

This procedure is supposed to transform the Korean into an American citizen, but this remains an incomplete and flawed national identity, because it remains an externally imposed identity and fails to transform Cha's internal identification as Korean. It bestows an 'unformed' identity (57). By repeating the naturalization oath, Cha

stages a 'drama of identity' (Wald, 1995: 300) in which even the
accumulation of all the accoutrements of official identity – photographs, passport, signatures, seals, evidence, documents – are not
enough to render Cha an American. Rather than conferring a new
identity, this oath robs Cha of her Korean identity. The emphasis
is upon the alienation that this externally imposed official identity
causes; it is 'their photograph'; as well as depersonalizing experience: '*some*where *some*one' (Cha, 1995: 56; emphasis added). Even
Cha's right hand is experienced as alien as it performs the bodily
ritual accompanying naturalization: '*the* right hand' (56; emphasis
added). Rather than conferring an American identity, the naturalization oath simply allows Cha to reflect back an American identity
that she does not possess, but can only mirror in 'their own image'
(57). Figured as an empty vessel at this moment, Cha has no identity herself. Her Korean identity has been 'taken', and she is able
only to reflect back someone else's identity.

The inefficacy of the naturalization oath in conferring a stable
national identity upon Cha is highlighted on her subsequent trip
to Korea. This ceremony has failed to resolve Cha's identity differences from both Korea and America:

> You return and you are not one of them. . . . But the papers give
> you away. Every ten feet They ask you identity. . . . They say
> you look other than you say. As if you didn't know who you
> were. You say who you are but you begin to doubt. They search
> you. They, the anonymous variety of uniforms, each division,
> strata, classification, any set of miscellaneous properly uniformed.
> They have the right, no matter what rank, however low their
> function they have the authority. Their authority sewn into the
> stitches of their costume. Every ten feet they demand to know
> who and what you are, who is represented. The eyes gather to-
> wards the appropriate proof. Towards the face then again to the
> papers. (56–7)

Cha's return to Korea emphasizes the connections between personal
and national identity. National identity is emphasized through references to uniforms, which are shown to possess the ability to confer
an official identity, an authority and the 'right' to commit acts in
the name of that identity, however pernicious they may be. Cha's
own national identity is shown to contrast with her personal identity: her papers – official documents – speak of her identity as

American, whereas her visual identity is Korean. Her papers 'give [her] away', thus illustrating that it is always the national identity that is the most dominant.

'Melpomene/Tragedy', the final section I shall discuss, addresses the division of Korea into two halves, North and South, and opens with a map of Korea divided. This section depicts the nation/woman as divided and broken down. Once again this figures the body and the body politic as one. This leads into a letter addressed to Cha's mother, in which Cha speaks of the war between the North and the South: 'yet another war', and attempts to tell the 'missing narrative' (81). This section, then, describes the division of Korea and war. Cha's version views America, and the American imposition of a division in Korea, as the enemy rather than the other half of the same country: 'We are severed in Two by an abstract enemy an invisible enemy under the title of liberators', she writes (81). In its extensive engagement with history, Theresa Hak Kyung Cha's *Dictee* protests against the effacement of both Korean and Korean American history and national identity in official chronicles. In order to express herself, Cha must tell her national story, which is not only the story of Korea, but extends across the world to describe the Korean experience of immigration to the United States (Kang, 1994: 79). The loss of Korean and Korean American national identity is viewed within *Dictee* as the result of repeated external intervention.

Indeed, the history of Korea is the story of foreign intervention. In 1894–5, it was the battleground of the Sino-Japanese war, and later the battlefield of the 1904–5 Russo-Japanese war. It was also subject to repeated Chinese intervention and aggression in the late nineteenth century. In 1910 Korea was invaded by Japan, and remained a colony (with tacit American approval) until the Japanese were forced to leave in 1945. In 1948 the country was broken into two and became North Korea and South Korea, and in 1950 war broke out between the North and the South. (An armistice was reached in 1953.) A student-led uprising in 1960 toppled the American-installed government. It is not difficult to see why many Koreans view their country's history as crucial to their own expressions of identity. The turbulent past also helps to explain the history of political activism of both the Korean people and their immigrant counterparts in America. However, in linking her personal identity with those of her fellow Koreans and Korean Americans, as well as with her country's national identity, Cha refuses any easy identification with a Korean national identity, insisting that there is no unproblematic relationship between self and state (Lowe, 1994: 48). Rather, in *Dictee*, for both Koreans and for Korean Americans, national identity is shown to be imposed. Through her exploration of enforced identification with Japan during the colonization of Korea, Cha demonstrates the alienation coercively imposed national identity produces in the individual and suggests that identity is actually far from natural, but is instead always mediated (Wong, 1994: 110).

The connections between individual identity and state identity are extensively explored in *Dictee*, making use, for example, of nationalist symbols such as flags and uniforms in order to do this. But the text's exploration of national identity, as I have suggested, is also located very firmly within the context of the recovery of a distinctly Korean/Korean American female identity. Women, as Elaine Kim has pointed out, have been erased from the national histories of Korea (1994: 14). *Dictee* restores their role by telling the women's stories, and relating their part in the wider struggle to liberate Korea from repressive influences in order to claim a national identity. Cha uses female narratives, including her own story, in order to question national versions (Korean, American and Japanese) of Korean history and identity. She tells the stories of herself, her mother and of the Korean female nationalist revolutionary, Yu Guan Soon, as well as relating events in the lives of other, nameless women whose acts of resistance and bravery in difficult circumstances are also eulogized. These personal and subjective accounts are juxtaposed with excerpts of official chronicles including: letters to governments, history book accounts and petitions. This juxtaposition serves to hold these female accounts in tension with other national versions (Kang, 1994: 78). The erasure of female roles in the struggle over Korean identity within official histories results partly because Korean history chronicles were traditionally written in Chinese, a language which has been off limits to women for centuries (Kim, 1994: 14). Cha's own rendering utilizes many languages, including Korean-Chinese, Korean (*Hangul*), French and English. Language becomes a political vehicle for the reconstitution of female national identity for Cha. This is one way in which she signals that her version differs from the more traditional exclusionary texts of Korean history.

Cha's mother is particularly crucial in the retelling of her history. *Dictee* acknowledges a debt to the mother-figure as a source of the daughter's subjectivity, since the mother is also figured in the daughter's text as metonymic of the nation (Lowe, 1994: 48). This not only affirms the mother's position as source of the daughter's national identity, but also indicates the damage that the conflicts have wreaked at both a personal and a national level. This metonymic figuration serves to express the explicit parallel at the heart of *Dictee* between the ravaged, ruptured and invaded female body and the colonization and bifurcation of the body politic. Thus, by telling the mother/body's story, Cha also tells the nation/body's story, which involves her in utilizing non-textual linking images too. For example, she depicts the break-up of the body by including illustrations of the body in parts, as well as including a map of Korea divided.

Cha also enlists the form of *Dictee* in her project to claim and inscribe a national identity. *Dictee* is a highly complex, multi-generic text; it uses photographs, calligraphy, graffitti, nameless inscriptions, diagrams and maps to supplement the textual content. Textually, it comprises letters, journal entries, scrawled personal notes, extracts from F. A. McKenzie's *The Tragedy of Korea*, language translation exercises and official texts, such as the American naturalization oath and the Catholic catechism.[2] The juxtaposition of personal and subjective forms of narration alongside official inscriptions of history and national identity serves a double function. Not only does it provide a critique of the omission of Korean female perspectives from the national story, it also highlights the elision of female Korean identity from official discourses. The non-chronological, anti-developmental structure of the text aids Cha's purpose too. The text frequently ruptures and, as we read, these ruptures become more and more frequent, until the chronological progression engendered by left-hand page to right-hand page reading practice breaks down and the reader finds that s/he must read all of the left-hand pages or all of the right-hand pages in order to follow the text. This structure formally patterns the ruptures and splits in Korean national identity caused by repeated onslaughts by foreign powers. The damage caused is not repaired either: textual wholeness and continuity never return. In fact, the division of the text into two at this late point echoes the division of Korea into the North and the South late in Korea's own national history. In addition, the occasional interposition of non-textual symbols such as the Korean-Chinese calligraphy for man and woman, or the photograph of a Korean nationalist, function as textual warnings to the reader of the interpellatory power of nationalist symbols, as well as the invidious uses to which they may be put.

Identity in *Dictee* is ultimately contradictory, both on a personal and a national level. The demands of the state and the role of foreign intervention together are seen to exert alien and impossible pressures upon the individual for national identification. Official 'Korean' identity is alien, changeable and out of reach. National identity affords the bearer an invidious authority, both to police the identity of others and the identity of places. This fundamental alienation is reflected textually through rupture and disjuncture. It is also figured lexically. Possession and non-possession of national identity are indicated in turn through pronoun shifts: non-possession through 'she', 'he' and 'you', and possession occasionally through the use of 'I'. Cha repeatedly experiences her identity as external: by turn as imposed, as lost and as stolen (Wald, 1995: 301). She refuses to depict her Korean identification in line with her country's current political identity. Indeed, as Kim notes, Cha's identity resides on both sides of the North/South border, as well as in both Korea and America (1994: 11). *Dictee* asserts the identity of its author not just in spite of the many attacks upon and schisms of a Korean national self, but *because of* and *through* those actions. It ultimately depicts a resistant and resilient female subject: in writing her self, Cha also writes her nation.

Notes

1 See, for example discussion in Wald (1995).
2 *The Tragedy of Korea* is footnoted in Cha (1995).

References

Cha, T. H. K. *Dictee* (Berkeley: Third Woman Press, 1995)
Cheung, K. (ed.) *An Interethnic Companion to Asian American Literature* (New York: Cambridge University Press, 1997)
Kang, L. H. Y. 'The "Liberatory Voice" of Theresa Hak Kyung Cha's *Dictee*', in E. H. K. and N. Alarcón (eds) *Writing Self, Writing Nation: Essays on Theresa Hak Kyung Cha's DICTEE* (Berkeley: Third Woman Press, 1994) 73–99
Kim, E. H. and Alarcón, N. (eds) *Writing Self, Writing Nation: Essays on Theresa Hak Kyung Cha's DICTEE* (Berkeley: Third Woman Press, 1994)
Kim, E. H. 'Poised on the In-between: A Korean American's Reflections on Theresa Hak Kyung Cha's *Dictee*', in E. H. Kim and N. Alarcón (eds) *Writing Self, Writing Nation: Essays on Theresa Hak Kyung Cha's DICTEE* (Berkeley: Third Woman Press, 1994) 3–30
——— 'Korean American Literature', in K. Cheung (ed.) *An Interethnic Companion to Asian American Literature* (New York: Cambridge University Press, 1997) 156–91

Kim, R. *Clay Walls* (Seattle: Washington University Press, 1994)

Kingston, M. H. *The Woman Warrior* (London: Picador, 1976)

—— *China Men* (London: Picador, 1981)

Lee, M. P. *Quiet Odyssey: A Pioneer Korean-American Women in America* (Seattle: Washington University Press, 1990)

Lowe, L. 'Unfaithful to the Original: The Subject of *Dictee'*, in E. H. Kim and N. Alarcón (eds) *Writing Self, Writing Nation: Essays on Theresa Hak Kyung Cha's DICTEE* (Berkeley: Third Woman Press, 1994) 35–69

McKenzie, F. A. *The Tragedy of Korea* (Seoul: Yonsei University Press, 1962)

Pai, M. K. *The Dreams of Two Yi-Min* (Honolulu: University of Hawaii Press, 1989)

Wald, P. *Constituting Americans: Cultural Anxiety and Narrative Form* (Durham, NC: Duke University Press, 1995)

Wong, S. S. 'Unnaming the Same: Theresa Hak Kyung Cha's *Dictee'* in E. H. Kim and N. Alarcón (eds) *Writing Self, Writing Nation: Essays on Theresa Hak Kyung Cha's DICTEE* (Berkeley: Third Woman Press, 1994) 103–40

3
Mary Kingsley: the Female Ethnographic Self in Writing
Lynnette Turner

Françoise Lionnet, in her important study of race and gender in acts of 'self-portraiture', asserts that the 'problematics of authorship' for women autobiographers turns on the splitting of the 'subject of discourse' into a 'narrating self and an experiencing self which can never coincide exactly' (Lionnet, 1989: 92). For Lionnet:

> The female narrator gets caught in a duplicitous process: she exists in the text under circumstances of alienated communication because the text is the locus of her dialogue with a tradition she tacitly aims to subvert. (93)

This chapter interrogates the proposition that the woman writer's mode of autobiographical address is that of 'alienated communication'. However, rather than focusing on an established tradition of self-writing, I wish to look at another 'experiential' form of writing, ethnography, and in particular at ethnography as a developing form of scientific writing attempting to forge a break with non-specialist writings such as the travelogue, diary and personal memoir. By examining the writings of the English traveller and ethnologist Mary Kingsley (1862–1900), my aim is to demonstrate the complex narrative strategies which position the late Victorian woman ethnographer within an emergent 'tradition' of writing struggling in its own attempts at representational legitimacy.

Although the ethnographic genre does not conventionally present the 'self' as its focal point – concentrating instead on communities other than the observer's own – it is none the less experientially based, and even in its formative moment appealed to 'participation' and 'I-witnessing' as its governing legitimizing criteria. The effort of masking the self in the pursuit of scientific credibility presents a complicated set of epistemological and representational hurdles to the ethnographer, and my purpose here is to examine the extent to which Kingsley's ethnographic writing discloses not only its *emergent* but also its *subversive* status precisely through what it does to, or with, the narrating and the experiencing self. My main argument is that the problematics of self-representation (the degrees to which the self is confidently expressed as a site and source of knowledge; the degrees to which the self is obscured, diminished, parodied or alienated) becomes, at this point in anthropological history, a crucial determinant in the claims being made to scientific status by this discipline. In addition, the readings that follow suggest that the *strategy* of self-modification constitutive of all experiential forms of scientific writing is at its most ideologically resonant when directly dealing with gender-based cultural practices. Thus by scrutinizing the shifting relations between gendered self and gendered other, this chapter demonstrates that the writing of the gendered self is the key strategy through which Mary Kingsley negotiates her claims to scientific status.

As a genre of writing, ethnography has remained since its inception formally unstable, being situated in ambiguous relation to a number of generic and critical canons. Its consistency as a genre stems not from a formulaic writing style, but from what George Stocking has noted as the 'special cognitive authority claimed by the modern ethnographic tradition' (Stocking, 1985: 71). Various anthropological traditions of ethnography are held together by the promotion and textualization of a '*stable* subjectivity, a standpoint for a self that understands and represents the cultural other' (Clifford, 1988: 112; emphasis added). Such an emphasis on objectivity means that the 'oddity of constructing texts ostensibly scientific out of experiences broadly biographical' which is, as Clifford Geertz argues, 'what ethnographers do' is 'thoroughly obscured' (Geertz, 1988: 10). Indeed, Geertz also points out that where the modern ethnography demands that the ethnographer convince us that what they say is a result of their having 'truly been there. . . . Explicit representations of authorial presence tend to be relegated, like other embarrassments, to prefaces, notes or appendixes' (4–6).

The early ethnographies of the 1890s anticipate the dissimulating strategies of the modern ethnography and similarly declare scientific impartiality through the removal of the author-observer-writer from the scene of ethnographic knowledge. As with the modern tradition, the experiencing self appears in prefaces, introductions and arrival scenes, but the need to convey on immediacy of experience and transparency of representation necessitates the ethnographer's removal from the immediate research field. Yet, in comparison with her male peers, Mary Kingsley's narrative style does not follow in any systematic way the ethnographic rules on the presence/absence of the observing self. In *Travels in West Africa* (1897), a narrative noteworthy for its interweaving of travel and ethnography, Kingsley seems to make an issue, not only of 'being there' in Geertz's sense, but of highlighting the *process* of producing objective description from 'experiences broadly biographical'. Indeed, the problem of self-definition and self-declaration in Kingsley's ethnographic work is not characterized by shifts between authorial presence and absence, but rather between masculinized and feminized identities. The self that Kingsley portrays is marked by gender shifts and slippages which slide between public and private versions. But in writing ethnography (as distinct from travel) Kingsley's self-representations are forced more often into masculine, chauvinist and imperialist modes, and transcultural identification (the key vehicle of ethnographic knowledge), is produced only in relation to Kingsley's active participation in masculine cultural practices. As I will now go on to discuss in detail, the self that Kingsley offers her readers – indeed the gendered self that she provides in her narrative – shows up clearly and with great complexity the particular pressures that an emergent scientific mode of knowledge imposes upon the woman ethnographer's identity and processes of transcultural identification.

As implied in Clifford Geertz's suggestion that ethnographers need to convince their readers 'that what they say is a result of their having actually penetrated (or, if you prefer, been penetrated by) another form of life' (Geertz, 1988: 4) the expression of an authoritative, that is, scientific, ethnography heavily appeals to models and images of liminality. And as Kingsley's statements of transcultural identification testify, the crossing of racial or cultural thresholds and boundaries form key tropes within the individual ethnographer's claims to authoritative knowledge of the communities studied. Her confident assertion to Anna Tylor that 'I have a mind so nearly akin to that of the savage that I can enter into his thoughts and follow them' infuses the language of ethnographic authority with the colonialist vocabulary of violation and possession (Kingsley in Birkett, 1992: 99). In the context of late nineteenth-century colonial West Africa – a prime landscape for degenerative fantasies and fixations in the wider public imagination – the structuring of scientific authority on models of intimacy and proximity inevitably produces a precarious and volatile authoritative grammar where good science always teeters between colonialist confidence and transgressive or atavistic intentions. Any declaration of intimate knowledge would always question and problematize the intersecting points between imperialist protocols of inter-racial contact and broader Victorian moral agendas preoccupied with sexual and gender propriety. So the risks for a woman writer to assert participation and intimacy were far greater than for male ethnographers. None the less, Kingsley's argument that 'Unless you live *alone* among the natives, you never get to know them' and her additional claim that she has the 'capacity to think in black' (Kingsley, 1897: 65) would potentially incur both social and scientific disapprobation. As Dea Birkett points out in her biography of Kingsley, 'women who challenged their [conventional] role within Britain could not be relied upon to convey truthfully their experience abroad. Their claims would always be met with suspicion' (Birkett, 1992: 60). Additionally, John W. Griffith has pointed out that uppermost in late nineteenth-century attitudes to moral degeneration was the 'idea that in transgressing national and ethnic boundaries, one inevitably transgressed moral boundaries as well' (Griffith, 1995: 126). Clearly, then, if there were any suggestions of Kingsley challenging her conventional gender role, the authority of her knowledge would be compromised.

It is unsurprising, therefore, that in *Travels in West Africa* ([1897] 1986), Kingsley's strategic evacuation of the first-person narrative position, together with her lack of attention to temporal specificity, are both signs of a discursive and epistemological slipperiness which serves to distance her self from prevailing sexual orthodoxies. In particular, Kingsley's discussion of the system of secret societies forms a noteworthy example of the complexity of her ethnographic discourse.

Kingsley opens her discussion of this aspect of 'fetish' with the claim that in West Africa the 'secret' societies are not essentially religious, their action is mainly judicial' (526). Her emphasis on their judicial purpose enables Kingsley to launch both an analysis of indigenous 'authority' and, significantly, a (broader) discussion of the relations between authority, knowledge and gender. Her starting point is the conventional nineteenth-century anthropological belief that analysis of the social practices of 'primitive' cultures would confirm that European patterns of gender organization are universal.

Not surprisingly, therefore, Kingsley's assessment of the 'broad lines of agreement between' the various secret societies observed is concentrated on segregationist gender practices ('there are no mixed societies'), a focus which allows her to adopt a crude essentialist discourse of sexual difference which is maintained throughout:

> Women are utterly forbidden to participate in the rites or become acquainted with their [the men's] secrets, for one of the chief duties is to keep the women in order; and besides it is undoubtedly held that women are bad for certain types of ju-ju [presiding spirit]. (526)

Any cultural specificity that Kingsley had initially intended is immediately offset by a comparative gender binarism that operates throughout the passage: one that secures the 'natural' equation of authority with masculinity, and disorder and contamination with femininity. Thus extending her account, Kingsley details 'an amusing case which demonstrates the inextinguishable thirst for knowledge, as long as that knowledge is forbidden, which characterizes our sex' (527). Here, Kingsley's brief identification with Ikun women through gender commonality ('our sex') suggests on one level that the whole passage might be ironic. However, a *clear* ironic stance would stamp the text – and the scene of ethnographic knowledge – with a marked feminine subjectivity: a marked or 'unstable' subjectivity which may well compromise the scientific value of Kingsley's observations.

None the less, the passage cogently dramatizes women's difficult relation to the source of authoritative knowledge. Unlike the male ethnographer's mode of asserting authority dependent on 'penetration', Kingsley's allusions to women's fallen state and 'rightful' exclusion from the masculine community of knowledge hints at the barriers preventing women's easy participation in the ethnographic will to truth. For women, the point of truth is never reached and their 'thirst' for knowledge remains 'inextinguishable'.

Earlier in the same passage, Kingsley describes an event in which a 'chief up the Mungo River deliberately destroyed his ju-ju by showing it to his women' and comments further:

> Probably the destructive action of women is not only the idea of their inferiority – for had inferiority been the point, that chief would have laid his ju-ju with his dogs, or pigs – but arises from

the undoubted fact that women are notably deficient in real reverence for authority, as is demonstrated by the way they continually treat that of their husbands. (526)

This small passage represents a remarkable allegory of the relationship of women to anthropological science. It takes on the proposition that authority is associated with men and probes for comic effect the structural implication that the 'segregation of women and the feminine from authority is internally connected to the concept of authority itself' (Jones, 1988: 120). In this way, Kingsley's account of women's exclusion from authoritative discourses presents women as deconstructive levers: as irruptive insurgents caught in the performance of 'rank heresy' (527); as figures, that is, who are always threatening to collapse the rules of the system.

Kingsley's women, naturally 'treacherous' and 'sceptical' (527), can neither get at the deep secrets, nor are likely to have any faith in them: women's scepticism, once mobilized, can spread 'to such an extent that nothing short of burning or drowning all the women could stamp it out and reintroduce the proper sense of awe into the female side of society' (527). Her account of women's proclivity for dissent and lawlessness, occurring as it does in a passage that comes so close to an allegorization of the gendering of anthropology as a system of knowledge, is highly suggestive of an obliquely stated sexual politics. Kingsley appears to be using her analysis of Ikun gender hierarchies and distinctions to launch a debate on the gendering of two forms of authority: as a category of anthropological analysis (in which women are disconnected from an authority that orders social existence) and as an ethnographical preoccupation (in which women are estranged from an authority that authenticates ethnographic writing); one enabling a critique of the other.

However, if any critique of anthropological bias is being intended – a suggestion which an ironic reading could indeed develop – it is immediately negated or contained by being advanced through an account of *African* femininity. As such, the passage could operate to confirm Kingsley's difference ('irreverence' as a trait of the 'primitive' female which 'civilized' femininity has eradicated), and therefore works to bolster Kingsley's claims to legitimate authority by constructing African women as the repository of a negative femininity. Indeed, if Kingsley is voicing a criticism of the politics of authority, then her technique of using African women as its vehicle brings to a focus the ambivalence of her assertions of gender commonality. Statements of identification which can also be read as disidentification highlight the tension in her writings between scientific neutrality and a feminine identity. Not only is Kingsley absent from the actual scene of female heresy (her evidence is largely anecdotal), but the governing framework of the secret society section is that of comic misrule, which suggests only a momentary and licensed inversion of the naturalized order.

A rather different approach to writing the ethnographic self emerges in an earlier section of the narrative where Kingsley details a day travelling from the coast into the forest with a group of West Coast porters and a group of Fan men. At this time Fans were widely recognized as the epitome of complete savagery: a treacherous, warring, cannibal people, dangerous, nomadic and resistant to conquest. Their uncontaminated primitivity made them superior ethnographic subjects, a fact not lost on Kingsley. According to Kingsley, the Fans 'will kill people, *i.e.*, the black traders who venture into their country, and cut them up into pieces, eat what they want at the time, and smoke the bodies for future use' (252). The style of much of this section alludes to the established tradition of imperial adventure. Yet the ethnographic demand that the Fans retain their autochthonous status, combined with the parallel obligation that Kingsley provide evidence of participatory knowledge, creates a generic tension in which the narrative of commercial travel and enterprise is punctuated with scenes of innocent non-travel. Once within the 'primeval' forest (261), Kingsley sets a scene of peace, tranquillity and natural beauty:

> When we got into the cool forest beyond it was delightful. . . . Here and there the ground was strewn with great cast blossoms, thick, wax-like, glorious cups of orange and crimson and pure white, each one of which was in itself a handful, and which told us that some of the trees around us were showing a glory of colour to heaven alone. (263–4)

The iconography of the pastoral is clearly identified in Kingsley's depiction of a rich and abundant nature; it is innocent, vibrant and as yet uncolonized by the definitional and cataloguing gaze of the natural scientist. Although this scene testifies to the 'fantasy of dominance' that Mary Louise Pratt regards as characteristic of African exploration writing (Pratt, 1986: 147), Kingsley's observations are not that of the prospector: her gaze does not rove across panoramic landscapes but instead produces the openness and receptivity of nature in an enclosed and delimited space. And it is within this secluded space of innocence and epistemological self-sufficiency that Kingsley is able to declare that:

> A certain sort of friendship soon arose between the Fans and me. We each recognized that we belonged to the same section of the human race with whom it is better to drink than to fight. We knew we would each have killed the other, if sufficient inducement were offered, and so we took a certain amount of care that the inducement did not arise. (264)

The passage represents a modified pastoral in the sense that harmony is achieved only through acknowledging the threat of conflict and chaos. As a model of mutual understanding which is predicated on (the absence of) manly combat, the scene presents also a modification of the adventure genre which conventionally offers a 'masculine world of risk and enterprise in the pursuit of fortune' (Dawson, 1994: 59). The bounty here might be knowledge, but both parties have reached an equal state of understanding. From this point onwards Kingsley declares that the 'Fans did their best to educate me in every way: they told me their names for things, while I told them mine ... They also showed me things: how to light a fire from the pith of a certain tree, which was useful to me in after life' (266). Throughout this section, Kingsley emphasizes an *exchange* of knowledge, actual conversation, mutual enchantment and a sharing of cultural codes. Although the entire scene is underpinned by the conventions of the modern adventure quest through its emphasis on the hazardous nature of the enterprise, the reciprocity of the activities described places the scene of participant-observation in an insecure temporal zone that disowns the register of modern colonial power relations.

The strategic blending of pastoral and adventure forms appears to offset any potential threat to Kingsley's integrity and authority which the romantic primitivism of the pastoral might imply. The swift shifts and slippages between the gender neutrality of Kingsley's pastoral scenes and the masculine world of danger and adventure once again marginalize the feminine self at the scene of transcultural knowledge. The ethnographic requirement of intimacy and objectivity, combined with the anthropological quest for the absolutely primitive, places pressures upon Kingsley's narrative style which see it searching restlessly for a genre or form that enables a white European woman to speak authoritatively about her unchaperoned experiences among so-called cannibal tribes.

But the fact that physical contact between Kingsley and the Fans did not arise is further emphasized in her argument that the 'cannibalism of the Fans, although a prevalent habit, is no danger . . . to white people, except as regards the bother it gives one in preventing one's black companions from getting eaten' (330). Her statement that 'my colour was some protection' (Kingsley in Tooley, 1896: 294) reinscribes the original scene of cross-cultural encounter with the visual codes of colonial relations (white vs non-white) and presents before the British public a vision of the Fans as deferential to European authority. In this version, what the Fans intuitively respect is the sanctity of the white imperial body. And what these strategies seem also to suggest is an awareness of the intense and widespread European fear of miscegenation, as a result of which any expression of physical contact between a black man and a white woman is liable to be interpreted as an admission of sexual liaison.

The main points that I wish to draw from my reading of these two sections of the narrative can be resolved into a discussion of representations of the gendered self. In the first extract, Kingsley ostensibly undertakes to eliminate herself from the observed scene, as good ethnography would demand, but she does so in relation to a passage that describes disruptive women. In the second passage, Kingsley freely asserts a participatory form of discourse, but does so exclusively with men. Expressions of gender commonality – that is, empathic identification with ethnically different women – are consistently surrendered in favour of forms of identification with ethnically different men, though this, in turn, is censored through the manipulation of formal and generic conventions. Thus, where Kingsley's travel narrative may indicate a self which conforms to models of the indomitable Victorian woman traveller, when confronted with the problematic of defining and speaking for different cultures and of producing an authoritative ethnographic discourse, Kingsley displaces and modifies her connection with women. Such manoeuvring confirms in a very specific way that the production of a satisfactory scientific presence is firmly associated with masculine forms of participation and is simultaneously anchored in the denial of sexual difference from the scene of participatory knowledge. The strange ways in which African women are admitted into

Kingsley's narrative further suggest that the very meaning of transculturality for a woman – where the self and the other are granted a degree of equivalence – is so problematic that Kingsley, as a good scientist, needs to display what she is not: undisciplined, lawless, untrustworthy, primitive. These are the roles that the ethnically different woman is compelled to assume.

References

Birkett, D. *Mary Kingsley: Imperial Adventuress* (Basingstoke: Macmillan, 1992)

Clifford, J. *The Predicament of Culture: Twentieth-century Ethnography, Literature, and Art* (Cambridge, Mass. and London: Harvard University Press, 1988)

Dawson, G. *Soldier Heroes: British Adventure, Empire and the Imagining of Masculinities* (London and New York: Routledge, 1994)

Diamond, I. & Quinby, L. (eds) *Feminism and Foucault: Reflections on Resistance* (Boston: Northeastern University Press, 1988)

Geertz, C. *Works and Lives: the Anthropologist as Author* (Oxford: Polity Press, 1988)

Griffith, J. W. *Joseph Conrad and the Anthropological Dilemma: 'Bewildered Traveller'* (Oxford English Monographs) (Oxford: Clarendon Press, 1995)

Jones, K. B. 'On Authority: or, Why Women are Not Entitled to Speak', in I. Diamond and L. Quinby (eds) *Feminism and Foucault: Reflections on Resistance* (Boston: Northeastern University Press, 1988) 119–34

Kingsley, M. H. 'West Africa from an Ethnologist's Point of View', *Transactions of the Liverpool Geographical Society*, 6 (1897) 58–73

—— *Travels in West Africa: Congo Français, Corisco and Cameroons*, 5th edn repr. (London: Virago Press, [1897] 1986)

Lionnet, F. *Autobiographical Voices: Race, Gender, Self-Portraiture* (Ithaca and London: Cornell University Press, 1989)

Pratt, M. L. 'Scratches on the Face of the Country; or, What Mr. Barrow Saw in the Land of the Bushmen', in H. L. Gates (ed.) *'Race, 'Writing and Difference* (Chicago and London: University of Chicago Press, 1986) 138–62

Stocking, G. 'The Ethnographer's Magic: Fieldwork in British Anthropology from Tylor to Malinowski', in G. Stocking (ed.) *Observers Observed: Essays on Ethnographic Fieldwork* (Wisconsin: University of Wisconsin Press, 1985) 70–120

Tooley, S. A. 'Adventures of a Lady Explorer: an Interview with Mary Kingsley', *The Young Woman*, 4 (1896) 289–95

Part II
Revising Genres

4

Traps Slyly Laid: Professing Autobiography in Harriet Wilson's *Our Nig*

R. J. Ellis

Our Nig has been persistently read as an autobiography with good reason.[1] Its title-page indicates that the book's author and the central protagonist are one and the same person, since its first and final words are, respectively, '*Our Nig . . .* by "Our Nig"'. The titles of the first three chapters reinforce the supposition that the book is autobiographical, since they are respectively entitled: 'Mag Smith, My Mother', 'My Father's Death' and 'A New Home For Me' (xxxi). Furthermore, in the 'Appendix', a testimonial writer, Allida, describes the text as an 'Autobiography' (75). Unsurprisingly, this led to a search for the identity of the anonymous author, Harriet Wilson, a search complicated by the fact that the text had lain largely unregarded from 1859, when it was first published, until 1983, when Henry Louis Gates republished a facsimile edition. However, whilst preparing his edition, Gates, and, subsequently, Barbara White, carried out painstaking research and managed to demonstrate that Wilson was an African-American living in Milford, New Hampshire, and Boston. Gates (1983) and White (1993) incontrovertibly established all discoverable autobiographical correspondences between *Our Nig* and Wilson's life.

Yet, just as often, the text has been described a novel. Again, the reasons are clear. The text is written not as a first-person but a third-person narrative. The central character, 'Our Nig', is named as Frado, and a series of literary devices is deployed to dramatize her experiences, most notably, Fido the dog she is given as a companion. The name parallel (Frado/Fido) and the way the dog is sited in the narrative indicate that Wilson's life has been fictionalized.

At one point, Frado, a violently abused, indentured black servant-girl to a white family, the Bellmonts, is instructed to eat from the same plate as her mistress. Before she obeys, Frado encourages Fido to lick the plate clean (38). This constitutes a complex piece of literary symbolism. In part, it is a calculated insult aimed at her white mistress: Frado would rather eat from the same plate as a dog, and she is beaten cruelly for her gesture. Additionally, Frado ironically recapitulates her own social situation: she is literally enduring a dog's life. The action of offering her plate to Fido cuts both ways. The irony is recursive, and the name parallel (dog/black servant) marks it out as a deliberate device.

Plainly the text is recurrently both autobiographical and novelistic. In representing this Northern black woman's life there is a constant circulation between these genres. The line between 'fiction' and 'fact' is consistently problematized. I see this problematization as strategic and constitutive, and in this essay I want to explore some of its parameters.

The text's extraordinarily sophisticated framing is a key source of this problematization. The complex self-referentiality of the title-page provides a good starting-point (Tate, 1990: 113).

OUR NIG;

OR,

Sketches from the Life of a Free Black,

IN A TWO-STORY WHITE HOUSE, NORTH.

SHOWING THAT SLAVERY'S SHADOW FALLS EVEN THERE.

BY "OUR NIG."

The constant circulation set up by this structure (*Our Nig . . .* by 'Our Nig') takes us repeatedly back through the embedded ironies. These are both overt (slavery's shadow falls upon a 'free black' in the emancipated North) and implicit (the Bellmont white house's cruel treatment of Frado rebounds upon the other, All-American presidential 'White House'). This Bellmont white house, situated in Singleton, is also a *two-story* house. It is a two-story of domestic agrarian (Jeffersonian) farm-life containing great cruelty, just as Jefferson's Declaration of Independence contains two stories – of guarantees of freedom made by a slave-owner destined to become president, who deliberately excised a paragraph prohibiting slavery in the Declaration of Independence that he drafted.[2] The title is far from standing simply as an indication of the text's autobiographical continuities; its also alludes to the conventions governing the slave narrative genre: 'Sketches from the Life of', 'Slavery', 'Free' – these foreshadow the text's use of the ingredients of slave narratives (respectively: individual testimony, oppression, desire for freedom), climaxing in the scene when Frado is finally compelled to resist her mistress, Mrs. Bellmont:

> 'Stop!' shouted Frado, 'strike me, and I'll never work a mite more for you;' and throwing down what she had gathered, stood like one who feels the stirrings of free and independent thought. (56)

This assertion clearly alludes to those moments of epiphany that feature formulaically in slave narratives (and, indeed, in Harriet Beecher Stowe's *Uncle Tom's Cabin*). The intertextual resonances therefore extend beyond Jefferson's Declaration of Independence. Echoes of Frederick Douglass's fight with his slave-master, Covey, and with George Harris's 'declaration of independence' as he fights off his pursuers in *Uncle Tom* complicate any reading of this as a moment of autobiographical record (Douglass, 1845: 107–13; Stowe, 1981: 298). Taking this wood-pile incident to be straightforwardly autobiographical neglects its intertextual complicities with slave narrative. These correspondences make Frado a representative of the Northern free black: her naming as Alfrado *Smith*, giving her the most common of second names, is thus part of this universalizing process.

However, the relatively straightforward emblematization found in slave narratives is absent. The problematic use of the word 'like' in this passage: 'she . . . stood *like* one who feels the stirrings of free and independent thought' introduces complications (Breau, 1993: 464). It is difficult to weigh the force of this simile. Resemblances with independence are established (she resists further *undeserved* beatings), but also differences (Frado returns to the farmhouse, continued servitude and further beatings). The statement becomes not only a measure of consciousness, but also of self-consciousness (Frado can be regarded as assuming a carefully *staged* posture: *just like* 'one who feels the stirrings of free and independent thought'). Frado is in this sense performatively staging a self-identity, rather than simply experiencing an epiphany in straightforward self-discovery. The use of a third-person narrative voice is crucial to the establishment of these complex resonances.

Whilst it is therefore possible to represent this wood pile episode as an autobiographical account of an epiphany, it is, in the same textual *movement*, fictionalized – a representation shifting between rhetorical figure, intertextual reference and complex, generalizing political intervention. Frado's life, generically, becomes like freedom but unlike freedom in the slave-'free', 'two-story' North. But what is 'really' happening in this representation of the wood-pile episode is problematized: the incident becomes quintessentially *textualized*. This difficulty is a concise replication of the problem besetting free blacks in the North: is their 'freedom' 'fact' or 'fiction', given their status as 'nigs'? The title-page's circulations preliminarily indicate this unending problem. In particular, the first-person plural pronoun performs a complex signifying function: 'Our Nig', the Bellmonts' label for Frado, becomes not only a label for all Northern whites to apply to the North's African-American population (*'our* nigs'), but also one taken up by Wilson herself as 'author', in a final recursive irony (one of 'authorization'): she *signs* ([as]signs) herself as 'nig' on her *title*-page.

This complex self-referentiality is intensified by the rest of the book's frame: the 'Preface', the final chapter, and the Appendix, ostensibly consisting of three testimonials to the authenticity of the text and the author's dependence upon public charity. It has been suggested that the testimonials were not written by actual people, but were rather the fictional creations of Wilson (see Breau, 1993: 458). Three points can be made in support of this idea. First, none of the three testimonial writers can be identified (in contrast to the conventional selection, in slave narratives, of socially prominent testimonial writers). Second, the names of the testimonial writers, Allida, Margaretta Thorn and C. D. S., carry symbolic connotations: 'Allida' > allied (cf., OED: 'united, joined; esp. by kindred or affinity'); 'Margaretta Thorn' is indeed a pain because of her constant recourse to Franklinian nostrums that hold no value for Wilson (Frado can only read 'Therefore, let us work hard while the day lasts, and we shall in no wise lose our reward' (78) ironically); the initials C. D. S. commonly stood for 'Coloured Indentured Servant' in the 1850s.[3] Third, there are congruences between the stylistic traits of the testimonials and the remainder of the text of *Our Nig*, particularly the 'Preface'. For example, where Allida states: 'He left . . . and embarked for sea' (134), Wilson earlier writes: 'He left her . . . – embarked at sea' (127); where Margaretta Thorn writes: 'I hope those who will call themselves friends of our dark-skinned brethren, will lend a helping hand' (140), Wilson earlier wrote: 'I sincerely appeal to my colored brethren universally for patronage, hoping they will not condemn this attempt' (3); where C. D. S. writes: 'I hope no one will refuse to aid her in her work, as she is worthy the sympathy of all Christians' (140), Wilson earlier wrote: 'Reposing on God . . . Still an invalid, she asks your sympathy, gentle reader . . . Enough has been unrolled to demand your sympathy and aid' (130).

These authenticating testimonials function as duplicit representational devices, designed to draw the novel into a conformity with slave narratives (which conventionally employ such testimonials), whilst also highlighting the way in which, even though slavery's shadow indeed falls upon the ante-Bellum North, patrons defending 'free' African-Americans from the two-story consequences have to be invented. What is 'fact' and what is 'fiction' are rendered ineradicably unresolvable, subject to a constant churning.

More fundamentally disconcerting, however, is the remainder of the narrative frame – the Preface and the final chapter, which both introduce motifs going beyond the precise limits of Frado's story. Again, the method of foregrounding this frame is textual recirculation. The final chapter speaks of 'professed abolitionists' (69) – a curious phrase echoing the words, 'professed fugitives', printed a few paragraphs earlier (68). Taken together, these *'professions'* highlight the extent to which double-values pervade the anti-slavery lobby, as abolition took hold. By the late 1830s, in the Northern states, support for abolition was rapidly becoming the social dominant, rather than a position of radical dissent. Indeed, a number of prominent Milford citizens formed a group in 1842 known as the 'Come-Outers', to encourage yet more people to make a stand against slavery (White, 1993: 11). The risk for African-Americans in this, as abolition became more common and even more open, was that since social and pecuniary advantage could flow from embracing abolition, as it became the majority position in certain Northern towns, 'professed' recruits might possess a bottom-line not of principle, but of profit.

This ties in with the central economic theme in the text: the worth of Frado. Noticeably Frado at the wood-pile threatens to withdraw her labour if she is struck ('I'll never work a mite more') – a critique of how puritan 'Yankee thrift' informs the slow 'progress' of abolition in the North (from chattel slavery to wage slavery). Such a focus on hypocritical 'profession' in the final chapter, however, also retrospectively glosses the sentence in the Preface which reads: 'I have purposely omitted what would most provoke shame in our good anti-slavery friends at home' (xxxi). The use of the adjective 'good', apparently a mere act of politeness ('our good . . . friends'), in hindsight also throws a distinction between 'good' and 'bad' anti-slavery supporters.

Even more disturbing is the difficulty of determining what the 'purposeful' omission might be, given the text's explicit representations of violent maltreatment. This problem is emphasized by the use of a first-person narrative in the Preface, which lays implicit claim to autobiographical truthfulness in the same section that undermines this status by highlighting how the third-person narrative that follows will be characterized by 'purposeful' omission. Two main lines of critical speculation exist as to what exactly is omitted. One suggests that Wilson was exercising necessary self-censorship, both to avoid alienating potential white benefactors (Wilson was impoverished) and to avoid providing succour to the opponents of abolition, who frequently stressed that Northerners' treatment of African-Americans was crueller than that of Southern slave-holders (such pro-slavery propaganda was rife in the decades leading up to the Civil War). This reading derives much support from the sentence appearing just before this statement of omission: 'I would not . . . palliate slavery at the South, by disclosures of its appurtenances North' (xxxi). For this reason, self-censorship based upon such strategic motives might be preferred over another proposal: that Wilson may be censoring some act of 'rape' – in the sense that the young Frado is befriended by the younger male Bellmonts, who seek her out, sometimes in secluded locations (barns) and on one occasion invite her onto the bed, in ways admitting to sexual constructions, where relationships of power (age, gender and race) introduce an element of structural coercion.

However, it is not necessary to endorse either reading of the identity of the text's 'omission'. Rather, it should be noted that the Preface invites such a speculation, by drawing our attention at the outset to Wilson's claim of narrative omission. This implicitly highlights how all autobiography ultimately inheres in a degree of self-censorship, as *Our Nig* problematizes autobiography's generic aspiration towards revelation. Beyond this the text suggests a necessary process of silencing is involved for 'free' blacks. Again, this is part of the circling between the Preface and final chapter, churning out conflicting meanings. Though the 'Traps slyly laid by the vicious to ensnare her' (70) are being eluded by the narrative's restraint, which enables it to broadcast details of racist mistreatments and the perils of the Fugitive Slave Act, there is also an accompanying assertion that Wilson cannot speak out forthrightly, in another form of coercive entrapment.

This, in turn, reinforces a main theme of the book: the process of silencing that Frado's story traces. When she speaks 'truthfully' (by denying a false accusation) she is not believed, and almost immediately is punished viciously and silenced so she cannot cry out.

'I didn't do it! I didn't do it!' answered Nig, passionately, and then related the occurrence truthfully.

The discrepancy greatly enraged Mrs. Bellmont'. . . . Turning to her husband, she asked,

'Will you sit still, there, and hear that black nigger call Mary a liar?'

'How do we know but she has told the truth?' I shall not punish her,' he replied, and left the house, as he usually did when a tempest threatened'. . . . No sooner was he out of sight than Mrs. B. and Mary commenced beating her inhumanly; then propping her mouth open with a piece of wood, shut her up in a dark room, without any supper'. . . . While the tempest raged within, Mr. Bellmont went for the cows, a task belonging to Frado, and thus unintentionally prolonged her pain. (16)

On two further occasions, Frado is similarly gagged (both times to prevent her crying out *whilst* being beaten). The effect always is to prevent her expressing the truth: her forcible silencings mean she cannot bear testimony. This links thematically to her announcement of her apparently voluntary silencing of herself at the start. The black servant girl cannot speak (14), though Wilson's text speaks both *of* this silencing ('she gave her a thorough beating . . . and threatened, if she ever exposed her . . . she would "cut her tongue out"' (38)) and *to* its silencing: it metatextually announces its successive elisions ('I have purposely omitted') and so draws attention to its own, as well as its protagonist's, status as culturally coerced and constrained. What cannot be voiced is the extent and viciousness of ante-Bellum Northern racism, which allows Mary and Mrs Bellmont to give vent to their sadism:

> Angry that she should venture a reply to her command, she suddenly inflicted a blow which lay the tottering girl prostrate on the floor. Excited by so much indulgence of a dangerous passion, she seemed left to unrestrained malice; and snatching a towel, stuffed the mouth of the sufferer, and beat her cruelly. (44)

> It is impossible to give an impression of the manifest enjoyment of Mrs. B. in these kitchen scenes. It was her favorite exercise to enter the apartment noisily, vociferate orders, [and] give a few sudden blows to quicken Nig's pace. (35)

'Impossible to give an impression': the text again falls silent at the point where the critique of the 'dangerous passion' informing racist mistreatments is laid bare. Mrs. B.'s threat to '"cut . . . out" Frado's "tongue"' if she speaks of her mistreatment self-reflexively informs on the text's deliberate omissions. It is characteristic of this text to have recourse to ellipsis at the point where the narrative could (quite conventionally) lapse into sentimental hyperbole when representing Frado's brutal silencings. This refusal to speak out matches the way its dangerous inversion of the sentimental's gender politics remains textually unhighlighted, for the sadistic maltreatment is meted out virtually exclusively by females. In a brilliant, and brilliantly *economic*, image, Mrs. B. is described as 'spicing' her mistreatment of Frado with blows, both suggesting that there is a racist recipe that is being adhered to, despite gender stereotyping (14), and, in an underlying reference, through the invocation of home economics, that monetary motivations lie behind these cruelties – the need to secure hard work from this labourer ('"I'll beat the money out of her, if I can't get her worth any other way," retorted Mrs. B. sharply', (48)). It is the text's refusal to speak out explicitly, but rather *economically* and obliquely, that keeps returning the reader to the Preface's announcement of 'purposeful' omission and its relationship to 'Southern principles'. It also persistently points forward, to the final chapter, where the 'maltreat[ments]' and 'Strange . . . adventures' (69) remain unspecified, as once more the black woman does not speak.

These elisions and restraints convey the particular socio-cultural atmosphere of the time, which symptomatically had witnessed in 1850 sanctioning of the peculiar provisions of the Fugitive Slave Act. This disgraceful Act is not alluded to directly but, once more, elliptically: the final chapter refers to the way Frado's movements are 'watched by kidnappers', presumably seeking to pounce on her under the aegis of the Act – one 'Trap' set by the 'vicious' (69–70). The novel, in these oblique allusions and silences, foregrounds the precarious narrative path taken between full exposé and the need to sustain the provision of ideological sustenance – 'humbugs for hungry abolitionists' (69). This is the charge that Frado levels at her husband, for passing himself off as an escaped slave to exploit the abolitionist lecture circuits. Reflexively, it could also be applied to her own omissions, but her rhetorical tropes, drawing attention to the text's silences, reveal how some types of 'humbugging' are systemically necessitated.

Our Nig, then, possesses real sophistication as fictionalized auto-biography – a claim supported by signs that the text was thoroughly revised. In particular, this would account for the strange reappearance of Henry, late in the text, after an early appearance, on page 29, as a villain, in league with Mrs. B., seeking the hand of her daughter, Jane, from pecuniary motives. First he reappears, inexplicably, where logic would lead us to expect Mrs. B.'s son Lewis to be named (62), and then appears again, even more unexpectedly, in the final chapter, apparently now motivated by love of Jane, who, the text implies, may eventually come to love him, after the death of her first husband. These strange reappearances suggest a quite different role existed for him in earlier drafts of the text.

Further acts of contrivance exist in the way that, at the heads of the chapters of *Our Nig*, quotations are selected from passages in which often the surrounding lines are even more germane to the themes of the text than the quotation actually used. Thus the title-page quotes, quite aptly enough, from Josiah Gilbert Holland's *Bitter Sweet*:

> I know . . .
> That gentle spirits on the rack of pain
> Grow faint or fierce, and pray and curse by turns;
> That Hell's temptations, clad in Heavenly guise
> And armed with might, lie evermore in wait
> Along life's path, giving assault to all –

However, in Holland's poem, even more aptly, these lines are followed by: 'I know the world is full of evil things, / And shudder with the consciousness' – lines which could serve well as *Our Nig*'s epigraph; yet the sentiment is 'purposefully omitted'.

The text, instead, signifies these 'evil things' at an indirect, referential level. In this way, *Our Nig* operates representationally as a 'converse parable': converse, because it establishes conversions of/ conversations with (converse/ations of/with) conventional autobiography's generic and ideological positions – its claimed openness. *Our Nig* as slave narrative converts autobiography into a fictionalized Northern slave narrative, re-presenting servitude, for such economic and domestic enslavement cannot be readily abolished; *Our Nig* as romance ends in desertion and deceit; *Our Nig* as sentimental novel possesses a gender-politics portraying violent, sadistic females and collusive or impotent males; *Our Nig* as autobiographical revelation repeatedly offers silence and ellipses. These converse/ ations undermine attempts to familiarize this text: it stands as a black woman's converse/ation of/with autobiographical norms.

It is wholly strategic that *Our Nig* also offers the 'converse' of a conversion narrative: a theme of the text is that Frado, despite prudently appearing to be 'serious', is never sure of white New England's Christian religion because of her experiences of its hypocrisy. This converse/ation of/with conversion climaxes when, in the Appendix, describing her 'dreaded' departure to the poorhouse, she explains that she leaves behind her Bible (72). Instead, she takes her pens, inkstand and paper. She implicitly recognizes the need to write out her own palimpsest (her converse parable), the story's 'without', exposing the depths and dimensions of Northern racism through elliptical significations. In this way the text converts the conversion narrative, declining its conventional closure. The facts of the text only go so far: the rest is represented in the techniques of fiction, used to expose the limitations of Northern abolition – not only in what the text says and what it is, but also, conversely, in the way these meld with what it does not say, and what it is not. Frado's biography and its indefinite and undefinable relationship to Wilson's autobiography orbit around these intersections.

The dissonances between the text's apparent first-person claims to autobiographical representation (*Our Nig . . . by 'Our Nig'*, 'My Mother'; 'A New Home for Me') and the third-person narrative that these entitlings frame, becomes a problematization of both the autobiographical narrative mode and its authority, tracing a shockingly unconventional, half-silenced message. Only the beatings are surely heard and only the beatings can be surely heard. This third-person narrative account of a life of silencing strategically elides the autobiographical 'I' in 'slavery's shadow', to expose the objectified condition of Black Americans in the Northern states in the second quarter of the nineteenth century, under freedom's complex servitude.

Notes

1 See Doriani (1993); Gates (1983); Russell (1990). *Our Nig*'s novelistic hybridity contrasts it to slave narratives, though these themselves subtly blend history, autobiography and fiction see Smith (1987).
2 These hypocritical circulations over slavery's continuation emerge in one of Jefferson's rough drafts of the Declaration of Independence: a bracketed section, condemning slavery, was finally omitted. Yellin (1972) frontispiece.
3 See Gates (1983).

References

Breau, E. 'Identifying Satire: *Our Nig*', *Callaloo*, 16: 2 (1993) 460–6

Doriani, B. Maclay, 'Two Women's Autobiographies', *American Quarterly*, 43:2 (1991) 199–222

Douglass, F. D. *Narrative of the Life of Frederick Douglass, An American Slave* (Harmondsworth: Penguin, [1845] 1982)

Gates, H. L. Jr. 'Introduction' to Wilson, *Our Nig* (New York: Random House, [1859] 1983) xi–lv

Russell, S. *Render me my Song* (London: Pandora, 1990)

Smith, V. 'Form and Ideology in Three Slave Narratives', in *Self-Discovery and Authenticity in African-American Narrative* (Cambridge, Mass.: Harvard University Press, 1987)

Spivak, G. C. 'Can the Subaltern Speak', in P. Williams, and L. Chrisman (eds) *Colonial Discourse and Post-Colonial Theory: A Reader* (New York: Columbia University Press, 1994) 66–111

Stowe, H. B. *Uncle Tom's Cabin* (Harmondsworth: Penguin, [1852] 1981)

Tate, C. 'Allegories of Black Female Desire; or, Re-Reading Sentimental Narratives of Black Female Authority', in C. A. Wall (ed.) *Changing Our Words: Essays in Criticism, Theory and Writing by Black Women* (London: Routledge, 1990) 98–126

Wall, C. A. (ed.) *Changing Our Words: Essays in Criticism, Theory and Writing by Black Women* (London: Routledge, 1990)

White, B. A. '"Our Nig" and the She-Devil: New Information about Harriet Wilson and the "Bellmont Family"', *American Literature*, 65:1 (1993) 19–52

Williams, P. and Chrisman, L. (eds) *Colonial Discourse and Post-Colonial Theory: A Reader* (New York: Columbia University Press, 1994)

Wilson, H. *Our Nig*, H, L. Gates Jr. (ed.) (New York: Random House, [1859] 1983)

Wilson, H. *Our Nig*, R. J. Ellis (ed.) (Nottingham: Trent Editions, [1859] 1998)

Yellin, J. F. *The Intricate Knot: Black Figures in American Literature, 1776–1863* (New York: New York University Press, 1972)

5

Lorine Niedecker: Auto/biography and Poetry

Lorna Jowett

Carolyn Heilbrun opens her book, *Writing a Woman's Life*, with the statement:

> There are four ways to write a woman's life: the woman herself may tell it, in what she chooses to call an autobiography; she may tell it in what she chooses to call fiction; a biographer, woman or man, may write the woman's life in what is called a biography; or the woman may write her own life in advance of living it, unconsciously, and without recognizing or naming the process. (1989: 11)

But there is a fifth way a woman's life can be written, which Heilbrun describes when discussing Adrienne Rich, whose 'autobiography is not to be found in a single book but rather in her poems and in diverse parts of her prose works' (Heilbrun, 1989: 66). Heilbrun briefly discusses the cross-fertilization between autobiography and poetry, concentrating on 'confessional' poetry written by white, middle-class, women poets after 1960. Lorine Niedecker (1903–70) does not fit Heilbrun's proposed model, since she did not write the kind of detailed, autobiographical, feminist poetry that Rich, Sexton and Plath are known for. Yet Niedecker's poetry can be read as autobiography, and we can find submerged in her poems the very problems about which the next generation of women were to speak out so strongly.

Traditionally, autobiography is written in prose, and 'the story of one's life' in poetry might be expected to be an epic of narrative poetry. However, in Niedecker's poems there is no sustained linear narrative, no story of her life with a beginning, a middle and an end. But whilst these might be autobiographical poems, do they constitute autobiography? In other words, how important is the autobiographical element, and how important is the poetry? These are some of the questions I will address in my discussion.

Niedecker was born in 1903 and spent most of her life on Black Hawk Island, a small peninsula jutting into Lake Koshkonong, about five miles from the small town of Fort Atkinson, Wisconsin. She attended college in Beloit but returned home after only two years because of family problems. In 1931, having separated from her first husband a few years before, Niedecker was inspired by Louis Zukofsky's guest editing of the Objectivist issue of *Poetry*. She wrote to, and subsequently visited, Zukofsky in New York. After a brief affair with Zukofsky and a terminated pregnancy, she again returned to Black Hawk Island. On the occasion of her second marriage in the 1960s, Niedecker moved to Milwaukee, but she returned to Black Hawk every weekend; after a few years the couple retired there permanently. Five collections of her work were published during her lifetime, and her death in 1970 caused hardly a ripple in literary circles. There is, as yet, no full biography of Niedecker.[1]

Whilst Niedecker deals with problems similar to those tackled by the female poets Heilbrun mentions, she does use the autobiographical 'I' in her poems. Nevertheless, one difficulty with reconstructing autobiography from Niedecker's poems is that she frequently uses transcribed 'folk' speech, so that a poem is spoken by an unidentified first person. Certain poems clearly *can* be read as autobiographical, and are verified as such in letters (the letters are particularly important in decoding Niedecker's poems), or because the connections are too strong to overlook. The autobiographical poems touch on several sensitive personal details, such as Niedecker's father's affair, her mother's death, her relationship with her working-class community, her friendship with Harold Hein and her second marriage to Al Millen.[2] For the purposes of this chapter, I shall discuss only her mother's death and her relationships with Hein and Millen.[3]

We know from Niedecker's letters that she spent a long time working on poems before they reached their final form: redrafting, condensing, cutting and finally re-positioning the words or lines. She once commented: 'For me the sentence lies in wait – all those prepositions and connectives – like an early spring flood. A good thing my follow-up feeling has always been condense, condense' (Letter to Corman, 18 February 1964; 1986: 33). Indeed she mentions this process in several of her poems: in 'Poet's Work' she wrote, 'No layoff / from this / condensery' (Niedecker, 1985: 54); elsewhere we read, 'What would they say if they knew / I sit for two months on six lines / of poetry?' (21).

Some of this effort might be read as 'poet's work', but translating an event from one's own life into a poem also means instilling the poem with a meaning for the reader as well as the poet whose experience it records. Autobiography is necessarily reflective, as with hindsight the writer imposes a structure or form onto past events, thus 'creating and not inertly remembering his [*sic*] past life in the present' (Cox, 1980: 125). Furthermore, as Gusdorf argues, it is clear that 'This postulating of a meaning dictates the choice of the facts to be retained and of the details to bring out or to dismiss according to the demands of the preconceived intelligibility' (Gusdorf, 1980: 42). This is similar to the process of composing a poem, the meaning of which will dictate what is emphasized and what downplayed or omitted. From her painstaking construction of poetry, Niedecker can be seen to be giving her life's events meaning in retrospect.

Niedecker often drew poems from 'folk' speech, and especially from her mother: she once commented 'Time for BP to write me a poem' (Letter to Zukofsky, 25 April 1949, *Correspondence*, 159).[4] Niedecker described her mother's natural 'folk' idiom thus: 'here was my mother . . . speaking whole chunks of down-to-earth (o very earthy) magic, descendent for sure of Mother Goose (I her daughter, sits and floats, you know)' (Letter to Cox, 10 December 1966; 1983: 36). In 'Well, spring overflows the land' (Niedecker, 1985: 13) the voice of Daisy Niedecker describes her family: 'My man's got nothing but leaky boats. / My daughter, writer, sits and floats.' Perhaps it was as a result of her relationship with her mother that Niedecker felt easy about transcribing 'folk' idiom, for Daisy Niedecker's increasing deafness (which became complete when Lorine was in her early twenties) meant that the two communicated by writing notes. Niedecker's father is also recognized as an important contributor to her 'folk' base in the poem 'He lived – childhood summers' (19).

When her mother died, Niedecker incorporated her last words into a poem. She described her mother's death in a letter to Zukofsky:

> BP died last Wednesday and was buried Saturday. Her last words may not have been of importance, she sat up for her supper an hour after we left and then fell back dead. But her last words to me were 'Wash the floors, wash the clothes and pull weeds.' BP

the ole worker. What a drudge she'd like to have made of her daughter! A clean drudge. (Letter to Zukofsky, 31 July 1951; 1993: 181)

The poem 'Old Mother turns blue and from us' (Niedecker, 1985: 17) translates this experience, using Daisy Niedecker's last words and a few phrases of Niedecker's own to present a bleak picture of the dying matriarch, her power denoted by the capitalization of 'Old Mother'. Significantly, Niedecker includes her own name in the poem '"Wash the floors, Lorine!"', thus placing herself as both child and poet. The insertions are kept simple to match the speech register. They provide the context and their very simplicity serves to emphasize the horror of the situation. The single word 'blue' is horribly graphic; the mother's 'turning from' her family demonstrates her movement towards death and away from life, perhaps her choice of this, as well as restless movement on her death bed. 'Death from the heart' implies pain and grief as well as the cause of death, while 'a thimble in her purse' continues the somewhat incongruous insistence on the domestic, pointing towards the final lines. The line-breaks, as usual in Niedecker's poems, are important, often leading to an unexpected conclusion, as in: 'Give me space. I need / floors.' The whole poem is keyed towards the last words – the last words of the poem, the last words of 'Old Mother', and of Daisy Niedecker – which appear with much more emphasis than in the letter: '"Wash the floors, Lorine! – / wash clothes! Weed!".' The poem confronts the daughter–mother relationship, implying something of its tension in the admonition to 'drudgery', seen by the mother as an essential part of her identity, but neglected by her daughter. As Clausen suggests (1987: 11), this poem shares some similarities with William Carlos Williams's 'The Last Words of my English Grandmother', and may be a conscious echo.

It is clear that the arrangement of material is particularly important to an autobiographical poem. However, Niedecker seemed to have particular reasons for cutting and redrafting certain poems. On more than one occasion she omits things which are 'too personal', implying that this would detract from her poetry. I would suggest that Niedecker was particularly concerned to omit mention of private relationships and the problems they brought to her as a woman. I would further argue that Niedecker often erases her negative feelings about her situation, and in this way she avoided drawing attention to her contradictory status as woman *and* poet.

Niedecker's relationship with Milwaukee dentist Harold Hein provides a personal subtext to several of her poems. Niedecker hoped
to marry Hein, whom she described as 'A simple person with innate goodness. Sensitive, warm, warm-hearted, terribly lonely since
his wife died 6 years ago. She was dying for 3 years – cancer.'
Niedecker later added to Zukofsky, 'Celia [Zukofsky's wife] is right
– marry him – wonder when he'll ask me' (Letter to Zukofsky, 27
June 1960; 1993: 264). Several poems were inspired by Hein, among
them: 'You are my friend' (Niedecker, 1985: 15). In this poem, the
'friend' brings gifts for the speaker and performs small services ('you
carry / my fishpole') as well as helping out with tasks the speaker
might be reluctant or unable to do for herself ('you water my worms /
you patch my boot'). This proof of friendship might imply that
there is no fear of rejection – the speaker asserts, 'You are my friend.'
Yet, given the autobiographical subtext to the poem, we realize
that this could be bitter irony, for the final lines of the poem ('nothing
in it / but my hand') suggest that while the relationship is only
friendship (there's 'nothing in it' to make us think otherwise), the
speaker wishes it was something more. The 'hand' could be her
hand in marriage. Hence, the opening line implies far more than
we may first have thought – longing, disappointment, regret. By
September, after spending more time with Hein, Niedecker was
prepared to admit: 'I suppose I no longer count on his marrying
me' (Letter to Zukofsky, 15 September 1960; 1993: 267). However,
Niedecker was uncertain about using her life for poetry in this way.
An early version of 'You are my friend' (Niedecker, 1985: 316–17)
had a third stanza, making explicit reference to Hein.

> The trouble of the boot on you, friend
> your dentist fingers
> an orchard to mow
> you also
> paint

This was cut later, with the comment: 'it shore [*sic*] bothers *me*
now, dead weight of that third stanza'; she explains: 'Sometimes I
can be so blind especially on something directly out of life. There's
a pitfall for poets – directly out of life' (Letter to Zukofsky, 18
December 1960; 1993: 271). Niedecker obviously sees this as dangerous ground and her condensation changes the tone of the poem,
offering resigned acceptance and regret, rather than frustration (the

first line originally read, 'Why do I press it: are you my friend?').
The problematic relationship with Hein is confronted more openly
in 'The men leave the car' (Niedecker, 1985: 49). Niedecker's description of the event which inspired this poem is confined to a
brief statement: 'We stopped in one place and the men rushed out
to pick Calla of the Swamp or Water Arum for us – greenish-white
lilies with heart-shaped leaves' (Letter to Zukofsky, 2 July 1961;
1993: 282). The incident is translated in the first lines of the opening stanza: 'The men leave the car / to bring us green-white lilies /
by woods.' It is interesting that the 'heart-shaped leaves', which
might have taken on some symbolic meaning, have been omitted
from the poem altogether. Jenny Penberthy comments on the 'em-
phatic rhythms and repetitions' of the final stanza, which culminate
in the 'clear' statement of Hein's intent: 'No marriage / no marriage / friend.' She also describes the last line, the single word 'friend'
as, 'In the context . . . chastened, muted (those soft words), meek,
confirming the opposition she [Niedecker] sees between male per-
pendicular strength and female floating irresolution' (Penberthy, 1993:
78). It is indeed 'the context' of the *poem* (not necessarily the life
event) which enforces these roles. The juxtaposition of 'large pine
spread' and 'swamp' is a figure that unifies the poem, and conveys
emotion. Niedecker's feelings about the incident are thus distanced
or translated, projected onto, and encoded within nature.

This is by no means an unusual poetic technique for Niedecker,
who uses it elsewhere. 'Club 26' (Niedecker, 1985: 47), for instance,
is charged with sexual energy and sensuality transmitted through
imagery of plants and flowers, culminating in the vivid last line:
'We stayed till the stamens trembled.' In using the natural world
as a figure for (female) emotion and / or sexuality, Niedecker takes
her place in a line of women poets which includes Dickinson, Rossetti
and H. D., who all employ the same strategy, though perhaps for
slightly different reasons. 'Unacceptable' aspects of women's lives
such as female sexuality, and especially female desire, are thus coded
in acceptable ways. In the case of 'The men leave the car' the technique might further act as a means of retrospectively controlling
the actual experience described. In the life situation she describes,
Niedecker had little control, but as a poet translating that autobiographical experience she arranges her material with confidence and
skill, and manages a successful outcome – the poem itself.

Another poem that reflects on Niedecker's life, 'I knew a clean
man' (20), features Al Millen, Niedecker's second husband, and

compares him with Hein. The poem demonstrates Niedecker's use of repetition, or repetition with variation. It begins 'I knew a clean man / but he was not for me' and ends 'He's / the one for me.' The unifying theme in this poem is the contrast between the 'clean man' (presumably Hein) and Al Millen. From a letter which comments, 'Sewing new slip covers for me new house chairs . . . so that when Al comes in from looking at a fish pole or cutting another tree down he can sit down without my worrying. He can cover himself with more sand and/or mud and new cut grass etc.' (Letter to Zukofsky, 25 August 1964; 1993: 348), Niedecker writes: 'Now I sew green aprons / over covered seats.' The first stanza breaks a new sentence after the first word 'He', leaving it hanging until we pick up the sentence in the second stanza. This runs on to the final statement, 'He's / the one for me', a positive repetition of the poem's beginning. Ending the first stanza here creates an ambiguity since we might assume that 'He' is the same 'he' who has been rejected in the second line. The word 'now' effects movement from one 'he' to another, from Hein to Millen, from one period of Niedecker's life to another. It seems significant that Niedecker identifies the book Al uses to 'smooth' his wet 'pay-check' as Whitman's *Leaves of Grass*, thus including him in her literary life, as well as linking back through both leaves and grass to the natural elements of 'muddy water' and 'sun'. It is interesting that this poem is often grouped with earlier poems, since it was published with the *My Friend Tree* collection (1961) and is thus not generally placed in proximity with other poems about Al, such as 'I married'.

Niedecker was uneasy about using her personal experience in 'I married' (Niedecker, 1985: 93), for she wrote to Cid Corman that she had composed the poem 'Just a few moments ago from a folk conversation and I suppose some of my own dark forebodings. We shd. try to be true to our subconscious? Sorry it is another *I* poem. My god, I must try to get away from that' (Letter to Corman, 20 July 1967; 1986: 129). It would seem that Niedecker was frequently inspired to write poetry by things 'directly out of life', but was not always happy with the end product, especially if she considered it had too much biographical detail. Or rather, she considered certain kinds of biography and personal reminiscence to be acceptable, while others were not, especially those connected with Niedecker's position as a woman. Niedecker often seemed uneasy about including such material and perhaps feared the disapproval of her male correspondents and publishers for doing so.

'I married' emerges from Niedecker's experience of her second marriage to Al Millen. It touches on some of the issues that later feminist poetry would address so forcefully, and also obliquely addresses the problem of being a woman poet. The reasons given for marrying in old age are more practical and realistic than romantic – 'for warmth / if not repose' – but what one has in the end is just 'someone'. The relationship seems uncomfortable, restricting – 'We lay leg / in the cupboard, head / in closet'. One specific problem is the husband's drinking ('he drank / too much'), but the whole marriage seems problematic and, as autobiography, the poem certainly suggests the difficulty Niedecker had in reconciling her marriage and her writing: note the juxtaposition of 'I thought / he drank'.

In fact, one of the misrepresentations Niedecker has suffered is that she was a childless spinster, with all its connotations of an unfulfilled woman who writes because she cannot find a man or have a family of her own. Indeed, this image persists despite her two marriages, and the relatively recent revelations about her early relationship with Zukofsky and subsequent abortion. As the number of rediscovered women writers proves, the idea that a woman either writes or marries is far from the truth; nevertheless, as 'I married' suggests, much of the tension in Niedecker's second marriage arose precisely from the fact that she continued writing. In one letter she anticipated the problems her second marriage would cause: 'I'll marry him. Somehow I'll work it out, time and space for poetry' (Letter to Zukofsky, 10 April 1963; 1993: 332), while later letters describe the problems her work faced after her second marriage when the couple lived in a small house with little private space. Niedecker had to rise early to write, and also mentions using ear plugs so that she could continue her work when her husband was watching TV. Thus we find Niedecker struggling against the same gendered misrepresentations, as well as the same conflict between work and marriage, that literary women have struggled with for many years.

We have seen that the concerns of Niedecker's life continually emerge in her poems. However, only in reading the letters can we fully grasp the autobiographical aspects of the poems, and the way in which Niedecker has re/written them as poetry. The tension between autobiography and poetry at times meant that Niedecker had to make choices for poetry's sake which affected the representation of her life. Hence the poems can be seen as transcribing a version of Niedecker's life, translations from the letters and from the events of that life. Given the nature of her literary correspondents (male), and the apparent lack of female support and friendship at home, poetry may have been Niedecker's only way to work through her concerns, and to confront, in however coded a manner, the nature of her own gender. The construction of autobiography in Niedecker's poems thus both reveals and conceals, and in doing so reflects on and critiques the life which produced both her self and her poetry.

Notes

1 Glenna Breslin began to write Niedecker's biography, but has never completed it. The privately printed Knox (1987) is available to visitors to Fort Atkinson.
2 For instance, Henry Niedecker's affair is mentioned in 'Paean to Place' and 'The Graves'; 'Old Mother turns blue and from us' deals with Daisy Niedecker's death; 'In the great snowfall before the bomb' is often quoted in discussions of Niedecker and her community; several poems refer to Harold Hein, notably 'You are my friend' and 'The men leave the car'; while among others, 'I knew a clean man' and 'I married' refer to Al Millen.
3 See Middleton (1997) for discussion of Niedecker as a 'folk' poet.
4 Daisy Niedecker was known to Niedecker and Zukofsky as 'BP', from *bellis perennis* (daisy).

References

Breslin, G. 'Lorine Niedecker: Composing a Life', in S. Groag Bell and M. Yalom (eds) *Revealing Lives: Gender in Autobiography and Biography* (Albany, NY: State University of New York Press, 1990)
Clausen, J. 'Lorine Niedecker', *Belles Lettres*, 2.5 (1987) 11
Corman, C. (ed.) *The Granite Pail* (San Francisco: North Point, 1985)
Cox, J. M. 'Recovering Literature's Lost Ground through Autobiography', in J. Olney (ed.) *Autobiography: Essays Theoretical and Critical* (Princeton, NJ: Princeton University Press, 1980)
Dent, P. (ed.) 'Extracts from Letters to Kenneth Cox', *The Full Note* (Devon, UK: Interim, 1983) 36–42
Gusdorf, G. 'Conditions and Limits of Autobiography', in J. Olney (ed.) *Autobiography: Essays Theoretical and Critical* (Princeton, NJ: Princeton University Press, 1980)
Heilbrun, C. G. *Writing a Woman's Life* (London: Women's Press, 1989)
Knox, J. S. *Lorine Niedecker: An Original Biography* (Fort Atkinson, WI: Dwight Foster Public Library, 1987)
Middleton, P. 'Folk Poetry and the American Avant-Garde: Placing Lorine Niedecker', *Journal of American Studies*, 31.2 (1997) 203–18

Niedecker, L. *From this Condensery: The Complete Writings of Lorine Niedecker*, R. Bertholf (ed.) (Highlands, N.C.: Jargon, 1985)

Niedecker, L. *'Between Your House and Mine': the Letters of Lorine Niedecker to Cid Corman 1960 to 1970*, ed. L.P. Faranda (Durham, N.C.: Duke University Press, 1986)

Niedecker, L. (ed.) *Niedecker and the Correspondence with Zukofsky 1931–1970* ed. J. Penberthy (Cambridge: Cambridge University Press, 1993)

6

Travel Writing as Autobiography: Rebecca West's Journey of Self-Discovery

Vesna Goldsworthy

A belief in the broader relevance of the individual voice, implicitly present in any (auto)biographical work, has meant that – until relatively recently – there were few purely autobiographical writings by women. Privileged 'historical' insight, such as that provided by high political office or military leadership, is still viewed as a prerequisite for memoir writing (see Swindells, this volume, chapter 1). It is hardly surprising that women writers continue to seek other outlets for a record of their own time and thought. Travel writing is one of the more obviously 'self-legitimizing' genres which has offered women a space in which to inscribe their experiences and views.

Given the paucity of personal memoirs, travel accounts written by women – from the earliest ones, such as Lady Mary Montagu Wortley's *Turkish Letters* (1763), to twentieth-century examples, such as Edith Durham's explorations of Albania or Freya Stark's adventures in Arabia and Asia Minor – have been examined as often for glimpses into their authors' lives as for their descriptions of remote corners of the globe. Indeed, particularly in the case of older travel accounts, those that reveal details of their author's personality and attitudes frequently seem more interesting than more impersonal, 'objective' descriptions of different lands and peoples.

Although written with an explicitly stated desire to offer a highly personal view of Europe in the late 1930s, Rebecca West's *Black Lamb and Grey Falcon. A Journey through Yugoslavia* presents a different case. While West's early life in particular has been subject of much – often prurient – attention, *Black Lamb and Grey Falcon*,

widely recognized as the most important work of one of the leading British women writers of this century, continues to be interpreted
almost exclusively by those interested in Balkan history.

Few travel books compare with *Black Lamb and Grey Falcon* in
the way that it still provokes controversy and heated debate in
newspapers and magazines more than 50 years after its original
publication. When it first appeared in 1941, West's half-million word
account of her Balkan journeys was welcomed by the reviewers as
one of the masterpieces of travel literature. In 1948, the historian
A. J. P. Taylor called it 'a work of genius' (Taylor, 1981: 294). As
recently as 1991, it was recommended as 'still one of the best introductions to the country and its people' (Finder, 1991: 195).

In the throes of Yugoslavia's disintegration, *Black Lamb and Grey
Falcon* was referred to, in a *New Yorker* article tellingly entitled 'Rebecca
West's War', as 'the key reference for the new generation of Balkan
commentators' (Hall, 1996: 74). One of the most influential ac-
counts of travel through the Balkans in the 1990s, Robert Kaplan's
Balkan Ghosts, which has counted among its admirers President
Clinton, his wife Hillary and the former chairman of the US joint
chiefs of staff General Colin Powell, described *Black Lamb and Grey
Falcon* as 'this century's greatest travel book' (Kaplan, 1993: 4).

In the 1990s, West's work sold tens of thousands of copies, but
also came under renewed attacks for what was seen as its 'unfash-
ionable' Serbophile and pro-Yugoslav attitude. New editions of *Black
Lamb and Grey Falcon* now provide a short introduction, explaining
how political developments in the 1930s encouraged West to believe that a union of small Balkan nations – in which the Serbs
would play a role analogous to that of Piedmont in Italy – was the
best defence against the imperialist aspirations of neighbouring states.

Useful though the debates between Balkan historians, journalists
and commentators have been in assessing the intricacies of West's
historical judgement, they have also, in a sense, annexed West's
travelogue to the realm of Balkan scholarship. *Black Lamb and Grey
Falcon* continues to be used, in the words of West's biographer Victoria
Glendinning, as 'an area of battlefield' (Glendinning, 1987: 168).
Seemingly reluctant to join in the 'Balkan' fray, English literary
studies have offered remarkably few interpretations of 'this century's
greatest travel book', despite the fact that it is the most reprinted
of West's many works. To cite a not altogether dissimilar example,
it is as if Byron's *Childe Harold's Pilgrimage* were still debated exclu-

sively as an eye-witness account of the rights and wrongs of Otto-
man rule in the Balkans.

For students of English literature, Rebecca West seems instead to
be frozen in an eternal late Edwardian moment, the dying summer
of 1912, as the fiercely outspoken young feminist who, on the pages
of *The Freewoman* magazine, called H. G. Wells 'an old maid among
novelists' and continued – 'as a measure of intellectual honesty' –
to dish out bad reviews of his work even after they became lovers
(Marcus, 1982: 64–9). The charismatic twenty-year-old suffragette,
embodied in the icon of 'Young Rebecca', the single mother of
H. G. Wells's son, has stood in the way of an appreciation of Rebecca
West as a mature writer. Some of her most important later work
remains neglected. Examples include *The Meaning of Treason* (1948,
and out of print), which examines the case of William Joyce (Lord
Haw-Haw), who broadcast Nazi propaganda during the Second World
War, and *The Birds Fall Down* (1966), set in pre-revolutionary Russia and described in a recent history of English literature as 'one of
the most stimulating novels of the latter half of the century' (Sanders,
1994: 580). West's attempt, in *Black Lamb and Grey Falcon*, to provide a personal insight into the political developments of the 1930s,
and, in particular, the role Britain and America should play in a
Europe threatened by Hitler's expansionism, is neglected, even though
it is a rare example of an explicitly political memoir by a British
woman writer whose record of anti-fascist activism spans the decade.

West was already a renowned journalist and author, with five
novels and two lengthy critical studies behind her, when she en-
countered the Balkans for the first time in 1936. She went to the
region on a British Council lecture tour, with no great prior knowledge
and no specific interest in Bulgaria, Greece and Yugoslavia: the
countries to which her first Balkan tour was to take her. She was,
however, acutely aware of the developments in Germany and recorded – as her biographer Carl Rollyson notes – her 'growing sense
of the apocalypse' in a series of articles written for the *New York
American* as early as between 1931 and 1933 (Rollyson, 1996: 130).
Black Lamb and Grey Falcon was to provide West with an outlet for
a vehement denunciation of new European nationalisms. In the
guise of travel literature and eyewitness account, she offered an
astute and early political analysis of the causes of the Second World
War, setting out her counterblast to the proponents of appeasement.

Perhaps because of West's gender, her most seminal work often receives less attention than some of her love affairs. Indeed, notwithstanding the recent wars in former Yugoslavia, a casual observer of television arts programmes and reader of the arts pages in newspapers might have concluded that her relationship with H. G. Wells was infinitely more significant than her longest and most deeply felt book.

While representing one of the most exhaustive literary and historical examinations of a Balkan country available in any language, *Black Lamb and Grey Falcon* is just as important as an attempt by West to redefine the boundaries of travel literature. British travel writing in the earlier part of this century tended to follow the traditions of Victorian travel narratives, which – much like the realist novel – claimed to be 'objective', unbiased, omniscient accounts of journeys, usually undertaken by intrepid male travellers in 'obscure' corners of the planet. As in the novel, the shift towards modernism increases the importance of the individual perspective. The individual voice which narrates the journey begins to be as important as the journey itself.

Rebecca West contemplated the changing philosophy of travel in her account of an encounter with D. H. Lawrence who, on reaching a new city, went straight to his hotel and proceeded to 'hammer out articles about the place, vehemently and exhaustively describing the temperament of the people. . . . This seemed obviously a silly thing to do', West thought at first, but later realized that he was writing 'about the state of his own soul', 'and the city of Florence was as good a symbol as any other' (West, 1978: 388).

Writing about Yugoslavia in the late 1930s, West similarly wrote about 'the state of her own soul'. Her journey to Yugoslavia forced her to face the increasing certainty of another European war, and she resolved to provide one of the most deliberately revealing and personal records of the intellectual anguish and soul searching undergone by a British woman writer in the late 1930s:

> This experience made me say to myself: 'If a Roman woman had, some years before the sack of Rome, realized why it was going to be sacked and what motives inspired the barbarians and what the Romans, and had written down all she knew and felt about it, the record would have been of value to historians. My situation, though probably not so fatal, is as interesting.' Without doubt it was my duty to keep a record of it. So I resolved to put on paper what a typical Englishwoman felt and

thought in the late nineteen-thirties when, already convinced of the inevitability of the second Anglo-German war, she had been able to follow the dark waters of that event back to its source. (West, 1982: 1089)

West's friend, the journalist John Gunther, characterized *Black Lamb and Grey Falcon* as 'not so much a book about Yugoslavia as a book about Rebecca West' (Hall, 1996: 76). Seeking to pay her an underhand compliment, Gunther pointed to one of the most abiding values of West's study. While the title defines West's work as a travelogue, 'a journey through Yugoslavia', *Black Lamb and Grey Falcon* is also a 'social autobiography' – that is, a very personal account of an important historical moment, described by its author as a record of 'what a typical Englishwoman felt' in the face of a war. Its Epilogue, written during the Blitz, while West watched the bombs falling over London and the sight of the burning city 'touched deep sources of pain that will not listen to reason', was a powerful mobilizing call directed at her readership in Britain and America. Brian Hall describes it as 'one of the most stirring and intelligent pieces of war propaganda ever written' (Hall, 1996: 74).

Combining as it does historical study, political essay, autobiography and elements of fiction, *Black Lamb and Grey Falcon* is a unique metatext. West does not observe chronology. She merges three journeys – the first lecture tour in 1936; the second, an Easter journey with her husband in 1937; and the final visit, which ended in the early summer of 1938 on the Adriatic coast – into one. In order to protect her Yugoslav friends whose country had – by the time when her book appeared in 1941 – been dismembered and occupied, she alters their names and identities.

West's primary concern is not the accuracy of her book as a record of her travels. She focuses instead on those insights into the Balkans which can help her make sense of British and European history. Her attempts to understand Yugoslavia are permeated with a sense of self-recognition. 'Nothing in my life had affected me more deeply than this journey through Yugoslavia,' she notes, adding: 'This was in part because there is a coincidence between the natural forms and colours of the western and southern parts of Yugoslavia and the innate forms and colours of my imagination' (West, 1982: 1088). She defines her efforts to understand the Balkans as an attempt to gain a deeper knowledge of herself:

But my journey moved me also because it was like picking up a strand of wool that could lead me out of a labyrinth in which, to my surprise, I had found myself immured. It might be that when I follow the thread to its end I would find myself faced by locked gates, and that this labyrinth was my sole portion on this earth. But at least I now knew its twists and turns, and what corridor led into what vaulted chamber, and noting in my life before I went to Yugoslavia had ever made plain these mysteries. (1088–9)

With its very personal insights, *Black Lamb and Grey Falcon* is quintessentially a modernist travel narrative. Introspection is the essence of West's journey. External descriptions of travel and people frequently end in moments of epiphany, when the country 'offers knowledge of itself.' 'Sometimes a country will for days keep its secrets from a traveller,' she wrote in Macedonia, 'showing him nothing but its surfaces, its grass, its trees, the outside of its houses. Then suddenly it will throw him a key and tell him to go where he likes and see what he can' (786). *Black Lamb and Grey Falcon* invites the reader to find such a key to the understanding of Balkan history. The book begins with a very private moment, as West urges her husband, Henry Andrews, a reluctant traveller to Yugoslavia, to expect a country in which 'everything was comprehensible', a country which, after one brief visit, feels like her 'mother country':

I raised my hand on my elbow and called through the open door into the other wagon-lit: 'My dear, I know I have inconvenienced you terribly by making you take your holiday now, and I know you did not really want to come to Yugoslavia at all. But when you get there you will see why it was so important that we should make this journey and that we should make it now, at Easter. It will all be quite clear, once we are in Yugoslavia.' There was, however, no reply. My husband had gone to sleep. It was perhaps as well. I could not have gone to justify my certainty that this train was taking us to a land where everything was comprehensible, where the mode of life was so honest that it put an end to perplexity. I lay back in the darkness and marvelled that I should be feeling about Yugoslavia as if it were my mother country, for this was 1937, and I had never seen the place till 1936. (1)

A similar, strongly personal tone permeates her travelogue right through to the Epilogue in which West's own country is facing Nazi Germany, alone and vulnerable. Britain's suffering, finally, makes her understand 'what it means to be Balkan'. The recognition of her 'mother country' in Yugoslavia comes a full circle in these final moments of the book. She had originally chosen Yugoslavia as her subject because of her interest in the relationships between small states and great empires – 'because I was born a citizen of one of the greatest empires the world has ever seen, and grew up as its exasperated critic' (1089). Before her journey to the Balkans, West had, as she explained to one of her Yugoslav correspondents, contemplated a book about a small country in a different corner of Europe:

> I went to Finland in 1935 and saw a lot of people there including the Communist leader, Vuoluoki, who seemed to me a superb woman, and I wanted to write a book on a small nation torn between the conflicts of greater powers. I meant to go back to Finland from time to time for a matter of years, but I went to Yugoslavia some months later on a lecture-tour for the British Council and realized that this was a far more exciting and noble subject. I went with some experience of Nazi Germany and Fascist Italy and a supreme loathing of both, and a great distaste for Austria, which I thought the nastiest of the old European powers and in her present phase very willing to hold the bag for Nazi Germany. (West, 1945: unpublished letter to S. Pribićević)[1]

Her initial, strong sense of identification with small nations whose destiny was controlled by the aspirations of imperial powers, perhaps typical of West as a woman writer, finally becomes a source of personal courage when Britain itself is threatened. The memory of South Slavs enables the author to face the destiny of her own country, whatever it might be, playing the music of Mozart on her gramophone ('Deh vieni, non tardar' – 'O come, do not delay' – Susanna's aria from *The Marriage of Figaro*) against the sound of bombs exploding over London. 'This has seemed to me at times an unendurably horrible book to write, with its record of pain and violence and bloodshed,' West writes, adding that 'perhaps the most horrible thing about it is that . . . I have to end it while there rages round me vileness equal to that which I describe' (West, 1982: 1126). While many recent autobiographical writings by women seem inspired by Simone de Beauvoir's argument that the personal is political, in West's work the political always becomes profoundly personal. Her moving account of the Blitz, with its deliberation on the redemptive power of art in moments of historical darkness – when there was 'no solid ground, only blood and mud poached to an ooze by the perpetual trampling back and forth of Judases seducing one another in an unending cycle of treacheries' (1126) – offers the most strongly autobiographical moments in the book. West's descriptions of walking with her husband through the rose-garden in London's Regent's Park, 'while France was falling, and after she had fallen', as Londoners sit among the roses under a heaven 'curiously starred with the silver elephantines of the balloon barrage . . . reading the papers or looking straight in front of them, their faces white', provide some of the most vivid evocations of the Blitz in English literature (1130). 'Let nobody belittle them by pretending they were fearless,' she urges. 'But their pale lips did not part to say the words that would have given them security and dishonour' (1130).

The sheer power with which West writes about this theme underlines the danger of seeing *Black Lamb and Grey Falcon* as exclusively a 'Balkan' travel book. Such a preoccupation neglects its value as testimony to a British woman writer's attitude to the Second World War – with its plea not in favour of mindless courage but against dishonour – written at a time when the war's outcome was far from clear.

Note

1   I am grateful to Aleksej Zorić and Kristina Pribićević-Zorić for allowing me access to Rebecca West's correspondence with Stoyan Pribićević.

References

Finder, J. 'Women Travellers in the Balkans: A Bibliographical Guide', in J. B. Allcock and A. Young (eds) *Black Lambs and Grey Falcons. Women Travellers in the Balkans* (Bradford: Bradford University Press, 1991)
Glendinning, V. *Rebecca West. A Life* (London: Weidenfeld & Nicolson, 1987)
Hall, B. 'Rebecca West's War', *New Yorker*, 15 April (1996) 74–83
Kaplan, R. D. *Balkan Ghosts A Journey through History* (New York: St. Martin's Press, 1993)
Marcus, J. (ed.) *The Young Rebecca. Writings of Rebecca West 1911–1917* (New York: The Viking Press, 1982)
Rollyson, C. *Rebecca West. A Saga of the Century* (London: Sceptre, 1996)

Sanders, A. *The Short Oxford History of English Literature* (Oxford: Clarendon Press, 1994)

Taylor, A. J. P. *The Habsburg Monarchy 1809–1918. A History of the Austrian Empire and Austria-Hungary* (London: Penguin, 1981)

West, R. *Rebecca West. A Celebration* (London: Penguin, [1977] 1978)

———. *Black Lamb and Grey Falcon. A Journey through Yugoslavia* (London: Macmillan, [1941] 1982)

———. Unpublished letter to S. Pribićević, 5 June 1945

7

'My Poor Private Voice': Virginia Woolf and Auto/Biography

Anna Snaith

For Virginia Woolf, writing and publishing women's lives was a crucial part of women's move from the private to the public sphere. This applied particularly to those 'lives of the obscure' as she called them, the Mrs Browns in the corner of the railway carriage (Woolf, 1967: 120; 1966: 319). Woolf wanted to reclaim women's lives, those lives found 'locked in old diaries, stuffed away in old drawers' or simply unrecorded (Woolf, 1960: 76). This concern was always synonymous with issues of representation: how one might write these lives, how the self might be recorded. These representations, in turn, entailed revision: Woolf's complex rethinking of auto/biography itself, involving her ideas on the contingency of self and the combination of fact and fiction.[1] Her redressing of patriarchal dominance, then, was intimately linked to generic, stylistic and conceptual revision.

The influence of Woolf's father, Leslie Stephen, his role as editor of the *Dictionary of National Biography*, as well as his own auto/biographical writings, meant that auto/biography featured prominently in her reading from an early age. From that same early age, however, she was questioning the purpose and methodology of conventional autobiography, particularly the linear, fact-based style of Victorian auto/biography. She marked herself clearly as a Modernist, indeed she was never to write a conventional biography of a woman. *Orlando*, *Flush*, *A Room of One's Own*, *Three Guineas* and *To The Lighthouse* all contain representations of real women's lives, but all reveal a Modernist concern with subjectivity and flux, a self-consciousness of the mechanics and methodology of representation and a questioning of history. Woolf's one conventional biography, of Roger Fry, which she was asked to write, caused her

much turmoil because she was obliged to stick to facts: accuracy
was a priority. She felt the work was 'too minute & tied down &
documented', and proposed something 'more fictitious' when she
entered the biography herself in 1909 (Woolf, 1984: 155). With
Roger Fry we see Woolf straining against the restrictions of the genre,
longing to mix accuracy with imagination.

In 1940 Woolf wrote to Ethel Smyth, asking her to remedy the
lack of women's autobiographies:

> I was thinking the other night that there's never been a woman's
> autobiography. Nothing to compare with Rousseau. . . . Now why
> shouldn't you be not only the first woman to write an opera,
> but equally the first to tell truths about herself?. . . . I should
> like an analysis of your sex life. . . . More introspection. More
> intimacy. (Woolf, 1980: 453)

Woolf, for many reasons, is unable to write this autobiography herself,
and avoided such explicit exposure. But her stylistic and imaginative vision took her to places other than the unequivocally stable
'I' of a conventional autobiography. Her autobiographical 'A Sketch
of the Past', for example, written just before her death, shifts between memoir and diary, focusing around an 'I' which is constantly
questioned, recreated and made contingent.

At the very beginning of her career, though, Woolf was incorporating autobiography, both real and fictionalized, into her short
fiction. In two early texts from 1906, 'Phyllis and Rosamond' and
'The Journal of Mistress Joan Martyn', Woolf exhibits this inter-
mingling of biography, autobiography, fact and fiction. The narrator
of Virginia Woolf's earliest short story 'Phyllis and Rosamond', written
in June 1906, meditates on the early twentieth-century interest in
biography, in 'pictures of people' (Woolf, 1985: 17). The emphasis
is on the veracity of these portraits, the accurate and faithful re-
porting of, for example, 'how the door keeper at the Globe . . . passed
Saturday March 18th in the year of our Lord 1568' (17). The narrator notes, however, the absence of such historical and biographical
portraits for 'those many women who cluster in the shade' (17).
Novelists and historians have only just begun to shine a 'partial
light' on the 'obscure figures' occupying the 'dark and crowded
place behind the scenes' (17), the narrator remarks, thereby setting
the premise for the story to follow. The story traces one day in the
lives of two daughters imprisoned in a repressive, Victorian,

Kensington household. The women, denied an education, play hostess and await marriage. That evening, however, the two women visit the Miss Tristrams in Bloomsbury and are exposed to a radically different way of life for women: 'if one lived here in Bloomsbury . . . one might grow up as one liked' (24).

The narrator presents the scenario as informative and representative: an essential addition to the many images of male experience. The story, then, is sociological: 'we intend to look as steadily as we can at a little group' and historical: 'which lives at this moment (the 20th June, 1906)' (17). The narrator refers to the 'facts' of the case, the 'excellent material' found in their situation and also to the topical phrase 'daughters of the home' which encapsulates their position (18). The women's lives are typical, a 'common case' and 'epitomize the qualities of many' (17). Woolf has set up a factual and historical framework for the piece, it will have the same function as the portrait of the doorkeeper at the Globe. Despite this clear historical agenda, Woolf, or Virginia Stephen, as she was then, also makes explicit the fictional element of the piece. The narrator picks the characters' names randomly: 'Phyllis and Rosamond, we will call them' (18).

On one level, the work is a short story, with requisite components, such as a narrator, characterization, imagery and plot. Yet, another layer of the story, the autobiographical element, is available to those readers aware that Woolf herself grew up in a Victorian home in Kensington and moved to Bloomsbury after the death of her parents. The story is about that transition: Woolf is both Phyllis and Rosamond, denied a formal education, existing as ornaments in the home, *as well as* the Miss Tristrams, whose party is reminiscent of Thursday evening gatherings at 46 Gordon Square, Bloomsbury. The reason that Woolf can so confidently present the piece as a sociological and historical case-study is that it is based on her own experience, but experience which she has reworked, transmuted and spread among the various characters. The story, although most obviously fiction, sits also at the intersection of autobiography, biography, history and sociology. Woolf fictionalizes fragments of her own life *and* a representative English, upper-middle-class woman's life in 1906 through a conceptualized and an actual crossover between fact and fiction.

In August 1906, just after she wrote 'Phyllis and Rosamond', Woolf was holidaying with Vanessa in Blo' Norton Hall in Norfolk where she wrote an unfinished piece, posthumously titled 'The Journal of

Mistress Joan Martyn', which continues the discussion begun in her first story about the representation of women's lives, reactions to those representations and concomitant negotiations between fact and fiction which were to preoccupy her throughout her life. The unfinished text is even more revealing, however, when viewed alongside her journal entries from August 1906. Finding herself in a new location, Woolf set out to represent the life of the land: its geography, its history, the social configurations of its inhabitants. The boundary between animate and inanimate blurs, and Woolf meditates on her characterization of Norfolk in biographical terms: 'strange, grey green, undulating, dreaming, philosophising & remembering' (Woolf, 1990: 312). Woolf makes explicit that the process of written description works the same 'for a place as for a person' (312).

Woolf goes further, however, figuring the land as 'some noble untamed woman conscious that she has no beauty to vaunt, that nobody very much wants her' (313). The largely uninhabited areas of Norfolk, through which Woolf spent her holiday walking, parallel the lives of the obscure, the undocumented lives of women. The land is described in terms of a woman's body through lesbian erotics: the 'undulating plains', the 'domesticities of the place' into which she is 'initiated', the land is 'so soft . . . so wild, & yet so willing to be gentle' (312 and 313).

The concern with the lives of women continues when she examines the gravestones at Kenninghall church. She copies down the inscription on a Mrs Susan Batt's tomb and meditates on the epitaph as an encapsulation of a life: a 'solid lump of truth' (314). Again Woolf has turned to the lives of obscure women and the process and means by which one might record those lives.

In August 1906, Woolf developed these ideas more fully in 'The Journal of Mistress Joan Martyn', technically a short story, but as so often with Woolf's work, a piece which crosses generic boundaries. The text deals with feminist historian Rosamond Merridew, who researches land tenure systems of the thirteenth, fourteenth and fifteenth centuries and who comes across the journal of a Miss Joan Martyn dated 1480. The piece is a double fictional autobiography in that Merridew writes herself and then the second half of the text is a transcription of Joan Martyn's journal.

Merridew introduces herself in terms of the 'lives of the obscure'; although her readers may find her obscure, she has 'won considerable fame' for her work: 'Berlin has heard my name; Frankfurt would give a soirée in my honour; and I am not absolutely unknown in one or two secluded rooms in Oxford and in Cambridge' (Woolf, 1985: 33). Woolf undoes the scenario she set up in 'Phyllis and Rosamond': here is a woman who is not in the shade. In order to do this, Merridew has 'exchanged a husband and a family and a house' (33). Her maternal passion is transferred to her 'fragments of yellow parchment' (33). Merridew's assertion of choices other than marriage and motherhood for women and her challenge to the then male world of academia is present not only in her career but in her methodology and independence. As an independent historian she is in competition with state historians and those attached to universities. The state system 'robs my poor private voice of all its persuasion' (33). Her private, female voice is up against the masculine conglomerate of the state.

However, the main challenge and obstacle Merridew both presents and faces is to do with her methodology and her subject matter. First, she is interested in women's history and second in the private, individual lives of her subjects. She wants the 'intricacies of land tenure . . . in relation to the life of the time' (34). Descriptions of Dame Elinor's stockings or 'Dame Elinor, at work with her needle' (34) are integral to her representation of medieval history. Her mixture of public records with private life, however, means a mixing of fact and fictional recreation, based on historical evidence. Merridew wants to present the time as 'vividly as in a picture' (34) and acknowledges that the absence of private documentation and records necessitates the use of imagination 'like any other storyteller' (35). Merridew in her historical research, just like Woolf with her Fry biography, wants to move beyond the strictures of facts. A bringing to life of the past necessarily means embellishment and creative imagining. Woolf, through Merridew, is questioning the boundaries of genre, the limits of historical research, the interplay of fact and fiction. This, of course, is where Merridew's critics object, claiming she has no documentation to 'stiffen these words into any semblance of the truth' (35). The masculine sexual image belies a philosophy alien to Merridew's feminist revision. She does not want the words stiffened, she wants them free-floating: suggesting, intimating rather than pointing. The fact/fiction combination in 'Phyllis and Rosamond' and the narrator who is implicitly a feminist historian is carried through to 'The Journal of Mistress Joan Martyn' and made more explicit.

This is particularly apt, Woolf knows, because if Merridew wants to include a female perspective on medieval history, she must include the private sphere: something which, in the absence of documentary evidence, she will have to imagine. In the text Merridew draws a line '————' in order to put the argument regarding truth and fiction behind her. She proceeds on her own terms. The dominating 'I' which is denounced in *A Room of One's Own*, the dark bar which casts a shadow on the page, is here laid on its side, casting no shadows. The line joins rather than excludes, it marks an ideological gap between Merridew and her critics, the dash moves the writing forward.

Merridew recognizes the value of Joan Martyn's journal, regardless of its owner, John Martyn's, dismissive comments. John, an expert regarding his ancestors, has time only for the male line. He values public achievement, and is scathing of Mistress Joan's diary. The Stud Book of Willoughby and the Household Books of Jasper make more interesting reading for John Martyn than Joan's private journal. When Merridew asks to borrow the journal, Martyn replies 'I don't think you'll find anything out of the way in her... as far as I can see, not remarkable' (45). His interest in his family history does not encompass women's experience.

The 'nobody very much wants her' which Woolf applied to the Norfolk countryside in her journal is extended to Joan Martyn. She is one of the 'lives of the obscure' which Woolf was so intent on recovering, be it in fact or fiction. Just as Woolf, in the journal, turned first to the epitaph on a woman's gravestone, so Merridew bypasses the books of records written by men, for the autobiographical recording of a woman's life.

The second half of the text is a transcription of Joan's journal, reinforcing the importance not just of noticing, but of publishing women's accounts of their lives. Joan feels herself trapped within Martyn Hall, and just as Phyllis and Rosamond found Bloomsbury liberating, Joan longs for the 'free and beautiful place' beyond the iron gates (45). She is soon to be married off and so retreats into fiction: stories of women such as Helen of Troy. Joan is a storyteller; she recreates her father's journey to London, as though making it herself. She finds inspiration in stories of 'Knights and Ladies . . . of whispers, and sighs, and lovers' laments' (56), but is forced to learn the management of the home and farm, the accounts and records, in readiness for her husband's absence. These will take precedence over her private journal, just as the household accounts did for John Martyn.

Joan needs privacy for her writing: 'confusion came over me when he asked me what I wrote, and stammering that it was a "Diary" I covered the pages with my hands' (60). Joan's father values her writing, but wishes that his male ancestors had done the same, and pulls her away from her journal to visit her grandfather's tomb. Her writing is secondary to the immortalization of her male ancestors as both her father and John Martyn make clear. Joan herself recognizes her talent and decides that she will write not of herself in future but of 'Knights and Ladies and of adventures in strange lands' (62). Writing can take her beyond the confines of the private home.

In this early text, Woolf, through Merridew, questions the inclusion both of fiction and of the private journal within the public, factual realm of history. Making the text half Merridew's autobiographical account of her work and the finding of the journal, and half a transcription of that journal, reinforces the importance of women's experience. Both Rosamond and Joan's accounts are historical documents, within the fictional framework of the text and both emphasize the importance of private narrative, within women's history in particular. This text, along with 'Phyllis and Rosamond' and Woolf's own journal from 1906, indicate how complex was her thinking about the need to represent women's lives, women's history, the mix of fact and fiction as well as generic mixture.

Moving forward to look briefly at Woolf's penultimate novel, *The Years*, we can see how central the issue of women's auto/biographies still were for Woolf in the 1930s and how she continued to rethink them. *The Years* started life as an essay, quickly became an essay-novel called 'The Pargiters' and then the essay sections were omitted. The evolution of the novel was a long, complex, six-year process, which included major generic and conceptual changes. The original idea, however, was a work 'about the sexual life of women' a work which was to be a 'novel of fact' (Woolf, 1953: 166; 1978: 9). Woolf conducted extensive research during the 1930s which produced, among other notes, three notebooks of cuttings and quotations, on the subject of women's experience and society's treatment of women. It is clear, then, that Woolf's intention throughout was to explore the lives of women – from the speech to the London and National Society for Women's Service out of which the work grew, to her feminist, pacifist essay *Three Guineas* which grew out of *The Years*. Also central is the factual base, her extensive research; she felt she had 'collected enough powder to blow up St Pauls' (Woolf, 1953: 179).

Much of that research came from women's auto/biographies. In 'The Pargiters', Woolf writes: 'There is scarcely a statement in it that cannot be [*traced to some biography, or*] verified, if anybody should wish so to misuse their time' (9). Even though Woolf omitted the essay sections, thereby excising direct quotation and exposition, the factual foundation remains. Her portrayal of the Pargiter women from 1880 to 1937, their lack of formal education, their imprisonment in the home, their treatment by their brothers, can, as Woolf remarked, be traced directly to biographies and autobiographies by and about women such as Mrs Humphry Ward, Anne Jemima Clough, Dorothea Beale and Mary Kingsley.[2]

Contrary to the critics who see the work as a battle between fact and fiction which failed,[3] when one acknowledges the continued presence of Woolf's research in *The Years*, it is clear how useful Woolf found the combination. As she wrote in her diary at the time, 'I am not a politician: obviously. Can only rethink politics very slowly into my own tongue' (Woolf, 1984: 114). The evolution of *The Years* is just that process of rethinking, it is her own way of representing women's lives, of conveying her feminism, preventing it from being propaganda, while incorporating the research she had conducted and the evidence she had accumulated.

Woolf was explicit about her fruitful combination of 'facts, as well as the vision' (Woolf, 1982: 151). However, Woolf does not view 'facts' as monolithic and permanent. In her two essays, 'The Art of Biography' and 'The New Biography' Woolf discusses her conception of 'fact' and the mixture of fact and fiction in biography. Facts, according to Woolf, are 'subject to changes of opinion. . . . Facts must be manipulated; some must be brightened; others shaded' (Woolf, 1967: 226 and 229). Facts are contingent, determined by context and in *The Years* where much of the fact comes from women's biography and autobiography, fact can be subjective and private. Woolf uses 'the creative fact; the fertile fact; the fact that suggests and engenders' (Woolf, 1967: 228).

Here then we return to 'The Journal of Mistress Joan Martyn' and Merridew's combination of fact and fiction. Woolf's fictional representations of women in *The Years* draw on many biographies and autobiographies, thereby mixing historical fact and experience with fiction, just as Merridew incorporated fictional elements into her historical accounts. Just as Merridew valued Joan's journal, an autobiographical text, so Woolf too values women's private and individual experience and women's recounting of that experience. Rather than dismiss women's accounts as subjective or non-historical, like Merridew's critics, Woolf never ceases to view them as political evidence.

At the end of 'The New Biography' Woolf writes that 'A little fiction mixed with fact can be made to transmit personality very effectively' (233), looking back to 'The Journal of Mistress Joan Martyn' and forward to 'The Pargiters' and *The Years*. She points towards a possible 'mixture of biography and autobiography, of fact and fiction' (235) when, of course, she herself has been enacting in her writing just such a complex negotiation throughout her life.

Notes

1 I refer to a fact/fiction dichotomy unquestioningly because Woolf herself, although she invariably combined the two, conceived of the terms as distinct.
2 Ward (1918), Clough (1897), Raikes (1908), Steadman (1931) and Gwynn (1932).
3 See Leaska's introduction to Woolf (1978).

References

Clough, B. A. *A Memoir of Anne Jemima Clough* (London: Edward Arnold, 1897)
Gwynn, S. *The Life of Mary Kingsley* (London: Macmillan, 1932)
Raikes, E. *Dorothea Beale of Cheltenham* (London: Constable, 1908)
Steadman, C. F. *In the Days of Miss Beale: A Study of Her Work and Influence* (London: J. Burrow & Co. Ltd, 1931)
Ward, H. *A Writer's Recollections* (London: W. Collins Sons & Co. Ltd, 1918)
Woolf, V. *A Writer's Diary*, L. Woolf (ed.) (London: The Hogarth Press, 1953)
—— *Granite and Rainbow* (London: The Hogarth Press, 1960)
—— *Collected Essays*, Vol. I (London: The Hogarth Press, 1966)
—— *Collected Essays*, Vol. IV (London: The Hogarth Press, 1967)
—— *Leave the Letters Till We're Dead: The Letters of Virginia Woolf*, Vol. VI
—— *The Pargiters*, M. A. Leaska (ed.) (London: The Hogarth Press, 1978)
N. Nicolson (ed.) (London: The Hogarth Press, 1980)
—— *The Diary of Virginia Woolf*, Vol. IV, A. O. Bell (ed.) (London: The Hogarth Press, 1982)
—— *The Diary of Virginia Woolf*, Vol. V, A. O. Bell (ed.) (London: The Hogarth Press, 1984)
—— *The Complete Shorter Fiction of Virginia Woolf*, S. Dick (ed.) (London: The Hogarth Press, 1985)
—— *A Passionate Apprentice: The Early Journals 1897–1909*, M. A. Leaska (ed.) (London: The Hogarth Press, 1990)

8
The Textual Contract: Distinguishing Autobiography from the Novel

Tonya Blowers

How is autobiography to be generically distinguished from the novel? It is often assumed that autobiography is based more emphatically on fact or reality, the novel on fantasy or imagination. Autobiography is a declared attempt to represent the life of the author; the novel may well represent that life to some degree, introducing characters who might be composites of aspects of the author's personality, but it makes no claims to correspond in any direct way to the author's life. However, we all know that many novels read like autobiographies and, indeed, much of the *frisson* of the writing depends on this close but unaffirmed identification. Philippe Lejeune's definition of autobiography as a pact between reader and writer, confirmed by the use of the author's name for both protagonist and narrator, is useful in that it gives a straightforward technical means of defining the genre, distinguishing it from the novel and allowing the critic to bypass endless discussions about truth, sincerity and intention (Lejeune, 1989: 3–30). However, in doing so, Lejeune's pact encourages the critic to ignore the fascinating points of intersection between the two genres. Here I will first look at what the categories autobiography and novel have in common and then attempt to pull them apart again. To this end, I call upon the French hermeneutic philosopher, Paul Ricoeur, and the New Zealand novelist, poet and autobiographer, Janet Frame.

In *Time and Narrative* (1984–8), Ricoeur describes the interwoven relationship between history and fiction, arguing that the tendency to force history and fiction into two separate categories belies their fundamental interdependence on each other. Thus, whilst it may be necessary to maintain history and fiction as two distinct and separate categories in order that we can talk meaningfully about them, it is impossible to define them in opposition to each other, to describe history as what fiction is not, or vice versa. Here I use Ricoeur's argument to examine the definition of autobiography (as a genre implicitly allied with history) and the novel (as a genre with a clear status as fiction). In particular, I take his notion that the structures of narrative (the sense of a story, of something to be told) underpin both fiction and history, as well as his argument that thinking historically requires a high degree of inventiveness.

History as Narrative: Refiguring Time

The main tropes through which Ricoeur draws fiction and history into an interdependent relationship are 'narrative' and the 'refiguration of time', since they are both narratives which seek to 'refigure' time. As Hayden White has argued:

> Historical stories and fictional stories resemble one another because whatever the differences between their immediate contents (real events and imaginary events, respectively), their ultimate content is the same: the structures of human time. Their shared form, narrative, is a function of this shared content. There is nothing more real for human beings than the experience of temporality. (1987: 179–80)

A successful narrative, be it 'imaginative' or 'historical', must represent time in a plausible and recognizable way. It is impossible to escape the strictures of time whether writing science fiction or biography, since without time there is no narrative and, subsequently, no meaning. Even when we are not writing chronologically, we still maintain a sense of time, which is inherent to the narrative or story or plot.

Although Ricoeur does not directly address the nature of autobiography as genre, he does state in a footnote: 'I ought not to avoid referring to [autobiography] in the context of the refiguration of time performed jointly by history and fiction. It is actually the only place that can be assigned to autobiography by the strategy operating in *Time and Narrative*' (1985: 183). He argues that rather than simply recollecting or re-presenting the past, the historian *refigures* time. 'Time' is an abstract concept and yet we talk about it as if it were a fact, an objective given. We can do this because we have the invention of 'historical time' which mediates between 'Universal time' (the sun rising, the leaves changing colour, the rings of a tree) and our experience of 'lived time'. Before the invention of historical time (hours, days and dates), the personal experience of time must have been highly subjective: we say even now that time passes quickly or slowly. Universal time is predictable: we know that it is a repeated pattern, that every day the sun will set, but if we have no watch or sundial we do not experience this passing of time in any objectively measurable, quantifiable way.

The arbitrary nature of this 'historical time' and its lack of correspondence with cosmological time (why we need a leap year, for example) is well illustrated by Nabokov's words in his 'revisited 'autobiography, *Speak, Memory*:

> Among the anomalies of a memory, whose possessor and victim should never have tried to become an autobiographer, the worst is the inclination to equate in retrospect my age with that of the century. This has led to a series of remarkably consistent chronological blunders in the first version of this book.…
>
> All dates are given in the New Style: we lagged twelve days behind the rest of the civilized world in the nineteenth century, and thirteen in the beginning of the twentieth. By the Old Style I was born on 10 April, at daybreak, in the last year of the last century, and that was (if I could have been whisked across the border at once) 22 April in, say, Germany; but since all my birthdays were celebrated, with diminishing pomp, in the twentieth century, everybody, including myself, upon being shifted by revolution and expatriation from the Julian calendar to the Gregorian, used to add thirteen, instead of twelve days to the 10th of April. The error is serious. What is to be done? I find '23 April' under 'birth date' in my most recent passport, which is also the birth date of Shakespeare, my nephew Vadimir Sikorski, Shirley Temple and Hazel Brown (who, moreover, shares my passport). This, then, is the problem. Calculatory ineptitude prevents me from trying to solve it. (1967: 10)

In this example, the ancient calendar introduced by Julius Caesar (where every fourth year lasted 366 days instead of 365) is replaced and corrected by the calendar in current use, originally introduced by Pope Gregory XIII, with very significant consequences.

The historical truth-fact of date-of-birth is exposed as not only ambiguous but also accidental, the real date almost impossible to resolve. Nabokov's listing of others (family and famous people) with whom he shares his birthday also highlights how such artificial inventions as the calendar cause us to identify arbitrarily with others with whom we believe we share 'historical' characteristics.

Through such temporal devices as calendars (which Nabokov reveals to be invented props), documents, archives and the conceptual props of successive generations, 'axial moments' and 'traces', we construct a sense of progression, of time passing and time past. For Ricoeur, an 'axial moment' is an event considered so pivotal that it is perceived as having changed the course of history: other events are then measured in relation to this moment. The invention of historical time allows us to measure time and to speak about it, from which we are able to place ourselves on a continuum and compare our lives with those who went before us, even to an extent immortalize ourselves by looking back to our 'forefathers' in one direction and towards our children (and our relatives' children) in another. The narrative structures (or ways of refiguring time) that we have invented for putting ourselves on this historical continuum are the same structures that we use to refigure time in fictional narratives.

Bearing this perspective in mind, it is fruitful to look at the extraordinary opening passage of Janet Frame's first volume of autobiography, *To the Is-Land* (1993a), which is presented as a self-contained chapter, set off from the rest of the book in form and style.

'In the Second Place'

From the first place of liquid darkness, within the second place of air and light, I set down the following record with its mixture of fact and truths and memories of truths and its direction always towards the Third Place, where the starting point is myth. (9)

Here, Frame presents historical time as a continuum: the first place interpreted as 'before birth'; the second place as 'the living present' that constitutes a life; and the third place an after-death zone, suggesting the cyclical nature of universal time. Truth and the historicity of time seem inextricably linked. Truth, facts and memories can only be associated with the trajectory of a life from birth to death: before and after all is either darkness or myth. Yet we need a sense of this before and after in order to validate the truth, facts and memories of what comes in between: the continuum of history validates our sense of who we are. As Bill Ashcroft has argued: 'clearly what it means to have a history is the same as what it means to have a legitimate existence: history and legitimation go hand in hand' (1996: 95).

Imagining the Past

How the historian uses or interprets historical time will depend upon how he or she relates to the past. The past is evidently not transparently and unproblematically available. For a start, much of our access to the past depends on fallible memory and unreliable, subjective documentation. We cannot remember everything that has ever happened, not even to ourselves. As St Augustine explained many centuries ago, the memory inevitably becomes a vast, immeasurable sanctuary, parts of which must be overlooked. This then becomes a prodigious philosophical problem: the individual is more than he himself can know: 'The mind is too narrow to contain itself entirely. But where is that part of it which it does not itself contain? Is it somewhere outside itself and not within it? How, then, can it be part of it, if it is not contained in it?' (Augustine, 1961: 216). Moreover, the process of recording what we can remember is no more transparent or accurate. Linda Hutcheon laments 'the paradox of the *reality* of the past but its *textualised accessibility* to us today' (1988: 114; emphasis original). Andreas Huyssen further articulates the problem in *Twilight Memories*:

> It does not require much theoretical sophistication to see that all representation... is based on memory.... The past is not simply there in memory, but it must be articulated to become memory. The fissure that opens up between experiencing an event and remembering it in representation is unavoidable. Rather than lamenting or ignoring it, this split should be understood as a powerful stimulant for cultural and artistic activity. (1995: 2–3)

Here, Huyssen crucially suggests that remembering is in itself a creative activity, thereby undermining the notion that historical texts are non-imaginative.

Paul Ricoeur tells us that while we are inclined to discuss 'history' as something real and transparent, the paradox is that the past no longer is – it has vanished – so to describe it is to narrate something that is no more. How do we do this? What mechanisms are needed? Even though the past may be backed up with documents and eyewitness accounts (apart from the obvious and relevant question of just how reliable such accounts themselves are), we still have to imagine ourselves into the past. It does not just exist out there for us to tell.

Using Plato's dialectic of 'leading kinds', Ricoeur outlines three broad ways of imagining the inhabitants of the past: as 'the same', as 'other' or as 'analogous' (1988: 142–56). If we see those who lived in the past as essentially the same as ourselves, we understand that the past persists in the present and leaves 'traces'; and it is only a re-enactment of the past that is necessary to bring it into the present. Alternatively, if we see those who lived in the past as 'other' we place a temporal distance between the past and the present, constructing the past as exotic. The historian who interprets the past in this way would be a kind of 'ethnologist of past times', emphasizing difference rather than similarity. Some historians, however, see the past as analogous to the present, wherein the past 'takes the place of' or 'stands for' the present. Each mode of looking back requires imagination; the past is not there, before our eyes; rather, we must imagine it, whether we believe that the inhabitants of the past were like us or completely different. The creative effort that is required to conjure up the past suggests that our 'will to history' – the need to see life as part of a continuous narrative – is itself the stimulus for creating fictional narratives.

Frame's second volume of autobiography, *An Angel at my Table*, begins with a passage similar in form, style and positioning in the text to the passage in her first work, 'In the Second Place', quoted earlier. What these passages suggest (at the very least) is an interest in the mechanisms of truth, memory, narrative, history and fiction. Moreover they function as 'bookends' which prop up the autobiography inside:

'The Stone'

The future accumulates like a weight upon the past. The weight upon the earliest years is easier to remove to let that time spring up like grass that has been crushed. The years following childhood become welded to their future, massed like stone, and often the time beneath cannot spring back into growth like new grass: it lies bled of its green in a new shape with those frail bloodless sprouts of another, unfamiliar time, entangled one with the other beneath the stone. (1993b: 11)

This passage is deeply resonant of one of the famous opening para-graphs of Karl Marx's *The Eighteenth Brumaire of Louis Bonaparte*, in which he analyses Napoleon III's *coup d'état* of December 1851:

> Men make their own history, but they do not make it just as they please; they do not make it under circumstances chosen by them-selves, but under circumstances directly encountered, given and transmitted from the past. The tradition of all the dead generations weighs like a nightmare on the brain of the living. (1954: 10)

Where Marx's theory of history describes the inescapable influence of the past on the present, Frame – in a complex inversion – focuses on the 'weight' of the future on the past; the past which is imag-ined through its future, a tense to be understood in grammatical terms as the 'future perfect'. For example, to write the sentence: 'In five years' time I will have lived in Oamaru for ten years', is to look into the future and imagine looking back in the past. Writing the narrative of a life from the perspective of the future (which is the author's actual present) enables the author to look back into the past, imagining her future when in fact she is writing already from that described future. Looking back on childhood is to simul-taneously look back knowing what happens next: the past is informed by its own future. As Frame says in the same volume:

> [The] invasion of the 'future' is inevitable in writing autobiogra-phy particularly after one leaves childhood and the circle of being fills time and space and the lives of others, separated now from oneself and clearly visible. (1993b: 143)

'The years following childhood', on the other hand, 'become welded to their future'; this past is 'the same', indistinguishable from the present. The author is too much like the protagonist to describe their differences and is thus unable to separate time into a con-tinuum of past–present–future: each tense has an impact on the other. 'Those frail, bloodless sprouts of another, unfamiliar time' is perhaps a reference to the future that informs all autobiographies

but is so little acknowledged: the inexorable movement towards death.
  Hayden White, discussing Ricoeur's 'philosophy of history', emphasizes how a narrative understanding of time is common to both
'historical' and 'fictional' accounts:

> To experience time as future, past, and present rather than as a
> series of instants in which every one has the same weight or
> significance as every other is to experience 'historicality.' This
> experience of historicality, finally, can be represented symboli-
> cally in narrative discourse, because such discourse is a product
> of the same kind of hypotactical figuration of events (as begin-
> nings, middles, and ends) as that met with in the actions of
> historical agents who hypotactically figurate their lives as mean-
> ingful stories. (1987: 179)

A 'hypotactic style' is one which uses words like 'when', 'then',
'because' and 'therefore' and phrases such as 'in order to' to express
the temporal relations between sentences (see Abrams, 1993: 204).
The mechanisms of narrative are fundamental to telling stories,
whether they are historical or fictional.
  In *To the Is-Land*, Frame elaborates her understanding of historicity and its relationship to writing autobiography:

> Where in my earliest years time had been horizontal, progres-
> sive, day after day, year after year, with memories being a true
> personal history known by dates and specific years, or vertical,
> with events stacked one upon the other, 'sacks on the mill and
> *more on still*,' the adolescent time now became a whirlpool, and
> so the memories do not arrange themselves to be observed and
> written about, they whirl, propelled by a force beneath, with
> different memories rising to the surface at different times and
> thus denying the existence of a 'pure' autobiography and con-
> firming, for each moment, a separate story accumulating to a
> million stories, all different and with some memories forever staying
> beneath the surface. I sit here at my desk, peering into the depths
> of the dance, for the movement is dance with its own pattern,
> neither good nor bad, but individual in its own right – a dance
> of dust or sunbeams or bacteria or notes of sound or colours or
> liquids or ideas that the writer, trying to write an autobiogra-
> phy, clings to in one moment only. (1993a: 161; emphasis original)

Here, the autobiography's narrative 'will to history' works against the whirlpool of memories that swirl in a disorderly fashion. Lived time is experienced as circular and chaotic, not linear and ordered: the order is imposed afterwards by both writer and story-teller in order to create a narrative that can be made sense of, recognized. In another passage that appears in *Angel*, Frame elaborates:

> The process of the writing may be set down as simply as laying a main trunk railway line from Then to Now, with branch excursions into the outlying wilderness, but the real shape, the first shape is always a circle formed only to be broken and reformed, again and again. (1993b: 143–4)

The Textual Contract: Having it Both Ways

Ricoeur's analysis applied to Frame's writing has allowed us to acknowledge the foundations of time and narrative that history and fiction and by extension, autobiography and the novel share. As Lejeune argues, autobiography links the narrator/protagonist overtly to the author: and this is to connect the outside of the text (its context), with the inside (its content); to highlight simultaneously both history (the author's life) and representation (the author's life as text). As Derrida has described it, writing autobiography is equivalent to 'put[ting] one's name on the line' (1989: 7). We can borrow his phrase and change its meaning slightly, seeing that line as the division between text and *hors-texte*, inside and outside, empirical and fantastic: the name of the author of autobiography simultaneously participates in both. How can we then find a way of talking about autobiography's intrinsic link to an historical, lived reality which incorporates Ricoeur's understanding that history itself is as much an invention as fiction is? In other words, is there a model of autobiography which can take on board autobiography's claims to 'truth' (rather than bypassing them as Lejeune does) whilst also highlighting the transformative processes inherent in recollecting and representing such truth? The model I propose is the 'textual contract', and I use Frame once more to clarify my meaning.

Shortly after writing her second novel, *Faces in the Water* (1961), Frame changed her name to Janet Clutha. It is ironic that she should have such an appropriate name by birth since so much of her art and her persona could be well described by the word 'frame' and the art of 'framing'.[1] To frame a work of art is to contain it, present it, determine its reception and delineate the boundaries between inside and outside: what is art and what is not art. Yet the 'frame' can also gesture to what is not contained within it: in a film, the viewer is often aware that there is a 'beyond the frame', parts of bodies, bits of scenery that the viewer can not momentarily see but can imagine. Here, then, the frame is metonymic, standing for the viewer's picture of the whole.

However, it is both characteristic and ironic that Frame should have made this reverse move: changing her real name rather than inventing a pen-name. Frame continues to use her birth-name (after her legal change of name) as the signature for all her subsequent writing. 'Janet Frame' is now obsolete inasmuch as the name no longer refers outside the text to a person with that name. Does this then disrupt the mechanism of 'naming' so crucial to Lejeune's pact? Furthermore, what does the choice of the name 'Clutha' suggest? The Clutha flows from the centre of the South Island into the Pacific Ocean on the south-east coast just south of Dunedin, the town in which Frame was born and where she attended Teacher Training College. It is uncannily suggestive that she should change her name from the static, rigid, unifying 'Frame' to the fluid and meandering 'Clutha'. Frame gives a clue to her intentions:

> After spending a year confined in the city, studying, writing, conscious always of boundaries of behaviour and feeling, in my new role as an adult, I now came face to face with the Clutha, a being that persisted through all the pressures of rock, stone, earth and sun, living as an element of freedom but not isolated, linked to heaven and light by the slender rainbow that shimmered above its waters. I felt the river was an ally, that it would speak for me. (1993b: 34)

Whereas the family inherited 'Frame' bounded her, closed her in and stopped her voice, the river 'speaks for her', substitutes its name for hers and stands for 'Janet Frame'.

Now I too make Frame's name-change speak for me by using it as a tool to bring together two seemingly contradictory perspectives: Lejeune's pact with its acknowledgement of the essential role of the author and the well-known cry that 'the author is dead'. The severance of her birth-name – 'Janet Frame' – with its patronymic reference to generations, time and place allows us to have it both ways: the gesture to a historical reality outside the text is there, but in practice it 'signifies nothing', it refers to a past that has passed. Instead, we can focus on the text.

If we bear in mind what 'Janet Frame' stands for, we can read the autobiographies as a *textual contract*, reading the signature that is common to author, narrator and protagonist, knowing that it implies a specific mode of reading: autobiography, not fiction. But we can also read that signature as a flourish that applies to no person, no thing, no history, other than that which it creates for the complicit reader in the text. Thus, the reader holds on to a sense of 'the real' outside the text whilst simultaneously aware of the representative nature of reality within the text. In other words, the textual contract provides a means of having our cake (there is a historical reality) and eating it (a text is pure representation).

Note

1 Barrington (1996) uses Derrida's elaboration of the word 'frame' or 'parergon' and Minh-ha (1992) to discuss at a more sophisticated theoretical level the implications and appropriateness of 'Frame' to Frame's project.

References

Abrams, M. H. *A Glossary of Literary Terms*, sixth edn (Fort Worth: Harcourt Brace, 1993)

Ashcroft, B. 'Against the Tide of Time: Peter Carey's Interpolation into History', in J. C. Hawley (ed.) *Writing the Nation: Self and Country in the Post-Colonial Imagination* (Amsterdam: Rodopi, 1996)

Barrington, T. 'Frame[d]: The Autobiographies', *Journal of New Zealand Literature*, 14 (1996)

Blowers, T. 'Madness, Philosophy and Literature: A Reading of Janet Frame's *Faces in the Water*', *Journal of New Zealand Literature*, 14 (1996)

—— 'Locating the Self: Re-reading Autobiography as Theory and Practice, with particular reference to the writings of Janet Frame' (unpublished doctoral thesis, University of Warwick, 1998)

Derrida, J. *Mémoires: for Paul de Man*, revised edn (New York: Columbia University Press, 1989)

Frame, J. *To the Is-Land: Autobiography* (London: Flamingo-HarperCollins, [1982] 1993a)

—— *An Angel at My Table: Autobiography 2* (London: Flamingo-HarperCollins, [1984] 1993b)

—— *Faces in the Water* (London: The Women's Press, [1961] 1980)

Hutcheon, L. *A Poetics of Postmodernism: History, Theory, Fiction* (New York: Routledge, 1988)

Huyssen, A. *Twilight Memories: Marking Time in a Culture of Amnesia* (New York: Routledge, 1995)

116 *Tonya Blowers*

44444444444
Lejeune, P. 'The Autobiographical Pact', in P. J. Eakin (ed.) *On Autobiography*, trans. K. Leary (Minneapolis: University of Minneapolis Press, 1989)

Marx, K. *The Eighteenth Brumaire of Louis Bonaparte*, third revised edn (London: Lawrence & Wishart, 1954)

Minh-ha, T. *Framer Framed* (London & New York: Routledge, 1992)

Nabokov, V. *Speak, Memory: An Autobiography Revisited* (Harmondsworth: Penguin, 1967)

Ricouer, P. *Time and Narrative* (3 vols), trans. K. McLaughlin and D. Pellauer (Chicago: University of Chicago Press, 1984–8)

Saint Augustine, *Confessions*, trans. R. S. Pine-Coffin (Harmondsworth: Penguin, 1961)

White, H. 'The Metaphysics of Narrativity: Time and Symbol in Ricoeur's Philosophy of History', in *The Content of the Form: Narrative Discourse and Historical Representation* (Baltimore: Johns Hopkins University Press, 1987)

Part III
Staging the Self

9
Staging Our Selves

Elaine Aston

In 'Gender, Sexuality and "My Life" in the (University) Theater', American theatre scholar and practitioner Jill Dolan includes a biographical comment on how her experience of being a lesbian undergraduate forced into a heterosexual programme of professional theatre training exiled her from the theatre, but also shaped her later desire to teach theatre practise in a way that took account of feminism, gender and sexuality (Dolan, 1993: 99). Similarly, Gayle Austin describes her 'personal journey' in theatre as moving through three stages: 'From the simple desire to see more female images on the stage and move more women into the mainstream of American theater, to a particular interest in women's playwriting, to a passion about the much broader issue of how drama and theater operate to represent women on the stage' (Austin, 1990: 3).

Like Austin, my 'personal journey' in the theatre academy has taken me from an interest in mainstream images of women in theatre, through the theory and practice of contemporary women's theatre, to the theory–practice engagement with the en-gendered apparatus of theatrical representation. '"My Life" in the (University) Theatre' is currently concerned with gender and devising: with finding ways of encouraging groups of young women to practise theatre in a gender-aware context; a praxis which, I shall argue, also invites them to identify, to explore and to define feminism and feminist issues for themselves.

In the course of working with women in feminist theatre workshops, I have been involved in the making of a number of auto/biographical projects, including, for example, devising feminist performances about the writing and lives of Susan Glaspell and Christina Rossetti (for details of the Rossetti project, see Aston, 1995).

In the brief space of this essay I cannot begin to cover all of this auto/biographical work, so I propose to focus on one particular project, *Self-ish*, which was made by six undergraduate women in the Spring of 1997 on the Gender and Devising course at Loughborough University. Through offering details of this project, I hope to illustrate how a feminist theatre practice can engage with theoretical and critical concerns central to the field of feminist auto/ biography, and contribute to the wide-ranging and interdisciplinary debate presented in this volume.

In recent years practical work in theatre studies has undergone a shift from working with scripts, to an emphasis on devising in which performers are responsible for creating and performing their own theatre. Alison Oddey states that 'devised theatre can start from anything', explaining that 'it is determined and defined by a group of people who set up an initial framework or structure to explore and experiment with ideas, images, concepts, themes' (Oddey, 1994: 1. For more on devising, see this volume, chapter 11). This is particularly significant for women because it offers them the opportunity to take responsibility for and control of the ways in which they are represented and the stories that are 'told'. It allows them to revise both dramatic form and content; to be seen and heard in ways previously denied to them. As Ellen Donkin and Susan Clement, writing on women's desire to 'construct' their own texts, explain:

> We wonder if traditional dramatic structure doesn't routinely impose certain distortions on women's lives and women's experience. There has been a lot of speculation about climaxes and male sexuality as they are inscribed in Aristotelian dramatic action . . . this is exactly the kind of male narrative that has systematically excluded women from the beginning of recorded literature, so it is hardly surprising that the dramatic forms of that narrative hold no particular appeal for women developing their own work and their own voices. (Donkin and Clement, 1993: 151)

Moreover, the devising-performer is actively encouraged to bring her/himself to/into the creative process. This is radically different from conventional actor training where the performer is invited to 'be' or 'to get into' a character which somebody else (usually a man) has created. This conventional 'method' of performing can be an alienating and potentially damaging experience for women, as Dolan describes: 'I . . . knew that my inability to do well in movement classes was somehow related to my alienation from my own body, which was somehow related to my thorough incompetence at the heterosexual role-play the professors in Boston University's theater program were casting me to do' (Dolan, 1993: 99). By contrast, in a gender-aware devising context, one that is premised on the assumption that gender, class, race and sexuality are important to how we work and to what we make, women have the opportunity to bring them 'selves' – their personal, social, political, cultural, sexual selves – to the making and performing process. Furthermore, in opting to 'construct our own texts', as Donkin and Clement describe, we can choose to make ourselves the subject of a performance.

It seems rather incongruous at first to think of ourselves as a subject on the drama syllabus alongside Shakespeare, Miller, Ibsen or Brecht. As the Personal Narratives Group have observed, 'far from encouraging our ability to think creatively about discovering the truths in personal narratives, our academic disciplines have more often discouraged us from taking people's life-stories seriously' (1989: 262). To make an auto/biographical performance like *Self-ish* we had first to address the issue of taking our life-stories seriously as a subject for theatre-making and academic study. Even more difficult than that, perhaps, was establishing the validity and value of making theatre by and about the lives of a group of young women.

Teaching theatre to young women in higher education in the 1990s means teaching women who do not connect easily or readily with issues of gender, race or sexuality, etc. (on the issue of race and drama teaching, see this volume, chapter 10). These are young women who have grown up under Thatcherism, and, until the recent advent of New Labour, have only experienced a right-wing government. As heirs to the 'top girl' ethos of the 1980s, feminism to these young women is consigned to history; it is something that happened before their lives and is no longer necessary in our spiced-up age of 'girl power'.

Preliminary discussions for *Self-ish*, therefore, took the form of consciousness-raising sessions in which the young women involved shared personal experiences with a view to developing an awareness of the social and political implications of their lives, so that gradually the 'girl power' age of the 1990s was perhaps not as empowering as it first appeared. At this discussion stage, it was also useful to introduce Julia Swindells on 'the project of using autobiography politically' and to state her two basic premises, which were kept as points of reference to come back to, namely: (i) 'to articulate the experience of oppression first-hand is a precondition for social and political change'; and (ii) 'collective testimony is one of the best means of achieving this, so that neither author nor reader [or, in our case performer and spectator] sees the autobiographical project as a matter of individualism' (Swindells, 1995: 213).

Working in a devising context means that the work is collaborative and generated not by a single author, but by a group of people. The collaborative group approach is important to resisting 'individualism'. In making *Self-ish*, for example, we were not trying to present one woman's personal, individual 'herstory' but were aiming to work as a group of women whose individual narratives would be woven together in a collective feminist exploration of representation. That said, it is important to note that the group did not set out to represent a universalising, cultural-feminist subject, one representative of all women; rather, it aimed to function as a collective subject capable of representing diversity and difference among its members.

The 'personal as political' discussion period was a useful prelude to practical work. Already, women were sharing autobiographical narratives and talking about feminism/s. There were a number of ways in which we began to move our discussion forward. In this short space it would be impossible to give an account of all of these, but I propose to outline some of the most fertile ways in which we went on to generate auto/biographical material on the *Self-ish* project.

In the forward to her autobiography *Bone Black*, bell hooks explains that she proposes to 'gather together the dreams, fantasies, experiences that preoccupied me as a girl, that stay with me and appear and reappear in different shapes and forms in all my work' (hooks, 1996: xiv). One way of bringing our 'dreams, fantasies, experiences' from childhood or teenage years to the surface in the workshop is to work with personal objects or possessions. We reached an agreement in the discussion period of *Self-ish* workshopping that the women would work on an autobiographical exploration of childhood and teenage memories. All the women were given time to go away and to find various possessions belonging to their formative years. These included, for example, items of clothing from when they were young, family photographs, music from teenage years, favourite childhood toys (for those who still had them), pictures of teenage pop idols, and so on.

In the first workshop after this period of personal research, the group improvised installations of their personal memorabilia. Each woman set up a 'display' of her objects and was given time to talk the group through her possessions, and the memories, experiences and feelings attached to them.

The photographs which were used as part of these personal 'displays' were a major talking point. We used ideas derived from the photographer Jo Spence on the family album (see Spence, 1995: 190–5) to encourage thinking about the personal histories portrayed in the private collections of photographs. Some women went on to make photographic displays of their lives which they used both in the workshop and in the final performance. These displays did not 'tell' a chronological, linear story, but collaged together different biographical time zones and forms of photography – childhood images alongside photographs of a contemporary, personal moment; an official school photograph juxtaposed with informal family snapshots. In particular these displays functioned as visual reminders of the ways in which we can never portray a 'complete' life; auto/biographical narratives re-tell lives through fragments, partial memories, special moments, but they never tell a 'whole' story.

Workshopping with personal objects was used extensively in the first part of the devising process to trigger more personal narratives. Participants improvised situations using clothing props from past and present lives; explored the gestures and images of former pop idols in freeze-framed body-sculpting, or read passages from teenage romance narratives alongside extracts from their own teenage diaries. Among the most memorable object sessions on the *Self-ish* project were those on bags and shoes.

Bags are excellent possessions for this kind of personal object play. So many stories come out of bags. Each woman on *Self-ish* had to find one bag that was special to her to work with. We started with the idea of using these as a ritualized way of beginning work: of arriving at each session with a bag full of stories to tell. In the end what happened was that the women brought in several bags over the workshopping period because they generated so much material. We had ballet bags from when some of them were young, university rucksacks, furry animal bags and carrier bags. Each bag had its own, very special story to tell.

Shoes are evocative of very strong childhood memories – particularly it seems about mothers. (We had personal narratives about mothers who always seem to choose for their daughters the most boring pair of shoes possible, and tales of coveting mum's high-heeled shoes for dressing-up games.) Improvising with shoes has the immediate effect of pulling the body into a particular shape or image. The minute we put on a pair of high heels changes how we sit down, stand up or walk. Working with shoes heightened the group's awareness of how they constructed identities for themselves, depending on the social situation they were in.

What began to emerge quite quickly from this kind of playing was a growing awareness of the social and cultural pressures of femininity which had conditioned girlhood fantasies of who to be like, how to dress or how to behave, and the disjunction between these representational strategies and the inner, real feelings which they often concealed. We pursued the gap between 'self' and 'representational self' in a session devoted to devising monologues on the theme of 'making a spectacle of myself'. Public occasions on which we try to present or to 'perform' ourselves in ways which go disastrously wrong tend to be vividly remembered. This is particularly true for women who tend to be more frequently objectified in social and cultural 'gazing' than men. A typical narrative to emerge from this session, for example, was about appearing in the 'wrong' dress at a teenage discotheque and being the object of laughter. As our aim was not to accept these experiences, but to re-present them critically, we workshopped these narratives using microphones in a stand-up-comedy register to amplify the voice; to create a resistant 'gap' between the playing and the telling.

Aided by Teresa de Lauretis's concept of being 'both inside and outside of gender, at once within and without representation', of being represented by the fictional construct of Woman whilst also knowing 'that we are not *that*' (De Lauretis, 1987: 10), we began to shape the workshopped material through a materialist-feminist performance register; a 'me . . . but not me' style of playing. The main prop for developing this transgressive 'me . . . but not me' register was a life-size version of our 'selves'. Each woman involved in the workshop had a fabric version of herself to play with, one which she in fact made herself. Working with mannequins or some form of puppet to make a point about the doll-like pressures of femininity on women is a device frequently used in materialist-feminist performance. To give an example: in Siren Theatre Company's *Now Wash Your Hands, Please* Tasha Fairbanks represented the mother of a typical 'nuclear family' in a ventriloquist act using 'a family-sized Persil packet with a smiley face on' (see Fairbanks, 1996: 104 and

Figure 2   Staging Our Selves in the Theatre Workshop

156 for photograph). What was different about the fabric 'selves', however, was that they were fashioned out of the individual bodies of the performers. Patterns were made by drawing around bodies on woman-sized pieces of paper. From the paper patterns we made cardboard 'skeletons'. The 'skeletons' were then assembled, jointed and inserted into white calico 'bodies' stuffed with wadding (full instructions are given in Aston, 1999). The 'selves' were further personalized as women individually chose different body parts to add on or to accentuate. One feature that they all shared was hair which was made out of strips of different, brightly coloured material. Hair it seemed was central to representations of femininity, and all of the women had narratives about hair they had wanted, longed for, but could not have.

When the 'selves' were introduced into the workshopped play they were used as a kind of canvas for trying out identities. The performers experimented with different 'identities' on their 'selves', ransacking wardrobes for different outfits from past and present lives to experiment with how they looked. To interrogate the 'feminine', they organized an installation in the studio space in which they set their 'selves' alongside dominant representations of women: images taken from women's magazines, from gender-encoded advertisements,

Figure 3   Working with a Fabric 'Self'

or from posters of female pop icons. As the 'selves' were jointed and stuffed, it meant that it was possible to use them to explore gesture and movement, so the women could also experiment with how they wanted to hold, to carry or to walk with their 'selves'. This kind of work generated a range of emotional responses – often angry, often tearful – as women explored their own 'bodies' in relation to socially constructed notions of the 'ideal' feminine body.

Out of the autobiographical material generated in the workshop and using the fabric 'self' as the *Gestus* to orientate a 'me . . . but not me' performance register, we were able to make a devised auto/biographical performance. As we had worked as a group of women we had a collection of shared memories: a collage of multiple memories which kept us away from the individual, singular narrative line and structure. A more apt description for the final organization of autobiographical material in *Self-ish* would be a quilt – a patchwork of images, memories, aspirations – in which the spectator was invited to see the seams, rough stitching and raw edges.

In print culture an equivalent model for this kind of performance might be the generational collection of autobiographical stories, such as Joan Scanlon's *Surviving the Blues*, a Virago collection which brings together personal experiences and stories by young women reflecting on the 1980s (Scanlon, 1990). However, where written examples of this kind require sequential organization – auto/biographical accounts are set out one after the other – an auto/biographical performance such as *Self-ish* offers the possibility of simultaneous narrative play. Individual narratives do not need to be sequential, but overlap, fragment or echo each other. When one woman tells her 'story' she shares the 'telling' with the group; her experience 'becomes' the collective experience of the group.

In her editorial introduction to *Surviving the Blues*, Scanlon argues that the young women writing about their experiences in the 1980s 'do not falsely presume that their personal histories might be representative of "young women's experience today", but show instead an acute awareness of both what is specific to them as members of a larger group, including their gender group – women' (1990: 4). Similarly, I would argue that the group of women who worked on *Self-ish* explored the politics of representation in a way which was both personal to themselves as individuals, to the group in which they were working, and to their 'gender group', whilst resisting the impulse to universalize. Through 'self-ish' workshopping in which they explored their personal lives, they also heightened

128   *Elaine Aston*

their awareness of the selfish 1980s in which they had grown up. Although too young to have understood the politics of the 1980s as they were living through the decade, the experience of the workshop gave the women the opportunity to reflect personally and politically on the material-girl pressures of the 1980s. The experience of gender-aware devising meant that feminism had ceased to be something outside of their lives to be studied on academic reading lists, but had become a 'subject' in the workshop, one which was creatively and politically explored, shaped and staged by them 'selves'.

References

Aston, E. '*Portraits of Rossetti*: Feminist Theory and Performance', *Studies in Theatre Production*, 11 (1995)
⸺ *Feminist Theatre Practice* (London: Routledge, 1999)
Austin, G. *Feminist Theories for Dramatic Criticism* (Ann Arbor: University of Michigan Press, 1990)
De Lauretis, T. *Technologies of Gender: Essays on Theory, Film, and Fiction* (Bloomington: Indiana University Press, 1987)
Dolan, J. *Presence and Desire* (Ann Arbor: University of Michigan, 1993)
Donkin, E. and Clement, S. (eds) *Upstaging Big Daddy* (Ann Arbor: University of Michigan, 1993)
Fairbanks, T. *Pulp and Other Plays* (Amsterdam: Harwood Academic Press, 1996)
hooks, b. *Bone Black: Memories of Girlhood* (New York: Henry Holt, 1996)
Oddey, A. *Devising Theatre: A Practical and Theoretical Handbook* (London & New York: Routledge, 1994)
Personal Narratives Group (eds) *Interpreting Women's Lives: Feminist Theory and Personal Narratives* (Bloomington and Indianapolis: Indiana University Press, 1989)
Scanlon, J. (ed.) *Surviving the Blues: Growing up in the Thatcher Decade* (London: Virago, 1990)
Spence, J. *Cultural Sniping: The Art of Transgression* (London & New York: Routledge, 1995)
Swindells, J. (ed.) *The Uses of Autobiography* (London: Taylor & Francis, 1995)

10
Performance and Pedagogy: the 'Signifying Monkey' and the Educative I/Eye

Nike Imoru

In the Drama Department at the University of Hull, year three students are invited to opt for their final year academic modules. There are a range of academic options available at any one time, most of which are linked to areas of staff research and specialization. In this way, academic modules are spaces in which staff are able to engage in processes of teaching, research and exploration alongside the students. Popular African American Theatre is one such academic option that I have offered. This chapter is an attempt to discuss the students' responses to the module, as well as my subsequent analysis of the dynamic inter relations between the subject matter of African American theatre history, the students and the lecturer. I am interested to explore the ways in which the pedagogic situation re-enacted various elements of theatre and theatre history which were under critical analysis on the module and, in particular, the ways in which I came to understand that the historian is not so dissimilar to the playwright, and the lecturer not dissimilar to the actor.

The idea that historical narratives, including 'theatre history', have become contested sites in scholarship is now well known. The notion of History, and the construction of the historical narrative, have been dismantled from their reified status of objective truth. There are, of course, many ways of reading and writing histories, and the historical narrative is as carefully and ideologically constructed as the dramatic text. Just as the narrative of the dramatic text is crafted to offer 'metaphysical or symbolic system[s] of representing the world' (Strong, 1978: 249), so too, as Hayden White argues in *Tropics of Discourse*, are historical narratives, fictions that are always of a 'contingent and provisional nature' (1978: 39). Consequently the strategy of re-writing (theatre) history becomes a drama of competing terms.

In order to ensure that students were aware of the process of narrative construction involved in the act of writing a history, the introductory session of the module began with a critical evaluation of (theatre) history and the construction of the dominant (theatre) historical narrative by academics. The module investigated nineteenth- and early twentieth-century African-American popular theatre forms from the development of minstrelsy to the musical comedy, and was structured to enable discussion and to develop a cultural, political and social understanding of the period in tandem with the popular theatre entertainment of the time. The aim of the course was to interrogate the construction of historical narratives with a view to understanding how we come to arrive at such categorizations as 'African-American theatre' or even 'American theatre'; its objective was to foster critical debate and to challenge generic terms within theatre history as an academic discipline.

However, in other more obvious ways too, this module made me realize that teaching drama or theatre studies inevitably gives rise to degrees of performance. As the seminars took shape, I became aware that there was also another dynamic at play: the dynamic of the self, my self as lecturer (as actor), in tandem with the material and the students (as spectators). I began to view the educative performance as a performance of the self, or a performance of the selves. I became aware of a critical other self that simultaneously taught and reflected on the teaching, and this gave rise to a process of ongoing reflection resulting in a form of an auto/biography. Indeed, if autobiography is an account of a person's life recorded by that person, then I began to experience the ways in which the autobiographical form is also contingent upon the ways in which the auto/biographer, comes to know, understand and interpret self-identity through the gaze of the onlooker or spectator.

In the seminar, the lecturer finds that both creative and pedagogical approaches are discovered and applied. Peter Brook reminds us in *The Empty Space* that: '[a] man walks across [an] empty space whilst someone else is watching him, and this is all that is needed for an act of theatre to be engaged' (1968: 9). In the seminar, it is the interactive space between the student and the lecturer that creates the forum for learning and teaching. On a very basic level, then, the seminar exhibits some of the precepts of a staged performance. Moreover, just as the actor becomes increasingly familiar with the process in rehearsals, and the director becomes more able to meet the demands and needs of the actor, so too does the lecturer become a more seasoned performer: aware of students as spectators, familiar with the latecomers, the shufflers, the coughers, those who retreat to the back row, and the empty seats that may or may not be filled after the break. However, it was the more complex interactions between lecturer and student around issues of race and gender that proved the most crucial in this particular theatre of learning.

The module in Popular African-American theatre began with an overview of slavery in order to contextualize the beginnings of minstrelsy. Historically, there are different narratives detailing the beginnings of minstrelsy but most are agreed on its progenitor – Thomas Dartmouth Rice – who, in the 1830s, heard a Negro singing a popular tune of the time: 'Jump Jim Crow'. Being an enterprising actor, he 'borrowed' the song, blackened his face with burnt cork, and created a jig to the tune of 'Jump Jim Crow'. T. D. Rice became famous in Britain and America for his Negro impersonations. By 1840, the popularity of the solo minstrel performer grew, resulting in travelling minstrel troupes. Over time, these travelling troupes became too large in size and too expensive to tour (some had up to 80 minstrel performers). By the 1880s, minstrelsy's form and content had been subsumed by new types of popular entertainment such as burlesque, vaudeville and eventually the revue and the musical comedy. However, it was T. D. Rice who earned the title of forefather of America's only indigenous theatre form: minstrelsy. In *Love and Theft*, Eric Lott notes that these early impersonations which masked the white actor and placed the Negro centre-stage were not, in the first instance, intended to ridicule (1993: 16). He argues that one might also view them as early anthropological studies of the negro. A number of troupes and solo minstrel performers, for example, became specialists at impersonating what they perceived to be regional physical and vocal negro traits. There was the Northern Dandy known as Zip Coon who wore an oversized garish suit, and also the slave plantation Negro from the South with his malapropisms of which the performers made great play. Thus, blackness, according to Lott, was disseminated by the white performer who travelled from province to province with what was considered to be an engaging popular art-form. Only later, he argues, did minstrelsy become a form of ridiculing Negroes and this primarily after the abolition of slavery in 1863.

As part of its intellectual content, the module examined the fascination with the negro during the early part of the nineteenth century and the ways in which popular Negro folk songs were compiled. It also looked at the obsession with dances which were influenced by the increasing presence of Scottish and Irish immigrants, and sought to discern the perceived fear of the Negro by the white population. Black performers, for example, were not allowed to appear on stage in front of white audiences and if they did, they were forced to black up, effectively to be masked by a grotesque representation of the Negro. The students' research into William Henry Lane, also known as Juba, a nineteenth-century African-American dancer and reputedly the best dancer of his age, led to further analysis of the Negro body and its status 'the world's body' (Lott, 1993: 112). I encouraged the students to question: Why was there this fascination? How did it manifest itself in the theatre of the time, and what was the corollary of this fascination?

Discussions that dealt specifically with the Negro body of the time along with the fear and fascination of the Negro unsettled the students in ways that I did not immediately comprehend. More detailed analyses and examples gave rise to more discomfort, to silences and averted gazes. This discomfort reached its zenith when we tried to discuss the pathologizing of the black woman's body in order to examine the responses to the black female performer on stage in the early twentieth century. We looked at Sarah Bartmann who was known as the Hottentot Venus. Between 1810 and 1815, Bartmann was on public display in exhibitions around Europe so that the public could view what was perceived to be her inordinately large genitalia and backside. When she died at the age of 25, she was dismembered and once more her genitalia were exhibited in a medical academy before being transferred to the Musée de l'homme in Paris, where they remain on display today.

It was at this point that a chasm seemed to appear between myself, as the actor, and the student spectators, giving rise to a sensation that was synonymous with being caught in the act! I realized that I had made two grave inaccuracies about my audience that rendered the module pedagogically problematic. I had assumed, whilst preparing the module, that my audience was the same, more or less, as me. However, on 'closer inspection', I saw that the group was exclusively white and predominantly middle-class. I also presumed that despite the newness of the module the students might well be familiar with some of the references, if only through popular culture. Most, of course, were familiar with rap and hard-core rap, but they had not necessarily made connections between the content of that popular form and an attendant history.

These observations led to a heightened awareness on my part of the dynamic between the students and the material, but they also gave me the opportunity to evaluate critically the space between lecturer and student – between actor and spectator. It was at this point that a critical process of autobiographical representation began to emerge: it became clear that as the black female academic in the guise of an actor presenting a history of racist and sexist subjugation of blacks by whites to an exclusively white audience, her/my own body began to re-present itself in ways that were beyond her/my control. Thus, as she/I referred to Bartmann, she/I too became a spectacle, and for a moment her/my physiognomy which, up until the module began, had remained 'unknown', became known. A curious form of revelation was enacted through history. Where before the actor was able to be invisible in performance, offering dispassionate if humorous accounts of African-American theatre history, suddenly she/I was caught in a curious bind. She/I became inextricably bound up in the history that she was narrating. At the same time, the audience was finding itself in a position, vis-à-vis the subject matter and the black actor before them, that was historically and perhaps psychologically untenable. By a gradual process of recognition the white spectators were positioned, by virtue of the historical narratives, in such a way as to see themselves as part perpetrators, by virtue of racial and/or cultural descent, of nine-teenth-century white supremacism even though they were not American but British and she was not African-American but Anglo-Nigerian. Student and lecturer, actor and spectator were caught momentarily in between cultures, narratives, fact and fiction unable to do anything more than stare unblinkingly at each other. This was an exciting moment because it exemplified Susan Bennett's view in *Theatre Audiences* that 'the spectator becomes a self-conscious co-creator of performance' (1990: 23). Neither the spectator nor the performance is value-free. Rather, the spectator comes to the performance with specific rather than general socio-cultural and political horizons thus influencing how they receive the performance.

In *Black Skin White Masks*, the Martiniquan psychologist Frantz Fanon states that 'to speak a language is to take on a world, a culture' (1952: 106). The effect of this has been reiterated variously by black scholars writing or recording a condition that acknowledges a plurality of identities which would seem to be an adjunct to immigrant status or a result of living in a diasporic location. Scholarship by African-Americans has frequently foregrounded a multiplicity of social, political and psychological identities. W.E.B. DuBois, a leading African-American scholar and black activist of the nineteenth and twentieth centuries, described a 'peculiar sensation resulting from the fact that one ever feels his twoness, an American, a negro, two unrecoiling strivings, two warrings ideals in one dark body' (1903: 2). Mary Church Terrell, the first president of the National Association of Colored Women, described the double enslavement of black women as both a woman question and a race problem (1904: 292); and Fanon, writing from a Freudian and cultural perspective, argued for the ways in which the psychic map of the (male) Negro is ever reactive so that:

> When the Negro makes contact with the white world a certain sensitising action takes place . . . if his psychic structure is weak, one observes a collapse of the ego. The black man stops behaving as an actional person. The goal of his behaviour will be the Other (in the guise of the white man). (1952: 136)

More recently, Deborah King has moved on from the binary model to describe: 'multiple jeopardies and multiple consciousness' (1988: 42). Whilst these scholars tend to stress the conflicts that such dualities create, one can argue for the way in which an awareness of such tensions can be positively and creatively harnessed so that the 'Other' does not endure, in seemingly endless fashion, the kind of 'collapse' that Fanon cites.

Indeed, there have been positive renderings of black female subjectivity and the notion of multiple identities both in literature and in dramatic writing, particularly in the United States, and interestingly, without recourse to the European critique of the subject within postmodernity. Fiction by black women tends to take as a given the multiple and often contradictory and conflicting roles that actually enact black female subjectivity. In her article 'Speaking in Tongues', Mae Henderson argues that black women writers speak from a multiple and complex social, historical and cultural positionality which, in effect constitutes black female subjectivity. She believes that black women enter *simultaneously* into familial, or testimonial and public or competitive discourses – discourses that both affirm and challenge the expectations of the reader. As such black women writers enter into testimonial discourse with black men as blacks, with white women as women and with black women as black women. At the same time, they enter into a competitive discourse with black men as women, with white women as blacks and with white men as black women. . . . It is the complexity of these simultaneously homogenous and heterogeneous social and discursive domains out of which black women write and construct themselves that enables black women writers authoritatively to speak to engage both hegemonic and (non) hegemonic discourses. (1992: 148; emphasis given)

In assessing my own teaching, I found that it had been easier to become an actor in the seminar in order to manoeuvre between the spectators and the subject matter. Not, however, a naturalistic actor, offering a slice of African-American life or even a realistic and truthful actor, in short not a twentieth-century actor but perhaps something in the mould of the renaissance actor who, according to Stephen Greenblatt (1980), engaged in complex processes of self-fashioning. This enabled me, to a greater or lesser degree, to distance myself from the gaze of the students/spectators without abdicating from the role of lecturer or facilitator. Arguably, I adopted Henderson's framework of discursive strategies to generate discussion and debate, to facilitate autonomous ideas whilst avoiding the pitfalls of the performed identities of 'honorary white' and/or 'victimized other'. Consequently, I entered into testimonial discourse (pastoral) with the students as their lecturer. In addressing the sexual exploitation of African-American slave women, I entered into a public discourse with white female spectators, as a black woman, whilst simultaneously entering into a competitive discourse with white male spectators, as a black woman. Finally, I entered into a competitive discourse with the white spectators, as a black woman, when examining issues around African American culture, history and politics.

These positions occurred simultaneously depending on the specific issue under debate. Given the discomfort I felt within the group it was important to keep the testimonial discourse in view. By the same token, the intention was not to clone student thinking in the shape of my own, but to encourage autonomous thought. In this way, I was attempting to find a way to respond positively to the mutual discomfort I sensed in the classroom; as lecturer/actor I was trying to stage the inter*play* of identities as a form of 'creative dialogue' (Barbara Christian in 1985: 147). However, this creative dialogue can also give rise to some confusion which is as comic as it is problematic. As the lecturer who was also self-spectating, in these moments, I wondered when or whether to refer to 'us' or 'them', to 'we' or 'they', when dealing with specific questions or discussions.

My pedagogic performance of these multiple selves was perhaps a dissembling form of auto/biography, one which gave rise to endless forms of playfulness, and which also resulted in a range of critical perspectives which continue to inform my pedagogy both positively and dynamically. Indeed, this process of dissemblance itself has a history that predates postmodern theories of subjectivity. In 'Blackness of Blackness', Henry Louis Gates Jr makes mention of a figure in black culture called the signifying monkey (1984: 285). The signifying monkey appears in black literature and culture descended from Nigerian (Yoruba) and Cuban mythology and may be considered as synonymous with Hermes in western culture. Briefly, the signifying monkey offers resemblance by processes of dissemblance, creates havoc and mayhem, is there and yet not there, sets up situations which are not always benevolent, and watches while those around her fall foul of her pranks. In the seminar, the signifying monkey, the lecturer, the actor and the spectator converged in one body, creating selves that were at once subject for as well as the object of a constantly shifting autobiographical form.

References

Bennett, S. *Theatre Audiences: A Theory of Production and Reception* (London: Routledge, 1990)
Brook, P. *The Empty Space* (London: MacGibbon & Kee, 1968)
Christian, B. *Black Feminist Criticism: Perspectives on Black Women Writers* (New York: Pergamon, 1985)
DuBois, W. E. B. *The Souls of Black Folks* (London: Longman, Green & Co., 1903)
Fanon, F. *Black Skin White Masks* (London: MacGibbon & Kee, [1952] 1968)
Gates, H. L. Jr (ed.) *Black Literature and Literary Theory* (New York: Routledge, 1984)
Greenblatt, S. *Renaissance Self-fashioning: From More to Shakespeare* (Chicago, Illinois: University of Chicago Press, 1980)
Henderson, M. G. 'Speaking in Tongues: Dialogues, Dialectics and the Black Woman Writer's Literary Tradition', in J. Butler and J. W. Scott (eds) *Feminists Theorize the Political* (New York: Routledge, 1992) 114–66

King, D. K. 'Multiple Jeopardy, Multiple Consciousness: The Context of a Black Feminist Epistemology', *Signs*, 14 (1988) 47–72

Lott, E. *Love and Theft: Blackface Minstrelsy and the American Working Class* (New York: Oxford University Press, 1993)

Strong, T. B. 'Dramaturgical Discourse and Political Enactments: Towards an Artistic Foundation for Political Space', in R. H. Brown and M. L. Stanford (eds) *Structure, Consciousness and History* (New York: Cambridge University Press, 1978)

Terrell, M. C. 'The Progress of Colored Women', *Voice of the Negro*, 7 (1904) 290–310

White, H. *Tropics of Discourse: Essays in Cultural Criticism* (Baltimore, MD: Johns Hopkins University Press, 1978)

11
Viglen's Revenge

Alison Oddey

'Viglen's Revenge' is the title for a future devised performance piece. 'Postscript Post-its' was devised specifically for the 'Representing Lives' Conference, pursuing an ongoing process of work, which was already examining the roles of academic, artist and mother within the author/performer's life. 'Postscript Post-its' is the beginning and end of both process and product, in being the final performance of 'Show and Tell: the delights of devising theatre' and the germ of an idea for 'Viglen's Revenge'.

Postscript Post-its

HELLO MR MUM!

AN ANGEL DOESN'T ALWAYS HAVE WINGS

SEEDS OF AN IDEA FOR AN AUTOBIOGRAPHICAL
PERFORMANCE PIECE IN 1998

A:\ACADEMIC

P:\PERFORMER

W:\WRITER

S:\SELF

M:\MOTHER

M:\MOTHER

    FOLDER: SYSTEM

In order to operate as the MOTHER, I must look after my SYS-
TEM, otherwise I will crash . . .

M:\MOTHER

    PROGRAMME ANTI-VIRUS

I must sort this out so that I don't become infected by Dr.
Spock's writings re: not smacking my child . . .

| APPLICATION UNINSTALL |

An uninstaller is like therapy; it's about chucking out all the
useless stuff. I need to uninstall the buggy now that he walks
everywhere; the potties – now that he can 'go to the loo' . . .

| APPLICATION WINZIP |

I must WINZIP my files into a smaller storage space, for example, the X FILE:
'MY MOTHER's WORDS OF WISDOM ON CHILDREARING!'

M:\MOTHER

    FOLDER: SYSTEM

    FILE: STROKES

If I haven't got anything in my STROKES file, I become a grumpy
mother full of low self-esteem . . .

M:\MOTHER

    FOLDER: CHILD

    FILE: CARE ARRANGEMENTS

I must sort out the Nursery's 'Summer Creche' arrangements
(fill in the form . . .)

>>>>> SCREENSAVER

'I need to keep moving; I need to keep animated . . .'

When I download SCREENSAVERS from the net, I must not BREAK
DOWN!

> **SLOGAN:**
>
> 'She's a woman, she's a lover,
> she's a worker, she's a mother.'
>
> 'What the slogan omitted to say was that she is also on the
> verge of a heart attack.'
> **Sharon Maxwell Magnus (The Guardian, 23 July 1997: 9)**

Post-its – things to do – competing identities, moving them around in relation to parts of my body. I want to devise an autobiographical installation, a gallery showing of all those DRIVES (those competing identities), using the map of my body to make the self feel better. What is written on these sticky labels is only part of the story, a reminder to myself to make childcare arrangements whilst I am at a conference or to phone U-Net (yet again), requesting my Janet CD-Rom of Netscape Navigator to browse the World Wide Web. Notes that can be re-used (stored in the SYSTEM), making the MOTHER DRIVE work. The 'Defrag' programme is essential to make the Mother Disk complete, to function efficiently, not to forget to do this or that. I am not lost; the 'ethernet card' is somewhere. How to devise a piece of performance which communicates a complete internal logic externally?

'What Shall I Do With My Amstrad?' originated as a piece of performance practice, which was given as a contributing paper to the SCUDD (Standing Conference of University Drama Departments) Annual Conference in Scarborough, on 21 April 1996. Following this, I received a number of invitations from various university drama departments to perform the piece to students studying MA Drama or Theatre programmes, as well as a request to publish the performance text in *Studies in Theatre Production* (Oddey, 1996: 105–8). I decided to develop the work further and commenced a tour of 'Show and Tell: the Delights of Devising Theatre' in Autumn 1996.[1] I gave the first performance at Exeter University on 24 October 1996 and the final one at Nottingham Trent University on 24 July 1997, as part of the 'Representing Lives' Conference.

It is interesting to note that it was a nine-month gestation period (to the exact date). Was I giving birth at the 'Representing Lives' Conference? I began and ended in one, unique final action with the creation of 'Postscript Post-its' (a woman's body randomly covered in yellow Post-its, each with their own inscribed message), sowing the seeds of 'Viglen's Revenge'. It was an act of fruition, realizing one journey, and yet, clearly consummating the start of another. I left the Amstrad afterbirth on a bed in a Nottingham hotel room. I threw it away, as though it were a discarded lover, a *fait accompli* and a symbol of both an effectuation and termination. Now, another nine months later, I reflect on the autobiography of 'Show and Tell: the delights of devising theatre' as a piece of performance. At the 'Representing Lives' Conference, I wanted to explore a spontaneous process in performance, in order to lay open the identities about my person. The text was there, but it was the overall, final visual image that mattered. The body as text: the possibilities of changing the status, positioning and interrelationship of particular Post-its to each other. What I discovered was an acknowledgement of the continuum of competing selves for playing space, and the need to accept a shifting of roles (and associated identities). This performance made me particularly aware of my interest in the body as a primary site for devising work, and of the breadth of audience that could relate to the specific concerns of the piece.

The 'Representing Lives' Conference audience consisted mainly of women academics from a wide range of disciplines, including sociology, women's studies, literature and theatre studies. It was a much more sophisticated rapport between performer and spectator, evident in the nature of discussion that followed the performance, when Professor Liz Stanley from Manchester University raised some fascinating questions about the work in relation to current issues within universities. The performance was shifting from the microcosmic world of the woman academic in theatre studies (operating as performance artist) to the wider debate of the macrocosmic world of higher education. The desire to perform this piece had dwindled over the year, and what became significant at the 'Representing Lives' Conference was the need to move on, transform and conclude. Ultimately, I was still interested in playing with the performing self, investigating the boundaries between being one's self 'in performance' and performing 'selves' for a particular audience. I was questioning and cross-examining the original text of 1996, rediscovering what I now wanted to represent as my 'performing self'.

My ongoing research in relation to performance practice is concerned with questions about why I, as a woman, want to perform; why women want to perform and how their personal history has contributed to their desires or dreams of 'performing'. As I write, I am currently editing a collection of interviews with leading women performers from different generations, cultures, perspectives and practice, which will provide a collective discourse about women performing at the end of the twentieth century.[2] These edited interviews also represent fragmented autobiographies of performers in particular moments of their lives, telling a collective story of what motivates them to perform and where they are coming from.

The performer (Alison Oddey) takes her nose ring out and places it on the table. She speaks:

Beginnings

WHY did I want to devise this performance paper in April 1996? The obvious answer is that I had made a commitment to Eric Prince and the proposed SCUDD Conference at Scarborough in January 1996. *I didn't know then what I was going to do.* It then became clear from a telephone conversation with Professor Baz Kershaw at Lancaster that he was going to write No. 2 in The Messy-stuff Dialogues, and the opening sentence, 'I had an E-mail from Aristotle today' sounded very impressive. So did his two props: a laptop computer and a mobile phone. *This certainly wasn't me.* I immediately thought of my Amstrad 1512, and the University of Kent's directive to staff to become computer-literate by 1997. The title, 'What Shall I Do With My Amstrad?' evolved out of a discussion with my husband (Ben Williams) about news that my application for a new Viglen computer had been approved, and would be arriving in a matter of days. My new equipment cost £2,500. Ben drew the analogy between purchasing a computer and it becoming instantly out of date with the ephemerality of performing devised theatre. The seeds were sown.

Alison takes the mouse out of her hair, and throws it on the ground.

THE PROCESS of devising this piece took place in the week leading up to the conference during the Easter vacation. *I didn't want to do it.* I was feeling particularly pissed off with the University of Kent, and with academia generally. I tried to think of ways of getting out of it – *constantly.* I suppose the starting ideas that mulled around in my head were to do with the new technology I had to encounter, my dissatisfaction with the workplace, and a preoccupation with trying to be 'super, superwoman' (as my aromatherapist once described me). The first breakthrough (or wave of enthusiasm) came from a conversation with a 'computing' friend, who laughed raucously when I naïvely read aloud the various computer courses and documentation sent to me. Experimenting with the sounds of computer jargon was fun. It reminds me of a project we once did in my undergraduate days at Exeter University, which was about Artaud and the 'isms': the enjoyment of discovering Marinetti's Futurist recipes, such as 'Devil's Roses' (rose petals fried in batter); reading aloud Tristan Tzara's *The Gas Heart* with its striking images of 'angels in helicopters', 'angels in ice', and 'I have necklaces of goldfish' (Benedikt, 1964: 138–9); and practically investigating Apollinaire's surrealist drama *The Breasts of Tiresias* (Benedikt, 1964). As Apollinaire says, 'The child is wealth and the only wealth that's real' (62).

On another occasion, my friend (Alison Packer) impressed me greatly when she fixed her computer by taking it apart with a special screwdriver and changing various component parts. The ease with which she did this, combined with her knowledge and expertise, created a hankering in me to investigate further. I asked her if the Computing Laboratory could provide me with any old models to prise open. A practical workshop took place at our house one evening, which proved to be a turning point. Various bottles of wine were consumed by all three of us (Alison, Ben and myself), as we handled the numerous old models offered up for exploration. It was here that I became excited at the prospect of making a costume out of the different items. What could I wear next? I dressed up in a range of artifacts, whilst Ben and Alison undid everything in sight! This was my devising team, and a vital part of the process.

Prior to the opening of the SCUDD Annual Conference in Scarborough (19 April 1996), I had written down anything and everything that had occurred to me during the week. The conference's theme of 'Identities and Realities: Issues in Research and Practice' had certainly uncovered another strand of personal enquiry, focusing on my life as a working mother. I was interested in exploring different identities, whilst portraying the realities of my lifestyle. I packed a bag with selected props that might prove useful (including the computer equipment), and trusted to instinct. It was on the six-hour train journey to Scarborough that I wrote much of the text, reflecting on the week's jottings and ideas. I worked intensively, knowing that my deadline was almost up. *I was hooked.* I

Figure 4   Show and Tell (i)

Figure 5   Show and Tell (ii)

Figure 6   Postscripts–Post-its

started to see how the various strands could intertwine – for example, the act of placing computer items about my person as a representation of various identities, and thus a structure was created.

On Saturday, I took time out to re-read the text and made some alterations. During Saturday evening, I went into panic – how could I perform this piece when I hadn't even rehearsed it! Not prepared to give up my one night of freedom, drinking and being alone, I returned to my room at two o'clock in the morning, completely drunk. It was then that I rehearsed. Picture the scene: I toppled about as I practised the attachment of floppy disks to my night attire with large safety pins, telling myself – as Oliver[3] frequently does – 'I'm just all right!' On Sunday morning (complete with hangover), I relaxed, allowing myself to be, to go with the flow, and thoroughly enjoyed myself.

As Alison unties the cable, removing the motherboard and plastic sheeting from her body, she speaks:

It was very important that Ben cut the umbilical cord when Oliver was born, but he's not here today, so I'll have to do it myself!

The Performer's Perspective

What struck me most when performing this piece was the electric atmosphere it generated. The sense of tension and horror when I threw the Amstrad to the ground, when I tore open the disks, and when I attached the floppies to my breasts with safety pins was overwhelming. How it affected people in differing ways was quite incredible. One drama professor was clearly upset by the action of throwing 'the battered baby' to the ground, whilst others spoke in shaken tones about watching their 'work' or 'books' being ripped apart. One colleague described the experience of the performance as 'Blue Peter on speed'. It was as though I had uncovered a multiplicity of fears and anxieties about the dominance of computer technology alongside the ever-increasing demands of higher education: research, publication, increased student numbers, less money, more administration, and so on. Colleagues were acknowledging the many frustrating and difficult aspects of the academic's role within the changing context of university institutions.

(Pause) *The influence of Thatcher*: institutions have been turned inside-out; 'communities' are gone; we function as individuals in a non-caring society. (Pause) How do we make sense of this? How can we nurture the talent of the future?

Alison takes out her 'Earth Mother' earrings and places them on the table.

Practice and Theory

The practice of devising and performing 'What Shall I Do With My Amstrad?' reinforces certain basic points that I make in my book *Devising Theatre* (1994), such as the importance of trusting to instinct, spontaneity, and being well organized: 'Devising is about thinking, conceiving, and forming ideas, being imaginative and spontaneous, as well as planning' (Oddey, 1994: 1).

This piece evolved out of a five-day framework, reflecting a typical devising process in terms of the use of time, for example, trying out of ideas, developmental experimentation, creation of deadlines, and lack of rehearsal time:

> Decisions about time are specifically related to the nature of the devised piece, the purpose and intention of the work. . . . What is essentially different for devised theatre is the company's need to plan and schedule its own time-scale according to the development of the work, and in relation to a flexible structure of potential change, shift of focus, and spontaneous decision-making. (Oddey, 1994: 12–13)

I made a spontaneous decision to hit Professor Michael Patterson on the head after breakfast on Sunday morning, when he enquired whether I would be 'getting my revenge on him' in light of the previous Saturday afternoon. (I should add here that it was during Professor Peter Thomson's paper [whilst I was playing a 'head in a well'], that the heroine of the piece [Professor Michael Patterson] had to draw water from me, which resulted in a hard blow to my head with a cardboard box.) A sequence of events; a spontaneous decision:

I AM – FIGHTING WOMAN
She walks in a 'Robocop' manner across the space to Professor Michael Patterson, who is sitting on a table at the back. She

threatens with her shield and brings it down on his head. The audience cheer loudly. She gestures acknowledgement as though she has just won an Olympic Gold Medal. She returns to the table. (Oddey, 1996: 108)

Although 'What Shall I Do With My Amstrad?' is a solo performance, collaboration with other people was a necessary part of the process, offering alternative perspectives to prompt the deviser/performer's thinking, to stimulate their creativity, and to provide opportunities to try out ideas, whether in discussion or workshop:

> The process of devising is about the fragmentary experience of understanding ourselves, our culture, and the world we inhabit. The process reflects a multi-vision made up of each group member's individual perception of that world as received in a series of images, then interpreted and defined as a product. Participants make sense of themselves within their own cultural and social context, investigating, integrating, and transforming their personal experiences, dreams, research, improvisation, and experimentation. (Oddey, 1994:1)

Alison carefully unpins the floppy disks from her breasts.

Knowing *who* you are making the work for – *the specific audience* – is a prerequisite for the devising performer. I knew that my audience at Scarborough was all Drama academics, facing similar problems and experiences. It is for this reason that I wavered when invited to visit various institutions performing the piece, aware of the real danger of repeating the same material with a postgraduate audience – would it have the same resonance? Indeed, even more so with the Waterstone's Bookshop invitation in January 1997 – knowing the potential breadth of this audience, fully aware of local interest! However, the chance to speak about the work after the performance provides a new 'package' to promote further discussion in the devising theatre debate. (I can also tell you that now, as 'a skilled mouse user', it gives me great pleasure to 'format my floppies' and 'Mount the home directory from Crane'.)

> Devised theatre is a contemporary reflection of culture and society. It is continually addressing new theatrical forms, making original contributions out of the existing interests and considerations

of the time. . . . Devising allows for a constant re-definition of
theatrical performance, and for the work to begin from any starting
point. (Oddey, 1994: 23)

The starting point for 'Viglen's Revenge' is the final visual image
created by 'Performance Post-its'. A woman's body covered in yellow
sticky labels with written instructions of what is to be done. Data
can be viewed, processed and communicated with each act of attachment to the body. The performer broadcasts a series of announce-
ments, warnings or advice, publicly sharing and transmitting each
label as an item of news. The form is a physical, visual installation, using both body and computer technology to enhance the
theatrical structure, process and product in performance. The concerns are still focused within the world of education. How does the
working mother address the new structures and system of the primary school environment, embracing and questioning the value of
base-line assessments for children aged four to five, as well as the
impending daily reality of a world which stops at quarter past three
in the afternoon?
The work will be devised when the 'performing self' has a need
to emerge again, when the 'inner child' wishes to come out to
play. There will be a need to speak through a visual, physical language of body imagery, as well as a compulsion to represent and
give forth on the next stage or journey of life:

> What is this constant appeal of wanting to begin from the germ
> of an idea, and develop it into a full-scale piece of theatre? It is
> the need to say something, to express oneself, to give a voice to
> ideas, thoughts, and feelings about the world. (Oddey, 1994: 200)

'Viglen's Revenge' will emerge from the woman performer's autobiographical *her*story, albeit in a different kind of narrative, and as
a result of wanting to share her story with others. The performer
will have a strong desire for some form of feedback or response to
that self-expression. The excitement comes from the unknown and
the exploration of the nature of being. Performing autobiographical
devised work enables the potential connection between performer
and spectator of a universal experience through a creative energy
and engagement, which is a way of understanding the human being, their experience and that universality. 'Viglen's Revenge' will
fulfil a desire to temporarily escape real life and enter a height-

ened, accentuated state of feeling alive in the attempt to discover truth and empowerment.

Notes

1 Drama Department, Exeter University, 24 October 1996
Drama Department, Reading University, 18 November 1996
Waterstones Bookshop, Canterbury, 29 January 1997
Workshop Theatre, Leeds University, 4 March 1997
The Open University, Milton Keynes, 7 April 1997
Nottingham Trent University, 'Representing Lives: Women and Auto/
Biography' Conference, 24 July 1997.
2 Oddey (Macmillan, 1999).
3 Oliver Williams, aged two.

References

Apollinaire, G. *The Breasts of Tiresias*, in M. Benedikt and G. E. Wellwarth (eds and trans) *Modern French Plays – An Anthology from Jarry to Ionesco* (London: Faber and Faber, 1964)

Oddey, A. *Devising Theatre* (London and New York: Routledge, 1994)

—— 'What Shall I Do With My Amstrad?' *Studies in Theatre Production*, 13 (1996) 105–8

—— *Performing Women: Stand-ups, Strumpets and Itinerants* (Basingstoke: Macmillan, 1999)

Tzara, T. *The Gas Heart*, in M. Benedikt and G. E. Wellwarth (eds and trans) *Modern French Plays – An Anthology from Jarry to Ionesco* (London: Faber and Faber, 1964)

Part IV

(Auto)Biographical Representations

12

Tupperware Ladies: a Story of Women and Tupperware

Vanessa Gill-Brown

> My mother in this history has no history. She lurks silently
> in the kitchen. She is safety. She is danger. She is the sub-
> urbs ... I cannot find her in my dreams because the kitchen
> is where I am most afraid to look.
>
> (Walkerdine, 1985)

I am interested in the way auto/biography is present but concealed
in so much writing about culture. The stories are often hidden,
squashed and disciplined; but as a reader I always have the sense
that experience, however unreliable, is somehow driving the research. I wanted to make an auto/biography – that could have
remained unwritten in my research – visible. Although my initial
intention to produce a cultural analysis of Tupperware stemmed
from the experience of attending a Tupperware Party, I was struck
by two observations which form the major themes of this chapter.
First, the continued need for women, feminists included, to perform to the expectations of other women; and second, the contrast
between the enormous distance I felt from the party, the products
and the other women, and the simultaneous pleasure, amusement
and familiarity I found in it. It was an enjoyable experience; we
passed the products around obediently and pretended to look impressed (as we felt we ought); we laughed, it was funny. Despite
our resistance, I came home with three *tropical serving cups* at £5.95
and my sister, Mandy, bought two *signature line* containers at £14.50
each. The fact that my mother (b. 1939) decided to take on the

role of 'Tupperware lady' for a short period after I was born (in 1970) reinforced my suspicion that all these feelings were rooted in the relationships between mothers and daughters that the second wave of feminism has interrupted.

Memories of my early childhood and relationship with my mum feature Tupperware props heavily. She always used it at family parties for things like rice salad and jelly. Indeed, if the large green bowl or the 'Party Susan' could not be found, I wondered how on earth the gathering could take place. A strong recollection is the strange sensation of biting on the perforated plastic stick of the lollies she used to make for me in Tupperware moulds. Sometimes we would make them together. My mother worked (part-time), often as a waitress at a posh restaurant or at the golf club, and whenever we had visitors her hostessing skills would come centre-stage. Mandy and I would get frustrated with her for 'plumping up' the cushions and behaving like a waitress in front of guests. We used to laugh and whine in irritation that it was all right, no need to bother, that she should come and join in, *sit down*. She never did, and still does not.

The jokes we made as adults at the party, my indignation and the frustration with which we looked at mum can all be seen as texts within wider discourses on domestic work and the myth of the 1950s housewife which address feminism and femininity. Here, I will trace some of the historical, political and cultural factors in the possible relationships between two generations of white, western women and examine the significance of Tupperware as a focus around which differing femininities can be articulated. My analysis draws on theory and other women's stories in order to tell the story of my mum and me, and the differing roles we have played as gendered subjects in our respective times.

The Tupperware phenomenon spans the postwar period and is strongly linked with ideal femininity; and yet, the products and marketing strategies have changed very little since the 1950s when it was invented and the party plan developed. This decade is often represented as a period of successful conspiracy to get women 'back to the kitchen' after the Second World War (see Rosen, 1975), with consumer goodies, 'New Look' outfits and promises of a drudgery-free future the principal agents of this ideological coup. The popular ideal of this consuming woman is the glamorous housewife of the 1950s advertising image. With her Hollywood set hair, lipstick and waisted apron she is the queen of all she surveys in her kitchen;

ideally, she has one hand on hip and the other draped on a refrigerator, vacuum cleaner or other appliance. She is Doris Day in the kitchen of the future – technology and woman in perfect harmony. These images structure my imagined memories of my mum's youth, but the oral histories of the 1950s told by my mum, and auto/biographies like Carolyn Steedman's *Landscape for a Good Woman* (1986) evoke a more complex reality for women in Britain. This was the period that promised future affluence, excess and technologically produced ease. The two 1950s photographs of my mum (Figures 7 and 8) show her desire to identify with Hollywood femininity. The poses, hair, clothes and make-up are a starlet's, but she was in fact a worker in the Pye television factory in Lowestoft.

This new femininity was represented by mainstream culture as progressive; and the commodification and modernization of the home and kitchen were seen as liberating to women. As Elizabeth Wilson explains: 'The installation of hoovers, refrigerators, electric mixers and washing machines was held to have given women equality' (Wilson, 1980: 2). Tupperware fits perfectly into this ideological framework. Made from new plastics, these containers would give women mastery over the materials and processes of their domain. The space-age materials, gravity-defying lightness and fashionable pastel colours seemed efficient and futuristic. It emphasized also the suburban social life with products like the 'Party Susan' – a circular polythene tray with compartments for nibbles, a sealable lid and a lacy plastic carrying handle.

Mica Nava sums up the 1950s as: 'The moment of the consuming housewife, locked into femininity, motherhood, shopping and the suburban idyll' (1991: 161). Feminists of later decades have responded with frustration to the apparent lack of resistance with which this ideology was met. Marjorie Rosen, author of *Popcorn Venus* (1975), ends a chapter on the female film stars of this period with an angry comment about what she sees as the 'foolishness of the bobbysoxer generation' who were seduced by these images. According to Sheila Rowbotham (1989: 41), the frustrations felt during the late 1960s towards the isolation and monotony of housework were in fact to kick-start the 'second wave' of feminist organization. From the concerted efforts to theorize housework,[1] to the everyday attitudes of feminists towards this work and those who do it today, the housewife's image and her duties are central to much feminist thinking. The symbols of housewifery remained in feminist consciousness; the equipment and technology once hailed

Figure 7. Vanessa Gill-Brown's mother (c. 1959) (i)

as women's liberators gradually became signifiers of our oppression. Rowbotham quotes the Peckam Rye Women's Liberation Group in their telling declaration of 1970:

> Our window on the world is looked through with our hands in the sink and we've begun to hate that sink and all it implies – so begins our consciousness. (Rowbotham, 1989: 3)

Figure 8. Vanessa Gill-Brown's mother (c. 1959) (ii)

A further reason for the revolt against housework is that popular emphasis was (and still is) placed on greater access to education, jobs and careers for women. It came to be perceived as a matter of *choice* between being 'just' a housewife or having a career or full-time job. Part of many women's identities is therefore constructed in explicit opposition to 'being a housewife'. However, the house-work has not gone away. According to Ros Coward, women in families are still largely responsible for the domestic work (Coward, 1992: 7). We should be forgiven for thinking it has disappeared though, because today's women's magazines – from *Woman's Own* to *Cosmopolitan* to *Homes and Gardens* – present their domestic features as a series of sexy, hyper-real *lifestyle* choices; as if you can have clean, well-pressed clothes and stylish individual houses without wash-ing, ironing and cleaning, as long as you make the correct *choice*. These representations collude with those ideas women once fought to change – that housework is not very significant, that house-wives and their cultures are less valuable.

If my mum were reading this she would know that these theo-ries and ideas are about her life and her investment in her family, and that hers is the lifestyle choice I and many others are busy trying not to make. There is no doubt my sister and I benefited from her efforts, certainly materially: clean clothes and beds, encouragement and money for degrees, yet we speak as if these things don't matter. 'Oh, I never vacuum', I lightly say as we eat the dinner she has cooked. She was too successful with us. We are different: more middle-class, more career-oriented, more 'left-wing', less 'feminine'. There's glib rejection on the one hand but – and here's the thorn in our side – guilt and longing on the other.

An article in *The Times* by Stephanie Calman (1984) expresses distaste for Tupperware which confirms its function as a symbol of despised domesticated femininity which stems from the 1950s ideal and the cultural significance of housework. She satirizes her own trip to a party and studiously distances herself from the product and the other women. The demonstrator is constructed as ignorant and lacking in linguistic style; and Calman carefully records her saying: 'Personally, myself, I like it very much'. She describes the products as 'totally superfluous' (Calman, 1984: 11), and the cheesecake made by the demonstrator as looking 'like bleached sick'. Calman claims to prefer the 'very best French oven-to-table which lasts you a lifetime'. She ends with a quip about the free gifts: 'Pauline showed me the gift she had got . . . it was a tiny white bowl with lid attached to a key ring. I looked in the catalogue but the "wee valium storette" wasn't there' (11). For Calman, the choice between a Tupperware Oval Server and a piece of French oven-to-table at a similar price is a choice between an object that currently connotes 'housewife/housework' and another whose major connotation was, at the time of writing, visual pleasure; its fashionability emptying it of the significance of its function. In this way, Tupperware has become a focus around which 'new women' can negotiate self-congratulation on the perceived degrees of distance from traditional femininity.

However, despite the negative associations, images and ideals surrounding Tupperware I have already stated that from the early stages of my research, I knew I also *enjoyed* and took *pleasure* in those images and ideals. The images of my mum were taken from my own photo album, watching a Doris Day film with her was a kind of 'truce'. Pleasure in Doris Day films has been explored by feminists before. Clarke and Simmonds (1980) and Williamson (1986) concentrated on her 'independence of mind . . . humour and self-respect' (Williamson, 1986: 151–2). I would add that the historical distance we feel is crucial to certain aspects of the humour and pleasure we find in it. I may be attracted to Doris Day, but I also feel irony and separation from her more typically feminine characteristics. However, I also enjoy films like *Every Girl Should be Married* (1948, RKO) and *Houseboat* (1958, Paramount), where resistant, progressive or alternative feminist readings are *much* less easily made, suggesting a more complex model of these pleasures. Safely in the past, perhaps those desires consciously denied – for our mothers, for continuation – can be indulged. A fantasy about being the ideal housewife in our own time frightens us; in the past perhaps it poses less of a threat and our desire for and identification with our mothers can breathe.

Having examined my own and other feminists' relationships with the feminine ideal, I wanted to find out why my mother had chosen to sell Tupperware. As she swept and I sat, she gave an unexpected response:

> Well, it was after I had you, you know, when I went all silly and I wouldn't go out or anything. I couldn't speak to more than one person at a time – I'd just freeze up! Anyway, one day I thought, 'This is ridiculous. I'm going to be like this for the rest of my life if I don't do something about it.' So I thought, if I did Tupperware I'd have to speak to people and go out; and I knew I wouldn't let anyone down; if I said I was going to do something I'd have to do it. . . . The first one was awful! My mouth went all dry and the spittle was like white cake I was so nervous. But after that I was fine. I used to do themes and recipes and it was really good. Have a laugh – if you got some good people there you could really have a laugh. But no one had much money and I used to think, crumbs, they're spending all their housekeeping on plastic pots to put things in. They asked me to be a manager, but I didn't want to. I wasn't taken in enough by it all. I used to laugh at it – 'You could earn this wonderful coolbox!' But it was good while I did it.

Far from locking her further into the problems of suburban house-wifery, Tupperware afforded her an escape, and her critical perspective sounds much unlike the foolish, oppressed female consumer of myth. Newer, more complex theories of consumption (see Fiske, 1989; and Willis, 1990) combined with histories of women involved with Tupperware, show that despite its many oppressive aspects it has been positive in many women's lives: from mild subversion in the all-female gathering (Clarke, 1990: 38) to confidence-building and economic independence.

In contrast to my mother's experience is that of my friend Elspeth, who was a Tupperware manager from 1991 to 1993. Her recollections underline the negative associations explored previously. As we chatted, I remarked that plastic was not very fashionable for kitchens at that time. Elspeth stopped suddenly (she was preparing dinner). 'Oh,' she said, 'Tupperware isn't trendy. But not just because it's plastic'; and she went on to describe the many benefits: fun, prizes and bonuses, a network of friends. Previously, she had always stressed how good the product is and how enjoyable it is to be a demonstrator. Following my fairly casual remark about plastic and fashion, she volunteered information about some less positive feelings and experiences:

> Sometimes I used to feel I wanted to say: 'Look, before I start, I have got a degree.' I always wanted to do something I could feel proud of and we used to have these meetings where they would say that Tupperware is a quality product and that we should feel proud to sell it. They used to make us feel brilliant . . . but sometimes we [Elspeth and her husband] would go out to a dinner party . . . and there'd be loads of young professionals there, and Bren would say he was a civil engineer, and that was OK, that was respectable, and then . . . I'd have to say, 'I sell Tupperware'. I did one party once that was awful. It was all young professional women – one of my friends had organized it – and they gave me a really hard time. . . . There was one girl with a Sinead O'Connor haircut who kept going [whispers behind hand and giggles] and when she came to choose something she kept saying 'I want something with Tupperware on it. Will it come in a box with "Tupperware" on it?' It was all right, I could still demonstrate . . . but I came home and I just burst into tears.

The strong feelings provoked in Elspeth are clearly related to matters of class. For young professional women there are acceptable and unacceptable femininities. The 'Sinead O'Connor haircut' appears significant since Elspeth pinpoints this woman as oppositional to her own femininity. Elspeth felt the signs of her lifestyle (Tupperware manager, wife, mother) signified a lack of intelligence or lack of commitment to 'worthwhile' (i.e. connoting 'public') work, and a contentment with playing the wrong kind of feminine role for her social group.

Ros Coward (1992) records similar feelings among women who,

despite many of the material conditions not having changed, feel that failing to live up to a particular feminist ideal is somehow their fault and something to be ashamed of 'avoiding being seen as a "stay at home wife" was a principal concern . . . others (full-time housewives) told me they dreaded parties when someone might ask them what they did' (77). It seems that Tupperware now, in the popular imagination of the contemporary woman, signifies traditional femininity, and is associated with the lower middle class.

I conclude that the critical attitudes expressed by some women (my laughter at the party, the frustrations with mum, the anger with the bobbysoxers) towards the apparently complicit practices of other women and the concrete symbols of these practices are masking a profound ambivalence towards traditional femininities and their representations. The everyday distancing techniques used show an allegiance to theories and ideas about mass culture, femininity and the private which have undermined the forms of work and consciousness of our mothers. They show that we often fail to recognize the uneven effects and partial extent of women's liberation from the material conditions that oppress us. This uneven development is consequently understood in the 1990s as a *lifestyle choice*. This distancing is also connected to the journeys of class which have often accompanied the desire for new roles. Furthermore, some of our more complex desires and pleasures show that these are classes and femininities that we have not broken with as easily as we might think. In a sense this chapter has been a conscious act of restitution (see Klein, 1988). The stories told here also demonstrate that we must keep a check on the housework – we either pretend our interest is about good design, condemn it and the women who do it, or attempt to ignore the fact that it is still here for us. We must dare to look in the kitchen and make small changes there. Incidentally, I can recommend those serving cups; and I still might see if I can get a set of the lolly-makers. Just for old times' sake, you understand.

Note

1 Feminist accounts of domestic work (see Delphy, 1984) made a case for the enormous contribution to society made by women and the lack of status afforded it. Shwartz Cowan (1983) demonstrated that while technology performs some domestic tasks, it also creates new work; thus, it is a false notion that housewives have little to do. These emphasize the oppressive nature of housewifery, but also show the importance and quantity of work to be done.

References

Calman, S. 'It's my party and I'll buy if I want to', *The Times* (11 June 1984) 11

Clark, J. and Simmonds, D. *Move Over Misconceptions* (London: BFI Dossier no. 4, 1980)

Clarke, A. 'The Tupper Echelons', *The Guardian* (27 September 1990) 38

Coward, R. *Our Treacherous Hearts* (London: Faber and Faber, 1992)

Delphy, C. *Close to Home* (Amherst: University of Massachusetts Press, 1984)

Fiske, J. *Understanding Popular Culture* (London: Unwin Hyman, 1989)

Heron, L. *Truth, Dare or Promise* (London: Virago, 1985)

Hine, T. *Populuxe* (London: Bloomsbury, 1987)

Klein, M. *Love, Guilt and Reparation* (London: Virago, 1988)

Nava, M. *Changing Cultures: Feminism, Youth and Consumerism* (London: Sage, 1992).

Rosen, M. *Popcorn Venus* (London: Owen, 1975)

Rowbottom, S. *The Past is Before Us: Feminism in Action since the 1960s* (London: Penguin, 1989)

Schwartz, C. R. *More Work for Mother* (New York: Basic Books Inc., 1983)

Steedman, C. *Landscape for a Good Woman* (London: Virago, 1986)

Walkerdine, V. in L. Heron (ed.) *Truth, Dare or Promise: Girls Growing up in the Fifties* (London: Virago, 1985)

Williamson, J. *Consuming Passions* (London: Marion Boyars, 1986)

Willis, P. *Common Culture* (London: Open University Press, 1990)

Wilson, E. *Only Halfway to Paradise* (London: Tavistock, 1980)

13

The Discourse of Selfhood: Oral Autobiographies as Narrative Sites for Constructions of Identity

Erzsébet Barát

Theoretical Framing

In this chapter, I analyse linguistic ways of constructing the self in oral autobiographies of Hungarian women. It is my argument that the existing auto/biographical research into women's lives could benefit from a systematic analysis of the narrative texture of the emerging life stories. My theoretical claim is that identity is an intersubjective, retrospective construction from within the existing, discursively mediated practices of writing and telling a life. Living as a human being inevitably entails reflexivity, and human understanding is narrative in nature. As Charles Taylor (1992) contends, we make sense of the world and ourselves in it from the stories we tell. Consequently, the auto/biographical story is a means for a reflexive understanding of the self. Furthermore, as representation is always intersubjective, it is necessarily located within a social relation to others. In this sense, auto/biography is a form of discursive practice that reconstructs the past as the major means of self/other understanding.

As defined by Norman Fairclough (1992), the genre of auto/biography is a mode of discursive practice the major function of which is to construct a continuous, unified personal identity at the intersection of the multiple discontinuous, fragmented and often contradictory socio-cultural positionings available. This construction is a process of articulating different narrated events together into a temporarily fixed coherence, providing a sufficient sense of identity through the narrative device of emplotment as defined by

Paul Ricoeur (1992). At the same time this process takes place in relation to others within the narrating of events. Thus, I also claim that oral auto/biography as a genre emerges in the dialectic of the narrated and narrating events. In short, to the extent that the various fragmented positionings (such as class, race, ethnicity, age, religion, sexuality, age and health) available in a particular socio-cultural context are constructed as meaningful in and through the unifying act of narration, identity is discursive in nature. Narration entails the search for a closure and self-narration the process of plotting a meaningful trajectory out of and for one's life. This search for a self-same identity over the span of one's life-time up to the moment of recollection was constructed by all of the narrators in my study around the resolution of a central dilemma in their life at the time of the narrating event. They all, despite the differences in their socio-cultural background informing their discursive repertoires, used the auto/biographical interview situation strategically, in order to resolve a dilemma of identity. Furthermore, this dilemma is equally formulated from a gendered position regardless of what and how 'being a woman' means for them in the respective life-stories.

This foregrounding of gender as an explanatory category does not mean that I disregard other socially salient dimensions of my collaborators' life-stories. In the same way as I am not arguing for a homogeneous category of Hungarian women, neither am I arguing for an essentialist category of 'woman'. What I wish to analyse is precisely the socio-culturally specific discursive ways of constructing its meaning. This latter qualification takes me to my other motivation for research. In my opinion, a discursive analytical approach to narrative texts – as worked out by Fairclough (1992, 1995) – should also contribute to the auto/biographical research regarding claims about the epistemological status of the genre. Instead of simply stating that the ways of knowledge production, as well as the knowing subject herself, are socially located, and thus inevitably partial, it could be more fruitful to analyse the collective identity categories in the making – that is, as constructed and interpreted during the course of their narrative emplotment.

The Origin of the Life-stories

I have interviewed twelve women in Hungary from two generations: the first, born after the Second World War, the second, born after the 1956 Hungarian uprising. These dates establish two important periods, entailing dramatic changes in Hungarian history: first, the introduction of Soviet-type dictatorship, and second, the disappearance and gradual deterioration of its most oppressive form. My assumption is that the two generations' lifespan should be significantly different as they are constrained by different sociopolitical conditions. Consequently, similarities in their discursive practices of (gendered) selfhood should be all the more telling. The fact that it is gender that turns out to be the most salient identity category for all the twelve women I have interviewed suggests that the most decisive dimension of social domination and unequal power relations for both generations is gender-defined.

For the purposes of this chapter, I have chosen only one interview, the one that seems to represent the most submissive position on the continuum of the gendered existences plotted along the heterosexual patriarchal norm which develops from the reconstructions of the twelve autobiographies. The chosen autobiographer is called Adél. She belongs to the pre-1956, first generation and was born in 1946, in a village. She is a dentist by profession and married with three children, all of whom are university students. Her husband, Kálmán, is also a dentist. They are the same age, graduates from the same university, currently living in a medium-sized country town, Szolnok.

In the course of all the interviews I tried to intervene as little as possible, constraining myself to the role of an attentive listener in order to minimize influencing what is told within the research framework inevitably imposed by my methodology. We agreed on no time limits and the women could switch off the taperecorder whenever and for as long as they felt it necessary. However, the women tended to talk for about three hours before finishing the reconstruction of their life story.

The Dilemma

As I stated earlier, a distinctive feature of the interviews was the staging of a specific dilemma. I shall begin my analysis by quoting Adél's dilemma itself in order to trace how the flow of the auto/biographical events is structured in terms of its re/occurrence. What I am interested in is the relevance of its structural location for the evolving process of identity construction and the importance of a possible resolution of the dilemma. Since all the interviews reach their end when the narrator finds a satisfactory resolution, what is at stake on the generic level is to construct a closure of the narrative and thereby to achieve a sense of guarantee of an equally successful closure of a future narrative, though of a different generic kind – that of a prospective obituary. This interpretation is supported by the other common feature in my interviews: the self-chosen theme of death, in whose context the respective different dilemmas are formulated. What is at stake for these women, then, is not only the construction of a temporarily self-same identity but a sense of knowing that they will have continued to live a life worth living in the future. The ultimate point of closure, that is the moment of death, functions as a self-chosen absolute measure of worthiness. This higher level of moral perspective seems to reinforce what Taylor (1992) contends when theorizing the self as the one that may be defined by the commitments and identifications which provide the frame or horizon within which one can try to determine from case to case what is good, or valuable, or what ought to be done. In short, each discourse of selfhood is informed by the values and beliefs the individual woman is oriented towards in her material and linguistic choices, be they conscious or otherwise.

Narrative Structure

In Adél's narrative, the dilemma is clearly centred on her retrospective evaluation of her life at the moment of the interview. However, it does not dominate the narrative and is verbalized only once, very briefly, towards the end of the recording:

> The thing that has meant or caused a big trouble in my life is the state of my career and my family. Right from the first moment on. That is, how can you do them both right? My father, when he told me how delighted he was that I was to become a dentist, because that is a very good profession, and I would be good at it, that's what he said. I don't know, the only thing he didn't take into consideration is that one needs such physical strength and condition so that . . . to do it on and on throughout the years, always with a lot of patients is a tormenting effort. . . . So that is my problem: where can I make concessions, after all it's impossible to do everything. To do my best here [in the surgery] as well as at home. . . . Then I thought that I . . . in the

family... [She can't help crying] I don't want to cry now but, you know, I must hold my ground there to a maximum extent. Switch it off.

The resolution is as follows:

> I have told you about this before, that, that ... in theory a lot of things, that is whatever in the theory could be learnt beside it [her family commitments], and and to participate in retraining, to go to conferences, and to exhibitions, So whatever could be soaked up I did but I didn't have the opportunity to practice them. And ... *I've had the role of a kind of fellow-traveller.*

In this narrative it is possible to trace Adél's strategic reference to her childhood family as a model for her own self. The repeated introduction of the parental model always indicates the end/beginning of a developmental stage in Adél's life, forming a structural unit. These are: the first recollections of the little girl; the end of primary school education; graduation from university; maternity leave with the first child; nine years of successful career-building in a village; formulation of dilemma and its subsequent resolution; current life without the three children in Szolnok; recount of the resolution.

This reference to her childhood family also functions as an evaluative comparison by which to measure her performance in her own nuclear family. These references are repeatedly formulated with the help of a generic noun, which in Hungarian means 'a human being'. Through this generalization, Adél assumes responsibility for any failure on behalf of her nuclear family members. In accordance with the formulation of her dilemma, to be a good mother and wife for her means to educate successful and happy children – as she and her three siblings were in her own childhood family – and to support her husband's career as a successful dentist so that he can be as successful as her general practitioner father used to be. It is also relevant that her father achieved his alleged excellence at the expense of Adél's mother never making use of her own degree as a teacher. This is also a parallel, though a modified, model in her mother's case. Adél does not have to give up her career from the very beginning but is to sacrifice her professional development and promotion prospects so that her husband can pursue his career. This life-story would seem to confirm Sylvia Walby's (1990) observation, that in spite of the apparent changes in the life of (white middle-class heterosexual) women, heterosexuality and patriarchy, through the reconfiguration of capitalist production in late modernity, have been reinscribed in systematic and oppressive ways, instead of being eroded.

The quotations above indicate another typical linguistic feature of Adél's speech: the predominance of the personal pronoun 'we' and the marked absence of 'I'. This strategic reluctance to reconstruct her life from the point of view of an 'I' means, on the one hand, that Adél may not feel an accountable individual, qualified to have her own voice heard. Seen from this point of view, then, her constant reference to her parents' family as the ultimate measure means that she feels obliged to justify her right, in front of them, to have a voice of her own. On the other hand, from Adél's point of view, the interpretation of this inclusive 'we', taking up 70 per cent of the interview, may mean a conscious use of the interview as an occasion for paying tribute. It is a chance for her to depict a family photograph with her as the invisible photographer, thereby performing her family duties in public. In fact, before we started the recording she mentioned how carefully she had thought about the family events so as not to leave out anything. Also, after the interview, she asked me to make a copy of it so that she could leave it for her own family once she is dead.

The distribution of the 'I' and 'we' narratives constitutes another possible structuring of the narration in so far as the self-reflexive 'I' explicitly evaluates her life in and through the dilemma, against the account of her life from within a 'we' position. The overall structuration of the narrative itself is thus hierarchical. The first level of the chronological life-events is imposed upon the developmental structuration of life, punctuated by the references to the parental model organizing the events into eight units. Onto this is imposed the third level as mediated by the 'we' vs. 'I' narrative voices: dividing the narration into only three units: the family photograph; the explicitly self-reflexive dilemma of identity; current events in her own family. I claim that this hierarchy in the textual body of the narrative provides a reformulation of Adél's dilemma from a critical point of view. Her original dilemma between career and family can be interpreted as a gendered dilemma between accepting one's submission to the patriarchal hierarchy – the will of her father and then her husband's career – and finding particular, differential ways of resisting it.

What makes Adél's recollection striking is the strategic use of non-verbal communication as an indirect way of self-evaluation. The crying resolves the tension generated by her self-chosen male figures of reference at the moment of the delayed formulation of her dilemma and its subsequent resolution. The proximity in narration of the dilemma and its resolution creates a tension, as if the narrator did not give herself time or space for a reasoned argumentation and deliberation. Thus, the tension of this narrative shortcut ruptures the even surface of the reconstruction and generates the sudden burst of tears.

On the one hand, Adél's model is her mother. At the very beginning of her interview Adél recollects her mother's account of her birth like this: 'My hands were wrinkled [when I was born] like hers from doing a lot of laundry.' In the light of the enfolding story this simile constructs Adél as a woman who is going to share her mother's gender role as the self-sacrificing family woman. In fact, the father's oppressive behaviour comes to be legitimized by his excellent performance as a surgeon, whereas its price, the mother's self-sacrifice, is never questioned. On the other hand, as a woman with her own career, she has male models to live up to: her father and her husband. However, although she would never explicitly say so, as a woman she is without the indispensable sacrifice of another to support her. The father not only made a choice for Adél regarding her university studies as a dentist, believing it to be the least demanding medical profession for a prospective wife and mother, but he also imposed the burden of his own professional measures on her.

Adél's dilemma shows that in her actual career as a dentist she also compares her performance with her husband's. They met at university and graduated together, but what she verbally refuses to formulate is that from the very beginning her 'choice' of workplace always had to be in favour of the husband's career. Added to this, she had three maternity leaves which inevitably left her behind. The point is that under the pressure of these patriarchal role models, Adél resolves their oppression by the non-verbal mode of communication of crying. The tears function as a 'voice' of criticism, as Adél's resentment over her acceptance of the traditional gender roles. As the metaphor of identity will show, on the verbal level, the reflexive evaluation of her life culminates in the reconciliatory, submissive and thus non-critical position of the 'fellow traveller'. Adél breaks down into at another point in the narrative:

'When he [the father] was dying, he asked me to take care of the children.' At this moment, the theme of death provides the interpretative frame through which Adél evaluates her life. However, as long as it is her father's death and career possibilities, not her own, through which Adél is evaluating her life, she is constructing herself as a traditional woman submitting to the patriarchal norm. On the other hand, as long as the crying is a relief for the emotional tension, she is indirectly questioning this submission, working towards an answer to her non-verbalized question of doubt addressed to her father and not to me, the listener: Is this what you meant by that last order of yours? Did I get your priorities of family over profession right? But why did you expect me to be a good dentist as well if they cannot go together?

Metaphors as Devices for Constructing a Unified Position of Identity

The metaphor of identity for Adél is mentioned only once, in the context her dilemma: 'I have fulfilled the role of some kind of fellow-traveller.' The discourses the metaphor brings to bear on the life-story are that of travelling and caring – a traditional image, but told from the point of view of a married woman who is split apart between the demands of her profession and her family. It constructs the female 'I' as a companion, a sacrificing assistant for her husband's journey, whose destination is neither negotiated by, nor known to, her. The only thing to know is that it will come to an end. Once embarked on this journey, her only duty is to stay by the man's side till death. The moral obligation of the family woman must override the needs of the professional woman. On the verbal level, there is no space left for negotiation or resistance.

Conclusion

Since in all interviews the metaphors of identity and the means of constructing a coherent self out of the multiple discursive positions are constructed from a gendered perspective, the women I interviewed evaluated their lives from a normative, gendered point of view: maintaining, contesting or trying to subvert the power of that norm against the interpretative horizon of gendered existence in the context of death. Regardless of their age, educational background, occupation or sexuality, the most salient dimension of life for all the Hungarian women I interviewed is gender as represented by the patriarchal heterosexual norm. That these auto/biographical narratives all construct and represent a gendered selfhood is suggestive of the continuation and stability of certain ideologies of being even during a period of enormous historical and political change.

References

Fairclough, N. *Discourse and Social Change* (Cambridge: Polity Press, 1985)
Fairclough, N. *Critical Discourse Analysis* (London: Longman, 1995)
Ricoeur, P. *Oneself as Another* (Chicago and London: University of Chicago Press, 1992)
Taylor, C. *Resources of the Self* (Cambridge: Cambridge University Press, 1992)
Walby, S. *Theorizing Patriarchy* (Oxford: Blackwell, 1990)

14
From Shaping Imperialism to Sharing Imprisonment: the Politics of the Personal in South African Female Missionary Biography

Deborah Gaitskell

The growing body of literature on western women and imperialism still tends to focus on the nineteenth century, despite welcome exceptions (see Bush, 1998). Detailed twentieth-century work is equally rare in the ongoing debate about missionaries and colonialism in Southern Africa. For both periods, researchers neglect female missionaries in favour of magnetic anti-colonial male pioneers (Etherington, 1996: 208–11). By focusing on a clutch of twentieth-century female missionaries from the Anglican Society for the Propagation of the Gospel (SPG) working in the southern Transvaal, this chapter seeks to redress this imbalance by showing that representing missionary women's lives can advance feminist historiography. Five 'mini-biographies' are outlined sequentially and analysed collectively in order to explore the relationship between gender and mission Christianity, from the imperial setting of early twentieth-century South Africa to the segregation and early apartheid years.

These biographical vignettes were inspired by Barbara Ramusack's (1992) portrayal of five British women activists in India, variously characterized as: 'cultural missionaries' in promoting British models of female education and modest dress; 'maternal imperialists' in their benevolent 'mothering' of 'immature' Indians; and, at their best, 'feminist allies' who collaborated successfully on a basis of equality and respect, 'to achieve the goals set by Indian women' (Ramusack, 1992: 134). That Jane Lewis (1991) likewise examined approaches to social questions in late Victorian England through a female quintet reinforced the value of collective biography where women share a social or religious project over time. Kumari Jayawardena provided further encouragement, with her sympathetic exploration of western women inspired by spiritual or secular 'universal causes . . . to live, and in most cases die, in South Asia' (1995: 8, 11).

Despite progress towards dominion status after the Union of South Africa was formed in 1910, church life continued its 'colonial' dependency on leaders recruited in Britain, including unmarried female missionaries, regularly employed by 'High Church' Anglicans. Transvaal mission leadership by celibate monks from the Community of the Resurrection (CR), to which the late Archbishop Trevor Huddleston also belonged, necessitated partnership with single women. This chapter explores three questions concerning the gendering of this metropolitan-dependent Christianity. What was seen as appropriate 'women's work' within the Anglican Church through this period? What sorts of relationships were forged between black and white mission women? Finally, how did female missionaries engage with, support or critique wider South African political processes of racial domination and subordination? Significant shifts and contrasts can be tracked across the half-century. No simple linear progression is posited, or sustainable. Different personal gifts and limitations mean that, for example, Dora Earthy perhaps forged deeper cross-racial ties than the later arrival, Dorothy Maud, who, by contrast, was far more assured in her municipal political campaigning. Frances Chilton's humble origins would probably, in Britain, have rendered her eventual diocesan responsibilities unthinkable. While Julia Gilpin enthusiastically cooperated with British forces trying to reconstruct and anglicize the Transvaal, effectively 'shaping imperialism', when Hannah Stanton was arrested, in the 1960 state of emergency, she was 'sharing imprisonment' with African National Congress (ANC) Alliance veteran, Helen Joseph, and other political detainees.

'The politics of the personal', exemplified in these life-stories, may apply to researcher as well as researched. As a white South African who cannot regard Christianity as an unmitigated blight on Africa, I am drawn by more than academic curiosity to thinking about possible ways of being a Christian woman in twentieth-century South Africa. Missionary biographies prompt assessment partly in terms of my own autobiography. Feminist researchers have suggested that 'most of us would probably be much less keen on doing' personal narratives if they couldn't be used as a mirror or guide to our own lives; certainly, we 'consciously and unconsciously absorb knowledge of the world and how it works through exchanges of life stories' (Personal Narratives Group, 1989: 238, 261).

Deaconess Julia

Julia Gilpin (1861–1948), with her prior nursing employment and ordination as deaconess in 1893 (Grierson, 1981: ch. 2), reflects two new sources of women's paid churchwork in Victorian times. After serving South London's urban poor, Deaconess Julia went to India as a missionary, returning to head the SPG Training Home in Wandsworth. In 1907, she responded to the call for female workers for Johannesburg, and never left, becoming 'by turns, nurse, teacher, social worker, and parish deaconess', with an impact also in Pretoria, Heidelberg, Cape Town and finally the George diocese, where she preached, took services and baptised with a near-priestly authority (Grierson, 1981: 100–1; *SWM Journal*, April 1944, November 1948).

Deaconess Julia certainly took initiatives in Johannesburg and was expected to, although the free rein she was given was clearly gender-specific. The CR 'Fathers' came out in the Milner era keen to put a stronger British imprint on Transvaal Christians. While they evangelized African miners and trained black priests, Deaconess Julia made a vital threefold contribution to 'devout domesticity'. She started devotional meetings for women on mine married compounds and in the slumyards of downtown Johannesburg. She founded St Agnes' Industrial School to give domestic training equipping African girls as servants for settlers and as élite Christian wives. Thirdly, for safe accommodation for African women working in town, she established a small hostel, later consolidated and expanded to act as a modest employment registry (Gaitskell, 1979; 1983; 1990).

So in terms of conceptions of women's role in the church, a lot of responsibility was vested in her. Politically, her South African work began in the heyday of 'imperial Christianity', when the head of SPG was seeking to build an ecclesiastical counterpart to the British empire (see Maughan, 1998). Personally, she seems to have been the most 'distant' of all five missionaries in her relationship with African women, viewing them through the imperial gaze as very weak, wayward and prone to fall. No friendships even approaching reciprocity come through in the letters, whereas the sudden death of a younger colleague, Marion Trist, her inseparable companion and nurturer, distressed Julia enormously (CWW, Gilpin to Miss Gurney, 9 January 1913). A warmer personality and more isolated domestic setting encouraged Dora Earthy, by contrast, to develop more intimate partnerships with the adult African women among whom she worked.

Dora Earthy

Mozambican scholars know Dora Earthy (1874–1960) for her monograph on Valenge women published by the International African Institute (Earthy, 1933), but she started as an urban missionary in the slumyards of central Johannesburg (1911–14), was transferred to the small Transvaal town of Potchefstroom, then moved to Maciene in southern Mozambique, where she lived from 1917 to 1930. An SPG visitor pronounced her 'charming, gentle, steady, persevering, daunted by nothing, acquiring the languages with great rapidity, loving her work, & a missionary out & out' (CWW, Miss Phillimore to Miss Gurney, 21 March 1913). An affectionate, jaunty tone marks out her reports on seemingly routine work, describing with gusto laborious journeys to isolated women's prayer groups, baptismal classes and confirmation preparation sessions. Some short-sighted male clergy viewed Dora Earthy simply as a female mission instructor, ignoring her venture to free Christian Mozambican widows from compulsory remarriage to serve the Church. Indeed, her priest-in-charge, positively hostile to any further anthropological research after her six months in 1928 for her book, spurned available South African finance.

Earthy had a much lower church profile than the pioneering Deaconess Julia, and colleagues suggested she was rather quiet and nervy; pinned to her personal file in 1931 was the note, 'Timid manner and low voice. Wd probably *write* much better than *speak*' (USPG Dossier 2640). She herself admitted: 'I find it easy to speak to natives, but of course it is a very different matter when one has to address a cultured "white" audience' (CWW, Earthy to Miss Saunders, 3 January 1917). This suggests that both race and missionary status empowered her self-perception in Africa. Her intellectual assets were nevertheless unusual: before offering to SPG at the relatively late age of 35, Dora's work cataloguing scientific papers for the prestigious Royal Society instilled a taste for research and employed her command of several European languages in translation. In South Africa, she learnt Dutch and Tswana; in Mozambique, Chopi and Shangaan, while improving her Portuguese; in retirement, she dabbled in five other languages (USPG: Dossier 2640).

Her warm attachment to Africa and affection for its churchwomen emerge in her words on leaving Potchefstroom in 1916, 'for I have loved the natives, and they have been so very sweet to me.' Showering her with little farewell gifts, one woman remarked, ' "She came from a far land to make herself one with us, we black people." ' En route from Britain to Mozambique, Earthy declared it was '*so* delightful to be back again in beloved Africa!' (CWW: Earthy to Miss Saunders, 26 November 1916; 17 July 1917). Deeper relationships grew during the 1920s with Christian widows resident at Maciene, all of whom were listed by name and their individual circumstances described in her correspondence. Dora was safeguarding their right to remain without men. Many of them were mature women closer to her in age, on whom she leant for material and emotional support. Rhoda and Mara travelled with her to outlying congregations, where sleeping in 'native huts' and eating 'native food' brought them 'into closer touch with the life of the women' (CWW: Earthy to Miss Saunders, December 1927). After Dora's contacts with the new academic anthropological community in South Africa expanded, the company and personal ministrations of Rhoda and Mara facilitated her field work (Gaitskell, 1998).

Dora Earthy's life requires the more subtle, sympathetic analysis of 'European women who tried to make a positive contribution in the colonies and who attempted to move beyond the ethnocentrism and sexism of their culture and period' (Strobel, 1991: ix). Her monograph engagingly documents the life cycle, daily work, cultural values and scientific insights of Valenge women. But her years in a foreign backwater and lack of powerful networks differentiate Dora Earthy from South Africa's notable women liberals and anthropologists of the 1930s, who could realistically expect to influence municipal and perhaps national policy towards Africans. Even when based in Johannesburg, she had shown little sign of being a political animal, but she nevertheless rooted herself deep in African society, offering a respectful evaluation of its culture.

Frances Chilton

Sharing Deaconess Julia's lack of ties to England, Frances Chilton (b. 1897) gave virtually her whole adult life to South Africa, arriving at 28 in 1926 and still there, a lively octogenarian whom I interviewed in 1978. Her candidates' papers throw into relief the class assumptions in which all her assessors were steeped and under-line how she found ecclesiastical advancement and spiritual responsibility through mission employment. Possibly illegitimate, previously employed as a domestic servant, her social origins would have made such status inconceivable back in Britain (USPG: Dos-sier 1562).

Frances offered for children's work in a school or institution, and children were indeed the central focus of her work for the first 20 years. While teaching domestic science at St Agnes' School, she was drawn into the mission-dominated girls' uniformed movement, Wayfarers, advancing to seniority as Commissioner, responsible for training many black leaders. Despite believing Wayfaring suited Africans better than Guiding did, Frances felt powerless to oppose the insistence on Guides by Dorothy Maud who, as bishop's daughter and bishop's niece, in the days when 'those things counted', had 'much more prestige . . . I was just a little ordinary missionary.' Frances continued with Sunday School work until her retirement in 1955, producing lessons which were translated into several African lan-guages for dissemination, and supervising classes all over the gold-mining Reef east and west of Johannesburg (Chilton, 1978).

For her first two decades on the Reef, Frances was living next to the church hostel in contact with younger women working as ser-vants, about whom she commented: 'They do still need a lot of mothering.' In 1946, the Mothers' Union (MU) presidency 'was rather thrust on' Frances, as convention still demanded white supervision. While giving advice where necessary, she largely left black clergy wives to run MU groups, conceding that Africans also questioned what she, as a single woman, could know about mothers. Her ref-erences to African women lack Dora Earthy's warmth and intimacy: her attitude was more distant, belittling their comprehension of the meaning of MU. Closer links with *male* clergy, via 25 years of weekly lectures to black theological students at Rosettenville, meant she spoke with generosity and certainty, rather than derogatory generalizations, of the African priests, asserting she got on well with the old ones because they knew she loved them (Chilton, 1978). While valuing African priests' paternal care for her safety, Frances Chilton was more at ease in the structured, hierarchical, maternal relationship of teacher than in the semi-sisterly, more egalitarian encounter needed in the MU – where her celibacy disqualified rather than empowered her.

Frances Chilton's career illustrates the striking expansion of Protestant mission activity among the growing numbers of Reef African schoolchildren in the inter-war period. Fearing secularization of the day schools, white mission supervisors encouraged burgeoning Sunday Schools and Christian youth movements, which Anglicans deemed primarily a female mission arena. She rarely commented on broader political issues, despite arriving as landmark segregation bills were published, and working on through the early years of apartheid. Questioned about the 1920s Joint Council of Europeans and Natives, she claimed intermittent attendance and little involvement because she was doing children's work. Education and class origins silenced her politically even more than they did Dora Earthy and her career illustrates to good effect the youth-training tasks then deemed suitable for women church workers.

Dorothy Maud

The Johannesburg mission career of Dorothy Maud (1894–1977) overlaps in time and focus with Frances Chilton's, but exhibits a distinctively broad social conception and racial self-consciousness. Under Dorothy's energetic leadership, two 'Settlement Houses' were built in black residential areas, Ekutuleni (Zulu for 'The House of Peace') in Sophiatown in 1928, and Leseding (Sotho for 'The House of Light') in Orlando (Soweto) in 1935. By 1943, when Dorothy left to become a nun, they housed some dozen white women doing social and church-building work reaching over 6000 African children. Two co-workers founded similar urban ventures: Tumelong in Pretoria (later run by Hannah Stanton, as discussed below) and Runyararo in Salisbury, Southern Rhodesia.

For the socially confident, articulate and charming Dorothy Maud, class position and race helped mitigate the disadvantages of gender. Her innovative project signalled the first institutional departure for Reef Anglican 'women's work' in the 20 years since the flurry of activity under Deaconess Julia. The fact that women missionaries deliberately built themselves homes in African areas in the very years when the city was implementing residential segregation – and quite against the trend of (married) white missionary practice – is perhaps the most striking aspect of their work. Singleness freed and empowered them to challenge convention, whereas it correspondingly limited their effective arena to urban children, rather than the adult women so frequently assumed to be their natural constituency.

Opened in February 1929, a large double-storey house with five bedrooms, sitting room, offices and chapel, with clubroom and playground close by, Ekutuleni was pronounced 'very clean and modern' by a visiting researcher, gaily artistic in its 'Oxford-English' decor. 'A cheerful crowd of women in bright linen aprons were preparing a Sunday School party, calling out to each other by their Christian names, all very happy and united' (Perham, 1974: 143). Dorothy wanted Ekutuleni to show that a new racial unity (rather than the cross-class bridge-building of London settlements) was possible through Christ, the peacemaker, who could assuage African bitterness and revolt (Ashley, 1980). Ekutuleni's emphasis on inter-racial harmony echoed the call for black–white cooperation by the Joint Council movement, to which Dorothy and her CR contemporary, Raymond Raynes, belonged.

'The children are our great hope and unfailing joy,' asserted Dorothy in 1929, delightfully amalgamating spiritual instruction with very 'English' recreational activities – teaching 'small people how to pray' but also 'how to do country dancing . . . make church kneelers out of oddments . . . play netball . . . bandage cuts.' The modern missionary, she concluded, needed an 'unfailing stock' of sports equipment, dolls and toys – not just a Bible and an umbrella (Maud, 1929a; 1929b; 1930). Though club work had become the foremost activity of British settlements, Ekutuleni also reflected Reef mission circles' lively interest in recreational provision to protect African children 'from the temptations of unoccupied leisure in a materialistic town'.

Work with children was both emotionally and spiritually rewarding, but the Mission had more difficulty relating to African clergy and married women church members. Spinsters lacked the authority of missionary wives active in the city. While pioneering four nursery schools and the necessary staff training, Ekutuleni also employed two African women as full-time evangelistic workers. Remembered with affection and respect for their deep spirituality or being 'quite brilliant' with children, they were especially praised for loyalty in times of anti-white suspicion. Nevertheless, it was hard for such inter-racial partnership to match the internal, egalitarian camaraderie of Dorothy's circle.

Margery Perham drove round the Western Areas of Johannesburg with Dorothy Maud to 'one long scream of greeting from waving children' (Perham, 1974: 144). By 1933, Ekutuleni's youth work had three facets: Christian teaching; developing African leadership; and giving scope for recreation, through clubs offering boys gym, games and boxing, while girls could do crafts, sport, singing, dancing, painting, acting, cooking, dressmaking and first aid. Leseding replicated this model. Missionaries also ran weekly preparation classes for over 80 day school teachers and senior pupils who taught Sunday school, a shepherding contact reinforced by encouragement and financial help to the academically gifted for professional training (*Ekutuleni Annual Reports*, 1931–4, 1937, 1939). Superbly organized Christmas parties offered a ritual climax and reward of the semi-maternal relationship between female workers and children. In Sophiatown in 1933, 900 were fed, entertained and given presents; while in Orlando by 1940, parties for guilds, clubs, youth movements and Sunday schools catered for nearly 1000 children (Ekutuleni Mission Committee Minutes, 6 October 1933; Orlando Log, 6–18 December 1940).

Raymond Raynes's successor, Trevor Huddleston, could still write of the Sophiatown child as 'the most friendly creature on earth and the most trusting' (Huddleston, 1957: 99). He paid strong posthumous tribute to Dorothy Maud's 'compelling' personality and love for God which had inspired 'a band of outstanding women missionaries ... to dedicate their lives to reconciliation between black and white', building up church 'witness against the oppressive forces of racism' (Ashley, 1980: Foreword). Canon Dick Norburn considered that the four missions under Dorothy's auspices offered a much-needed 'central community', affirming urban Africans as 'members of the Family of God ... The mission became almost a parent to many of these people and their families' (*Partners*, 1980). The parental metaphor is particularly interesting, as Maud's work was so child-focused, unlike Stanton's.

Hannah Stanton

Working in Pretoria not Johannesburg, Hannah Stanton (1913–93) also stands out in her university education and late entry to mission work. She particularly merits inclusion because her detention in 1960 suggests more outright church–state confrontation. Hannah Stanton became a hospital almoner in Liverpool after graduating in English and Social Work from London University, then took a postwar theology degree at Oxford. While visiting her CR brother in South Africa in 1956, she was asked to become warden of the Ekutuleni offshoot, Tumelong, 'The Place of Faith', in the African township of Lady Selborne, Pretoria (Stanton, 1961: 16–30, 210). Tumelong's standard repertoire of activities then (which echoed Ekutuleni of the 1930s) was at odds with Hannah's considerable professional training and employment history: she 'had never taught a Confirmation class', had 'very little experience in Sunday School work', her Girl Guide knowledge was 'twenty years out of date' and she 'certainly wasn't a trained Nursery School teacher'. She shrewdly lamented that inappropriate white South African charitable spirit which expected gratitude for anachronistic 'slumming', but was blind to 'modern Africa . . . knocking at the door' (Stanton, 1961: 26, 29, 24, 140). Nevertheless, Hannah was drawn by the chance to live among and work with the people, getting to know them as friends, sharing hardships like 'dust, heat, flies, bucket sanitation, some of the insecurity of the future.' In the end, the intense shock of an early political confrontation decided her (Stanton, 1961: 31–5, 38–40, 147, 203–4), crystallizing her mission vocation round commitment to the African cause, rather than church-building or evangelizing. In part, this reflected the passage of time both politically and ecclesiastically.

Hannah Stanton's theological training was soon put to good use as she took a far-sighted initiative which shows up changing attitudes to female leadership in even the very male-dominated Anglican structure. Half a century after the CR began training African men for ordination, Tumelong started giving a handful of African women intensive residential theological training, both biblical and practical. The spiritual demands were also rigorous, with daily attendance at six religious offices, plus 20 minutes' private prayer and meditation (Stanton, 1961: 96, 103–5). This venture further provides a window into the politics of female personal relations. Writing with candour and generosity about white predecessors and colleagues at Tumelong, Hannah also pays brief tribute to African female staff, but offers fuller, more considered reflections on the students. Mary Molatedi, for example, a mother of eight children, unable to afford high school but active for years in the National Council of African Women, ran the local Sunday school. The greatest evangelist among the students, Mary had charm, fluency and tireless energy in visiting, as well as organizational skills. 'In these women I put much faith and trust', Hannah commented, for their training gave 'great point to the rest of our life in Lady Selborne' (Stanton, 1961: 63–71, 117, 112–13). Respect, affection and aspirations towards egalitarianism emerge, rather than the daily intimacy of Dora Earthy's

Mozambican companionship or the unrestrained warmth of Hannah's later effusions about Helen Joseph.

Stanton's brief political prominence may owe more to National Party jitters than to sustained anti-apartheid activism on her part. Two days after the Sharpeville shootings, police confiscated some mildly political publications in a dawn search of Tumelong. A week later, at 3.15 am on 30 March 1960, Hannah was arrested; the whole township was ablaze with car headlights as others were suffering the same fate (Stanton, 1961: 179, 183–5). Imprisonment was tough, even though she wrote loftily afterwards of the privilege of suffering 'with one's friends and for one's Faith'. Under strain, isolated and bored, she was excited by the unexpected appearance of another white woman in the jail – Helen Joseph, Congress Alliance activist. Relishing each other's company, they successfully pleaded to share a cell where, supplied with flowers and chocolates, nightly hot drinks, and the company of Matron van Onselen's cat, Hannah Stanton's 'political education started. . . . Now the whole story of the ANC came to life for me.' When other women detainees, unbelievers, came to their prison, Hannah wished the church had taken a stronger political stand (Stanton, 1961: 187–225).

To her 'great horror', on 21 May 1960, her release was negotiated, but only on condition that she left the country. 'At last, completely shaken and distrusting my own judgment', she weepily agreed these unwelcome terms with, ironically, Dorothy Maud's brother, British High Commissioner (Stanton, 1961: 215–16, 242). She kissed them all goodbye, 'my darling Helen among them'. Taking consolation from Helen's injunction to tell the story, Hannah promptly published *Go Well, Stay Well*. Thus autobiography became political vindication, as she was seeking to represent the lives of others and the deserving 'African cause', more than her own life.

These five women, divided by class, not equally secure in church employment, identifying with Africans to varying degrees, only fit the triple ascription coined by Ramusack in part. Julia Gilpin was a 'cultural missionary' and a 'maternal imperialist', drawn to the Transvaal by a project of the English church, and of all the women, most concerned with notions of domesticity and 'proper' Christian motherhood. Frances Chilton and Dorothy Maud trained and tried to 'mother' inter-war urban mission children. Dora Earthy and Hannah Stanton worked as 'female allies' ('feminist' would perhaps be taking

it too far) with Transvaal and Mozambican women. Earthy contributed to a new valuation of the riches of African culture and tried
to build on existing spiritual desires and understanding in her sharing
of Christianity. Both Dorothy Maud and Hannah Stanton made bold
and noteworthy interventions in broader political struggles.

The many issues opened up by this biographical approach more
than justify it as a scholarly tool for the historian. These life-stories
should prompt some rethinking of South African mission history,
gender relations and church–state interaction in the twentieth
century. In fact, because of the very particular way in which female
Christianity and mission piety were worked out through a 'politics
of the personal' in South Africa this century, as female exclusion
from ordination necessarily constrained their formal, institutional
church role, the biographical approach proves essential to a measured judgement of the shifts and stages in the gendered building
of the black church.

References

Ashley, A. *Peace-Making in South Africa: The Life and Work of Dorothy Maud*
(Bognor Regis: New Horizon, 1980)

Bush, B. '"Britain's Conscience on Africa": White Women, Race and Imperial Politics in Inter-war Britain', in C. Midgley (ed.) *Gender and Imperialism*
(Manchester: Manchester University Press, 1998)

Chilton, F. Interview with Frances Chilton, 2 February 1978, Bloemfontein

CPSA Archives of the Church of the Province of South Africa, University of
the Witwatersrand, Johannesburg

Earthy, E.D. *Valenge Women: The Social and Economic Life of the Valenge Women
of Portuguese East Africa. An Ethnographic Study* (London: Oxford University Press, for the International Institute of African Languages and Culture,
1933)

Ekutuleni Annual Reports (Johannesburg)

Ekutuleni Committee Minutes, CPSA

Etherington, N. 'Recent Trends in the Historiography of Christianity in
Southern Africa', *Journal of Southern African Studies*, 22, 2 (1996)

Gaitskell, D. '"Christian Compounds for Girls": Church Hostels for African
Women in Johannesburg, 1907–1970', *Journal of Southern African Studies*,
6, 1 (1979)

—— 'Housewives, Maids or Mothers: Some Contradictions of Domesticity
for Christian Women in Johannesburg', *Journal of African History*, 24, 2
(1983)

—— 'Devout Domesticity? A Century of African Women's Christianity in
South Africa', in C. Walker (ed.) *Women and Gender in Southern Africa to
1945* (Cape Town: David Philip, 1990)

—— 'Religion Embracing Science? Female Missionary Ventures in Southern

African Anthropology: Dora Earthy and Mozambique, 1917–1933', paper presented to conference on Science and Society in Southern Africa, IDS, Sussex University (1998)

Grierson, J. *The Deaconess* (London: CIO Publishing, 1981)

Huddleston, T. *Naught for your Comfort* (London: Collins-Fontana Books, 1957)

Jayawardena, K. *The White Woman's Other Burden: Western Women and South Asia During British Colonial Rule* (New York & London: Routledge, 1995)

Lewis, J. *Women and Social Action in Victorian and Edwardian England* (Aldershot: Edward Elgar, 1991)

Maud, D. 'Ekutuleni Sophiatown', CPSA, faB 396 (1929a)

—— 'The Church at play in Johannesburg', *The Mission Field* (February 1929b)

—— 'An adventure in peacemaking', *SPG Overseas*, 41 (1930)

Maughan, S. 'Imperial Christianity? Bishop Montgomery and the Foreign Missions of the Church of England', North Atlantic Missiology Project paper, Cambridge, 1998

Partners, [periodical of Transvaal, Zimbabwe and Botswana Association] XXV, 3 (1980)

Perham, M. *African Apprenticeship: an Autobiographical Journey in Southern Africa, 1929* (London: Faber and Faber 1974)

Personal Narratives Group (eds) *Interpreting Women's Lives: Feminist Theory and Personal Narratives* (Bloomington: Indiana University Press, 1989)

Ramusack, B. 'Cultural Missionaries, Maternal Imperialists, Feminist Allies: British Women Activists in India, 1865–1945', in N. Chaudhuri and M. Strobel (eds) *Western Women and Imperialism: Complicity and Resistance* (Bloomington: Indiana University Press, 1992)

Stanton, H. *Go Well. Stay Well* (London: Hodder & Stoughton, 1961)

Strobel, M. *European Women and the Second British Empire* (Bloomington: Indiana University Press, 1991)

SWM [Society of Women Missionaries] Journal, CPSA

USPG: Archives of the United Society for the Propagation of the Gospel in Foreign Parts, Rhodes House, Oxford University.

—— Dossiers: Candidates' papers of individual missionaries

—— CWW: Correspondence of Committee of Women's Work

—— Orlando Log

15
Constructing the Subject? Emmy Ball-Hennings's Autobiographical Texts

Christiane Schönfeld

Between 1935 and 1948, the poet, actress and performance artist Emmy Hennings (1885–1948) wrote three autobiographical texts, namely *Blume und Flamme* (*Flower and Flame*), *Das flüchtige Spiel: Wege und Umwege einer Frau* (*The Fleeting Game: A Woman's Ways and Deviations*) and *Ruf und Echo* (*Outcry and Echo*).[1] In this chapter, I shall attempt to trace Hennings's life and explore the tension between reality and fiction in her autobiographies by comparing her autobiographical self with the multifaceted, contradictory personality that presents itself in her letters and diary entries and those of her contemporaries. Of course, tension is to be expected, since autobiographical selves are always constructions; however, a marked teleological tendency in Hennings's autobiographical texts at once veils and unveils a marked difference.

During the 1950s, critics such as Georges Gusdorf and Wayne Shumaker emphasized the necessity to differentiate between the author and the autobiographical selves, arguing that 'autobiographical selves are constructed through the process of writing and therefore cannot reproduce exactly the selves who lived' (Shumaker, 1954: 45, in Friedman, 1988: 34). During subsequent years, we have read Roland Barthes' declaration about the 'death of the author' and accepted Jacques Derrida's deconstruction of even the possibility of 'presence' or a 'full subject'. We are aware of the difference between past and present selves, between narrating and narrated subject; we know it to be an impossible task to overcome the distance between now and then; and consider it naïve to mention the word 'truth' within the context of de(con)structed autobiographical selves in an era of, albeit rather exhausted, postmodernism. However, this chapter is also the account of a struggle with a biography in the making, and with my own position as a biographer. Since the genre of biography essentially lays claim to authority and authenticity, the biographer is painfully forced into a crusade for the 'real' as soon as she accepts responsibility for the representation of someone else's past. Whatever I say about Emmy Hennings in a biography is not only a representation but somehow representative. But, to represent a woman's life in all of its richness, poverty and creative chaos seems an impossible task. Perhaps it is exactly this impossibility that feeds our desire to unveil and discover. Yet the more we unveil, the further Hennings's autobiographical narrative seems to drift towards fiction and the more fragile our biographical subject becomes.

Hennings was born Emma Maria Cordsen in Flensburg on 17 January 1885. Her mother, Anna Dorothea Zielfeld had married Ernst Friedrich Matthias Cordsen, a sailor, who brought his daughter Rebecca into the marriage (Werner-Birkenbach, 1993: 198). She grew up in Flensburg where she attended school until she was 14 years old, and then worked as a domestic help in a number of different households. On 13 January 1904, she married a typesetter, Joseph Paul Hennings. Their son, who was born in the same year, died in infancy while Hennings was already working as a singer and actress in a travelling theatrical group. Separated from her husband, in 1906 she gave birth to a daughter, Annemarie, who remained in Flensburg with Hennings's mother until 1916. Between 1910 and 1915 she performed in several cabarets including the 'Olympia-Theater', the 'Lindenkabaret' in Berlin and the 'Simplizissimus' in Munich. Hennings also worked as an artist's model and a writer, and published her first booklet of poetry in 1913. Since she wrongly assumed that it would remain her only publication, she entitled the small volume *Die Letzte Freude* (*The Last Joy*).

In the autumn of 1913, Hennings met the writer Hugo Ball, with whom she emigrated to Switzerland in 1915. Shortly before their departure, Hennings was arrested and forced to spend a couple of months in a Munich prison. The reason for her arrest remains unclear – ranging from her self-proclaimed complete innocence, to prostitution and theft. In February 1916, Hennings and Hugo Ball opened a cabaret in Zürich together with Tristan Tzara, Hans Arp, Richard Hülsenbeck and Marcel Janco. The 'Cabaret Voltaire', as they called it, became the birthplace of 'Dadaism': the revolutionary movement in art and literature which proclaimed itself as nonsensical anti-art or non-art and the only true art at the same time. Although today Hennings is seldom acknowledged as one of the founders of Dadaism, she seems to have been one of the driving forces among these artists and writers. In 1917, for example, Hennings and Ball opened the Galerie Dada, but retreated to Magadino, in the Ticino, the same year. Both continued to write, despite their financial difficulties and insecurities. In February 1920, they married and settled, with Emmy's daughter Annemarie, in Agnuzzo near Lugano. The writer Hermann Hesse, who lived close by, became a life-long friend. After Ball's death in 1927, Emmy Ball-Hennings continued to live in different towns in the Ticino (Agnuzzo, Cassina, Magliaso), doing manual labour to survive and writing or editing her late husband's work whenever she found the time and strength. She died in Sorengo near Lugano on 10 August 1948.

If this brief biographical sketch already points towards a highly unusual life for a woman of her class and time, it does not do justice to the multifaceted character that we encounter in her letters to Hugo Ball and others, as well as in the letters and diaries of her contemporaries. Her existence as a writer, a Catholic, a bohemian, a proletarian, a single mother, an actress and singer, a prison inmate and a wife cannot be properly reflected by merely chronological detail. But can we gain access to her via her own work, namely her autobiographical novels *Flower and Flame*, *The Fleeting Game* and *Outcry and Echo*?

In the Preface to the second part of her autobiography (1940), Hennings wrote:

> Already many years ago I planned to write a confession of my life. I took many notes, which I discarded time and again. Why? Although what I expressed seemed in parts quite entertaining, it was not truthful, not honest enough. For example, I tended to embellish, skate around or exclude my most prevalent negative traits. Therefore, the portrayal of my life became unclear and incomprehensible. The ability to be sincere is not only a matter of good will. . . . Whoever is about to make a confession, first of all has to overcome an inherent sense of shame. This might be even more difficult for a woman. Instinctively one shies away from unveiling the abyss. (Ball-Hennings, 1940: 9)

Here, Hennings claims the veracity of her autobiographical text, and the reader is not only encouraged to trust the author and her account, but also feel sympathy when the abyss is exposed. But the abyss turns out to be a gentle valley, and the reader turns again to the introduction with suspicion. Why is the author so eager to let us know that this is *really* what happened? Moreover, by claiming to offer a confession rather than an account of her life, the author clearly identifies the aim of the narrative to be the production of an authentic self (Felski, 1989: 87).

It is difficult to verify most of the dates in Hennings's biography via her autobiographical texts, as the first two parts of her autobiography avoid any sort of chronological specificity and most of her letters and scripts are undated.[2] The uncertainty created by this absence of dates is further encouraged by the curious lack of contradiction in this autobiographical narrative by an author who considered herself often highly contradictory in behaviour and even character, a trait many of her contemporaries confirm. On 23 May 1929, Ball-Hennings wrote to Hermann Hesse: 'I cannot tell you how much I would like to present myself as a harmonious human being, at least on paper. But the story [of my life] cannot even be reduced to ten different common denominators' (Ball-Hennings, 1956: 115). But she did, in my view, succeed in her aim when writing her autobiographical novels: she is an autobiographical subject we hardly recognize. In all her three autobiographical texts she appears as the rather harmonious and balanced character she was so eager to be. There is, for example, no hint at her quite drastic transformation that took place sometime between 1911 and 1915. This break which had such an influence on her behaviour and lifestyle coincides with her conversion to Catholicism, her imprisonment and her departure from Germany as Hugo Ball's partner. Contemporaries who knew her before and after her emigration describe the astonishing change from the wild, sexually liberated, nervous and extravagant bohemian to the tender, deeply religious, calm wife of Ball. However, in her autobiographical texts the life with Ball is presented as the logical conclusion to the biography which never lacks idyllic atmospheres; even physical abuse in school is presented in a positive light as the beatings made her appreciate literature and poetry (Ball-Hennings, 1938: 53).

In the portrayal of her youth in *Flower and Flame*, Hennings describes herself as an innocent child. But in contrast to her actual life, she remains an innocent, God-loving child throughout her autobiography. Pain, fear, poverty and marginalization all become transfigured. A tranquil and harmonious state of being seems to have become Hennings's objective, and the wish to uphold the idyllic guided her hand while writing her autobiography.

The account of her time as a singer, actress and artist's model in Munich is a case in point. Hennings describes her time in Munich in *The Fleeting Game* in only a few pages, assuring us of the import- ance of her years in Munich spent with educated and important artists and writers. Their very positive influence on her both awak- ened and strengthened her interest in art and literature, and she learnt to absorb 'what was good and beautiful' (Ball-Hennings, 1940: 263). The years she spent as a bohemian and actress only serve to contextualize Hennings's encounter of her soul-mate Hugo Ball a few pages later. The author's interest in a positive portrayal of her years in Munich is obvious. She describes the beginning of her career as a writer, her success as an artist's model and her popular- ity in the 'Simplizissimus' cabaret (Ball-Hennings, 1940: 267): only when she mentions in passing that she met Hugo Ball while sell- ing her postcards in the cabaret do we understand that her career as a singer did not provide sufficient financial security.

How different is the account given by the anarchist writer and editor, Erich Mühsam, of those days and nights in Munich, which he confided to his diary.[3] In entries starting from 1911, Hennings is described as Munich's avant-garde circle's erotic centre of atten- tion and the muse of Johannes R. Becher, Jakob van Hoddis, Erich Mühsam and Ferdinand Hardekopf (to name but a few). Erich Mühsam, also one of her lovers, calls Hennings 'an erotic genius. She wants constantly and every man, and any situation suits her' (Mühsam, 1994: 36). He describes her appearance, thus:

> Emmy with her boyish short golden hair, and a black cap, a silky green rag ... violet stockings, which she put leisurely on the opposite seat so that I would be able to caress her legs. This is how we drove through the busiest streets of Munich, which caused quite a stir on this beautiful Sunday afternoon. (Mühsam, 1994: 39)

Mühsam gives an account of Hennings as a very sexually active and self-confident woman, a depiction that is supported by Jakob van Hoddis and Erwin Loewenson (see Loewenson, 1958: 107). And she did not only absorb 'what was good and beautiful', if we trust

Johannes R. Becher's reference to Hennings's morphine addiction and a sexually transmitted disease in 1915 (Kühn-Ludewig, 1987: 72). In her autobiographical text, however, Hennings is deeply and exclusively devoted to Hugo Ball from their first meeting in the spring of 1914. Their love is presented as the ideal and perfect relationship between two human beings and only her love for God is more divine.

This example illustrates the abyss between Hennings's autobiographical writings and the way she has been perceived by others. The problem with the few descriptions of Hennings by contemporaries regarding her time in Munich is that almost all the authors claim to have had a sexual relationship with her (see Hornbogen, 1986, 37 and 91ff.; Mühsam, 1994: 40). These male accounts, therefore, refer mainly to her outer appearance and her 'liberated' behaviour. Nevertheless, in an effort to approximate some kind of 'reality', the biographer must rely on additional information, such as the accounts of contemporaries. Mühsam's diary, never having been meant for publication, could be assumed to be more honest, even though it cannot lay claim to greater objectivity than Hennings's own accounts.

Of course, every autobiography is predicated on the author's ability to remember, and memory is always already a reconstruction from the original incident. The ability to remember rests on the distance between long past and present forms of the self. As Friederike Eigler put it: 'The distance between narrating and narrated self cannot be overcome' (Eigler, 1988: 61). On the other hand, the distance between the past and the present forms of the self as we encounter them in the context of Hennings's autobiography seems minimal. What we find in these texts is not distance but rather an extreme closeness between the definition of herself as a child and that as an older woman. It is exactly the tender innocence and delicate purity of the child Hennings seeks to recreate throughout her autobiographical writing. Child-like innocence as well as Catholic devotion and perfect love become the prominent leitmotifs of her autobiography. This causes an apparent continuity of self-definition throughout the text and a harmonious closure between beginning and end, childhood and old age. By omitting disturbing events which could contradict the portrayal of the self and by concentrating on what was, retrospectively, truly meaningful (namely, her love for God and Ball), Hennings achieves what could be called a belated harmonization of a life full of contradictions, tension and chaos. Even negative experiences such as her first marriage simply serve as encounters leading up to the perfectly symbiotic relationship with Ball, which gains an ever more exuberant quality by comparison. Her autobiography ends with the death of Hugo Ball in 1927.

Emmy Hennings's autobiographical texts exhibit a clear teleological tendency, presupposing that developments are moulded according to an overall design and purpose. In autobiography it is always the present form of the self that gives meaning to its past forms. The past self still incorporates a multitude of possibilities; the present self knows of the choices that were made. Nothing can liberate the author from his/her knowledge of what or who he/she has become (see Aichinger, 1970: 423), and this awareness feeds into the construction of past selves in any autobiographical narrative. Therefore, a character appears unified, since every event is merely another step towards the present form of the self. At the same time, every step brings the reader closer to an understanding of what turned out to be the meaning and aim of the life presented. The knowledge of the retrospectively dominant experiences and the recognition of the 'meaning' of life – in Hennings's case her conversion to Catholicism and her relationship with Ball – leads to an ordering of all experience within this particular context and therefore to unity and coherence of the narrated life as a whole.

Hennings's autobiography certainly falls into the category of self-representational writing. But it is a post-1936 form of the self, or rather the *metaphor* of the present form of the self, which is represented here. In this metaphor, 'the self in the text transcends its materiality and becomes an emblem for a person's striving' (see Gilmore, 1994: 67). But still, it is not a unified self, but one split in two. As Roland Barthes, Adrienne Rich and others have pointed out: autobiographical writing always splits (or doubles) the I into the narrating and the narrated self which is yet again mirrored in the biographer herself and/or myself.

The split or doubled biographer is only unified in her desire for an unambiguous real, and can never claim a 'true' understanding of the past selves of the subject of her interest, since her understanding is always already based on a representation of these past selves, whether they take the form of autobiographical texts, letters or photographs. Biography is just as much a construct as autobiography, as Liz Stanley, among others, has argued (see Stanley, 1992: 77; Iles, 1992; Beer, 1989: 67ff.). Thus, the biographer remains a distant spectator, observing and reflecting upon the traces unveiled. Ideally, the biographical text could be forever in the process of becoming and in all its instability and fragmentation reflect what this woman was 'really' about.

Notes

1 All translations (including translations of titles) are my own.
2 Hennings's letters and unpublished works are held at the Robert Walser Stiftung, Zurich; the Hugo Ball Sammlung, Pirmasens; and the Literaturarchiv, Marbach. Her daughter tried to date the letters in her transcriptions, but many dates remain contradictory.
3 This diary had been kept under lock and key for decades until it was finally published in 1994.

References

Aichinger, I. 'Probleme der Autobiographie als Sprachkunstwerk', *Österreich in Geschichte und Literatur*, 14 (1970) 418–34
—— 'Selbstbiographie', in W. Kohlschmidt and W. Mohr (eds) *Reallexikon der deutschen Literaturgeschichte*, vol. 3 (Berlin: de Gruyter, 1977)
Beer, G. 'Representing Women: Re-presenting the Past', in C. Belsey and J. Moore (eds) *Feminist Reader* (Basingstoke: Macmillan, 1989)
Eigler, F. *Das autobiographische Werk von Elias Canetti. Verwandlung, Identität, Machtausübung* (Tübingen: Stauffenburg, 1988)
Felski, R. *Beyond Feminist Aesthetics: Feminist Literature and Social Change* (Cambridge, Mass.: Harvard University Press, 1989)
Friedman, S. S. 'Women's Autobiographical Selves: Theory and Practice', in S. Benstock (ed.) *The Private Self: Theory and Practice of Women's Autobiographical Writings* (London: University of North Carolina Press, 1988) 34–62
Gilmore, L. *Autobiographics: A Feminist Theory of Women's Self-Representation* (Ithaca, NY: Cornell University Press, 1994)
Hennings, E. *Die letzte Freude* (Leipzig: Kurt Wolff, 1913)
—— *Blume und Flamme. Geschichte einer Jugend* (Einsiedeln: Benziger, 1938)
—— *Das flüchtige Spiel. Wege und Umwege einer Frau* (Einsiedeln: Benziger, 1940)
—— *Ruf und Echo. Mein Leben mit Hugo Ball* (Einsiedeln: Benziger, 1953)
—— *Briefe an Hermann Hesse* (Frankfurt: Suhrkamp, 1956)
Hornbogen, H. *Jakob van Hoddis. Die Odyssee eines Verschollenen* (München: Hanser, 1986)
Iles, T. (ed.) *All Sides of the Subject. Women and Biography* (New York: Teachers College Press, 1992)
Kühn-Ludewig, M. (ed.) *Johannes R. Becher, Heinrich F.S. Bachmair, Briefwechsel 1914–1920: Briefe und Dokumente zur Verlagsgeschichte des Expressionismus* (Frankfurt: Lang, 1987)
Lacoue-Labarthe, P. and Nancy, J. L. *The Literary Absolute*, trans. P. Barnard and C. Lester (Albany, NY: SUNY Press, 1988)

Loewenson, E. 'Jakob van Hoddis. Erinnerungen mit Lebensdaten', in P. Pörtner (ed.) *Jakob van Hoddis: Weltende. Gesammelte Dichtungen* (Zurich: Arche, 1958)

Mühsam, E. *Tagebücher 1910–1924* (München: dtv, 1994)

Shumaker, W. *English Autobiography: Its Emergence, Materials, and Form* (Berkeley: University of California Press, 1954)

Spengemann, W. *The Forms of Autobiography* (New Haven, Conn.: Yale University Press, 1980)

Stanley, L. *The Auto/biographical I: The Theory and Practice of Feminist Auto/biography* (Manchester: Manchester University Press, 1992)

Werner-Birkenbach, S. 'Emmy Hennings: A Woman Writer of Prison Literature', in B. Keith-Smith (ed.) *German Women Writers 1900–1933* (Lewiston: Edwin Mellen Press, 1993)

Part V

Recovering Lives – Revising History

16

'My Mind on Paper': Anne Lister and the Construction of Lesbian Identity

Anira Rowanchild

Anne Lister (1791–1840) of Shibden Hall near Halifax, kept a diary for 34 years. It eventually extended to over four million words, in 27 quarto volumes, about a sixth of which are in code. In this chapter I argue that Lister's coded diary was an important tool in the construction of her sexual identity. By providing her with a safely enclosed textual space, it gave her the ability to assert a desire for women that offers a challenge both to the alleged absence of discourse on female homosexual experience and identity in the early part of the nineteenth century, and to the categorization of intimate relations between women of this period by the asexual term, 'romantic friendship'. Lillian Faderman notes that the eighteenth-century fashion for romantic friendship 'dictated that women may fall in love with each other, although they must not engage in genital sex' (Faderman, 1981: 74). She concludes that 'most love relationships between women during previous eras... were less physical than they are in our times' (19). However, Lister's explicit documentation of her sexual activity provides a refreshing alternative to what Terry Castle calls 'the lugubrious myths of lesbian asexuality' embodied by the idea of romantic friendship (Castle, 1993: 106). The conceptual possibility of physical relations between women has been problematized as much by the historical suppression of female sexuality in general, as by epistemological concerns; as Martha Vicinus warns, lesbian history consists largely of 'nuances, masks, secrecy, and the unspoken' (Vicinus, 1996: 235).

Jill Liddington's research has shown that Lister's lesbian experience was effectively silenced for nearly 150 years after her death.

Despite the existence of a key to her code, the sexually explicit subject-matter of coded entries was considered too controversial for publication until 1988, when a selection, transcribed by Helena Whitbread, was published, revealing that Lister's diary provides evidence of a flourishing discourse on woman-to-woman sexual relations in the early nineteenth century. Lister's code dated from her attendance at a fashionable boarding-school in York from 1805 to 1806, where she became friends and lovers with girls from well-to-do professional or aristocratic backgrounds, whose acquaintance fuelled her social ambitions (see Whitbread, 1988: 57). When Lister left the school, she and her lover, Eliza Raine, developed their 'crypt hand' for use in diaries and letters to discuss sexual and financial affairs, social gossip and grievances. Lister's own parents were poor gentry, and her three brothers, on whom the revival of the family fortunes rested, died young; but her social status improved considerably in 1815, when she went to live permanently at Shibden Hall, near Halifax, with her wealthy unmarried uncle. It reached its peak in 1826, when, on her uncle's death, she inherited his entire estate.

The coded diary provides graphic details of Lister's erotic encounters and relates her search for the origins of her sexual identity. Her accounts of the former are littered with sexual slang like 'grubble' [grope], 'queer' [female pudenda] and 'kiss' [orgasm]. By 1821 Lister had resolved that she 'love[d] and only love[d] the fairer sex and thus, beloved by them in turn, my heart revolts from any other love than theirs' (Whitbread, 1988:145). Such 'conduct & feelings', she argued, '[are] natural to me inasmuch as they were not taught, not fictitious, but instinctive . . . I had met with those who could feel in unison with me' (297). The existence of a sophisticated discourse on female homosexuality is suggested by the distinction she makes between her 'natural' feelings and what she refers to as the artifice of 'Saffic regard' (Whitbread, 1992: 49). Sapphism (derived from the ancient Greek poet, Sappho, regarded as the founder of a lesbian tradition) was variously associated with dangerous foreign practices, decadence of pre-Revolutionary France and exoticism of Mediterranean cultures. The following diary entry for 1824, recounting a flirtatious conversation between Lister and a woman she met in a Paris guest-house, indicates the range of assumptions about lesbian sexuality shared by women of the period:

[Mrs Barlow] began talking *of that* one of the things of which Marie Antoinette was accused of was being too fond of women.

I, with perfect mastery of countenance, said I had never heard of it before and could not understand or believe it. . . . I said I believed that when reduced to the last extremity – I was going to mention the use of phalli but luckily Mrs Barlow [interrupted] . . . I said I had read of women being too fond of each other in the Latin parts of the works of Sir William Jones. (32; emphasis original)

The tendentious phrase, 'too fond', implies excess and lack of control, but is at the same time knowing and suggestive. Lister's attempt to disguise knowledge of Marie Antoinette's rumoured proclivities hints at the perils of an open declaration, while signalling a seductive disingenuousness. Her humorous reference to the 'use of phalli' complicates the model of romantic friendship by acknowledging genital contact between women, and offers an alternative to what Castle calls 'the kind of depressingly chaste female–female bonding' emblematized by the famous Ladies of Llangollen, whose relationship was considered the paradigm of romantic friendship (Castle, 1993: 93). Lister herself was doubtful about the Ladies' much-vaunted celibacy, remarking after visiting them: 'I hesitate to pronounce such attachments uncemented by something more tender still than friendship' (Whitbread, 1988: 210). Her mention of 'the Latin works of Sir William Jones' is one of many similar references in her diary to the study of homosexuality she conducted through her reading of medical, scientific and classical texts. Lisa Moore has noted how Lister 'pillages male-authored texts . . . in order to authorize her desires, transforming those accoutrements into . . . the conditions of production of female homosexual character' (Moore, cited in Vicinus, 1996: 33). Through her reconstruction of the conversation with Mrs Barlow, Lister locates herself within the discourse and monitors her own part in it.

The use of code was common practice in private diaries from their emergence in the late sixteenth century. Samuel Pepys famously used shorthand in his diaries, and women diarists often disguised their sexual and emotional secrets with code. Elizabeth Roper, in the mid-eighteenth century, records in cipher her flirtations and love-making. In the late nineteenth century, Beatrix Potter kept her entire journal in an elaborate code, even though the entries themselves are occluded. In Lister's coded writings both the social and sexual figure significantly, for, as Lister observed, 'acquiring more importance' would enable her to 'do with impunity what I could not do now' (Whitbread, 1988: 298). Thus, her diary was not a family document like, for example, Dorothy Wordsworth's journal which was mediated through her brother, or Fanny Burney's diary which turned into a letter journal for her sister. Although she occasionally read aloud extracts to her lovers, Lister considered her diary strictly private and was vexed when it was discussed during a tea-party (see 96). Paradoxically, however, Lister did not keep the key to the cipher exclusive to herself. As well as sharing it with Eliza Raine, Lister gave copies of the 'crypt hand alphabet' to lovers and even casual admirers: to Isabella 'Tib' Norcliffe, for example, a friend and lover from a wealthy York family, and to Mariana Belcombe, a York doctor's daughter whom she met through Tib, and who, despite marriage to a Cheshire landowner, was her lover for many years. More startlingly, Lister passed on the key to women with whom she had only the briefest flirtation, like Miss Vallance, whom she met during a stay at the Norcliffe home. After an evening when she had flirted shamelessly with an entire roomful of women, Lister wrote:

> All up late & none of us went to church. . . . Miss Vallance put, in one of my drawers, a sealed parcel of spills to light candles with & a note enclosed . . . very affectionate. She certainly likes me & is very low & nervous about my going. . . . Gave her the crypt hand alphabet which M[ariana] – has . . . but was not very tender. Indeed, I get lukewarm about her. (142)

The code thus began to provide the rudiments of a secret language shared not only by Lister and Eliza Raine but among a network of 'women who are too fond of women', with Lister at its pivotal point. Those so privileged could use the code in communications with each other and in their own private writings, and in the process gain and allow access to each other's most intimate feelings and thoughts. In their diaries and letters, the change from uncoded to coded communication, clearly delineated in the text, signalled the moment of entry into the clandestine world of lesbian experience and identity.

Lister writes often about her desire to be an author and the self-consciousness of her written production suggests that she may have regarded her diary as a forcing ground for her literary talent and perhaps intended to publish some version of her travel journal. At intervals, she retrospectively re-examined, annotated, ordered, indexed or even destroyed her papers, gaining increasingly close command of her literary self-presentation. For example, an inventory of her letter-drawer for 1822 notes a 'List of . . . letters before burning them' (see Liddington, 1994: 58). She appears to have been aware of the autobiographical impulse, explaining in 1817: 'tis high time to begin if I mean to get it done in my lifetime' (Whitbread, 1988: 16). The private nature of the diary would seem to undermine its power to articulate and establish authorial identity, but Lister allowed the possibility of a readership by giving out copies of the key to her lovers, who, if not authorized to read the text, had the potential, creating an exciting relationship between subject/writer and putative reader. Lister positions her reader as a participant in an apparently spontaneous relation to the subject, while maintaining tight control of that imaginative experience. At the same time, there is little doubt that part of her editorial concern was with the construction of her sexual identity: 'Burnt Mr Montagu's farewell verses that no trace of any man's admiration may remain' (145).

The production of such a meticulous personal archive must have been time-consuming within Lister's daily schedule. All her life she pursued a relentless autodidactic programme, rising at 6 a.m. to study maths, French, classics, science or philosophy; breaking at noon for a light meal; visiting her mines and quarries, directing farming and gardening activities, or driving her gig in the afternoon; engaging in the necessary round of social engagements in the evening. Despite this busy programme, Lister wrote 20 or so business and personal letters a week, some over 70 pages long, and produced daily diary entries often of several thousand words. The physical writing of the diary thus became itself part of Lister's self-narrative. Carolyn Steedman has pointed out that written self-narration frequently 'placates and subdues the writer' by 'draw[ing] into a chronology the inchoate items of a life sequencing it, in some kind of order, to some kind of end' (Steedman, 1996: 62).

Knowing that you are going to write about an event or an idea encourages you to frame, construct and interpret it, in the same way that carrying a camera on holiday shapes your visual experience. Charles Taylor has described this self-narrating process in *Sources of the Self* in the following way:

> The life at any moment is the causal consequence of what has transpired earlier . . . [and] since the life to be lived has also to be *told*, its meaning is seen as something that unfolds through the events. (Taylor, 1989: 289)

Anne Lister, in her daily life over the 34 years in which she kept her diary, told and retold her story to herself, and, in the telling of past events, constructed the meaning of the next. This tendency may be discerned, for instance, in her narration of two episodes. In March 1808, Lister wrote enthusiastically to Eliza Raine of a book she had read about revolutionary Paris. She was impressed by its account of a beautiful and fanatical girl who kept in her room a pike, a dagger, a sabre and a brace of pistols and who 'headed a body of Pikemen against the king . . . and was so distinguished for her bravery and presence of mind' (SH: 7/ML/10). In 1809, she recounted in her diary how she defended her household from attack:

> About $\frac{1}{2}$ past [midnight] when Sam was in bed and I was just getting in, my mother came in violent agitation to tell us that there was a man in the garret . . . I with nothing on but my night jacket over my Shift . . . took the pistols loadened with ball which were ready under my pillow & a sword . . . he took the candle. (Liddington, 1994: 27)

The intruder turned out to be a servant's boyfriend, and loaded pistols were surely unusual bedfellows for a young woman, but Lister constructs a heroic account, emphasizing her readiness to defend the young or weak. The sword adds a final touch of swashbuckling glamour.

Lister's appearance was equally carefully contrived. She had adopted as her customary day attire the distinctive black riding-habit favoured by the Ladies of Llangollen. This deliberate act of resistance to gendered norms was regarded with open hostility by the working people of Halifax, who jeered at her in the street with cries of 'That's a man' and 'Does your cock stand?' (Whitbread, 1988: 48–9). The local gentry were more covert in expression of their disapprobation of Lister's sexual liaisons. Her diary was demonstrably valuable as an aide-mémoire in defending herself from gossip and insinuation, which Lister describes as 'a friend that . . . by never forgetting anything, is always ready to compare the past & present' (154). For example, in 1816 Lister heard of rumours circulating that she was not fit society for young people, having been seen being 'too fond' with another young woman. Using evidence from her diary, she wrote grandly to the sister of one of her accusers that she could call witnesses to the fact that she had *never* been seen in any 'fondling circumstances' whatsoever (SH: 7/ML/76/2). The crypt hand clearly allowed her to record, interpret and conceal her experience whilst at the same time providing her with a means to monitor, control and analyse the potential dangers she faced.

A code both presupposes and contrives a reader. The act of burying may be all that is needed to construct what is buried as treasure, and to produce and encourage a seeker. In Lister's detailed documentation of her life and thoughts, there is a presumption that an omnipotent reader of posterity lurks ahead of the text to survey Lister's writing sympathetically, and who will resurrect the self encrypted in its secret code and allow it to integrate with the diary's subject. Harriet Blodgett, in her study of Englishwomen's diaries, writes that:

> The existence of the diarist, presented in numerous if fragmentary entries, becomes the reader's imaginative experience of participating in the diarist's life as, day by day, in the same formless manner as life, the story unfolds. (Blodgett, 1989: 7)

The contemporary reader's experience, my *own* experience, is that the effect of Lister's code is to invite decipherment, to excite interest and to disarm by placing the decoder in a privileged position in relation to the text, its writer and subject. Each time I transcribe or decode a sentence from the diary, I feel I enter into an intimate, possibly dangerous, and certainly thrilling, relationship with its subject, while the process of reading and decoding enters my own self-narrative.

Lister's coded diary, then, supplied several functions: it concealed diary entries from casually prying eyes, whilst giving access to the privileged holders of the key; it signposted to writer and reader movement into a different textuality *and* sexuality, a metaphorical page turned down; it created an intimacy between writer/subject and reader and bestowed value on its contents; and it provided a site within the diary for the development and production of Lister's sexual identity, and, among the keyholders, for a discourse on woman-to-woman sexuality. The code, far from repelling the reader, rather encouraged unauthorized access to what was apparently hidden, revealing its secrets only to those in the know. The uncoded diary was itself theoretically secret, but the crypt hand signalled a deeper kind of secrecy, like the hidden compartment within a locked casket. As Gaston Bachelard remarks:

> The moment the casket is opened ... the outside is effaced with
> one stroke, an atmosphere of surprise and novelty reigns. The
> outside has no more meaning ... [and] a new dimension – the
> dimension of intimacy – has just opened up. (Bachelard, 1994: 85)

But while the diary may appear to reveal the individuality of the
writer/subject through this intimacy, it also exposes its opposite:
the fragmentation and divisibility of the self. Lister's use of the
word 'crypt' to describe her code, where the more common contemporary term would have been cipher, is perhaps significant, for
it connotes the tomb, a place of preservation, of ghosts, and of
silence. In their work on the assimilations and transitions of psychic
development, Nicolas Abraham and Maria Torok have investigated
silence and its various forms, arguing that:

> The untold or unsayable secret, the feeling unfelt, the pain de-
> nied [may result in] the individual's forcible creation of a psychic
> tomb, arising from his or her inassimilable life experiences.
> (Abraham and Torok, 1994: 22)

They go on to suggest that 'the objectal correlative' of the unsayable
loss is 'reconstituted from the memories of words, scenes, and
affects, [and] is buried alive in the crypt as a full-fledged person'
(130). Anne Lister's crypt hand diary, I would argue, created just
such a secret textual space to protect the sense of loss constituted
principally by the intense level of negotiation, self-surveillance and
vigilance necessary to maintain her sexual identity without being
outlawed or destroyed. It is possible to perceive in the closely written pages of the diary a 'visual sign', as the text breaks from a
cramped, but conventional, early nineteenth-century script into the
faintly familiar but unreadable crypt hand, of that 'full-fledged' but
buried-alive person who haunts the diary; the presence, perhaps,
of what Terry Castle has called the 'apparitional lesbian' (Castle,
1993).

   The part Lister's textual mediations played in her self-construc-
tion as lesbian is set in relief by the pitfalls that lay in wait for
those who failed to negotiate the constantly shifting divisions between their public, private and secret selves. The fates of Lister's
childhood lover, Eliza Raine, and her partner, Anne Walker, provide salutary reminders that Lister's nineteenth-century Yorkshire
neighbours would not tolerate any slippage. Eliza Raine, an Anglo-

Indian heiress, was committed to a mental asylum by her guardian in 1814, aged 23, for little more than rudeness and bad behaviour. She never regained control of her fortune, which remained in the hands of trustees. In 1843, three years after Lister's death, Anne Walker, to whom the Shibden estate was bequeathed, was forcibly removed from Shibden Hall by a local constable, a doctor and the Lister family solicitor (Liddington, 1994: 11). Walker was also committed to an asylum as 'of unsound mind', where she remained until her death in 1850. I cannot help noting that when the constable arrived at Shibden, he found all the rooms locked and was only able to enter the Red Room, where Walker had closeted herself with Lister's diary papers, by taking the door off its hinges. Walker, with probably unconscious irony, had hidden all the keys.

Abbreviations

SH: Shibden Hall Muniments (Calderdale Archives)

References

Abraham, N. and Torok, M. *The Shell and the Kernel*, vol. 1 (Chicago: University of Chicago Press, 1994)

Bachelard, G. *The Poetics of Space* (Boston: Beacon, 1994)

Blodgett, H. *Centuries of Female Days: Englishwomen's Private Diaries* (Gloucester: Alan Sutton, 1989)

Castle, T. *The Apparitional Lesbian: Female Homosexuality and Modern Culture* (New York: Columbia University, 1993)

Faderman, L. *Surpassing the Love of Men: Romantic Friendship and Love between Women from the Renaissance to the Present* (London: The Women's Press, 1981)

Liddington, J. *Presenting the Past: Anne Lister of Halifax 1791–1840* (Hebden Bridge: Pennine Pens, 1994)

Steedman, C. 'Linguistic Encounters of the Fourth Kind', *Journal of Victorian Culture*, 1.1 (1996) 54–75

Taylor, C. *Sources of the Self: The Making of the Modern Identity* (Cambridge: Cambridge University Press, 1989)

Vicinus, M. *Lesbian Subjects: A Feminist Studies Reader* (Bloomington: Indiana University Press, 1996)

Whitbread, H. *I Know My Own Heart: The Diaries of Anne Lister 1791–1840* (London: Virago, 1988)

—— *No Priest but Love: The Journals of Anne Lister from 1824–1826* (Otley: Smith Settle, 1992)

17
Promoting Herself: the Representational Strategies of Georgina Weldon

Helen Nicholson

From the age of 15 until her death at the age of 76, Georgina Weldon kept a diary; by the time she died in 1914, this comprised of 28 leather-bound volumes and a handwritten index.[1] Although the index is all that now remains of Weldon's private autobiographical project, there are nevertheless numerous public documents that tell the tale of the 'notorious Mrs Weldon' and her *cause célèbre*. Weldon's notoriety came from her highly publicized campaign against her husband Henry, and the alienist Dr Lyttleton Stewart Forbes Winslow, who had conspired with him to commit her to a private asylum. However, even before these events, she had successfully promoted herself, her choir and her orphanage through, amongst other things, the national press and her own public lectures. She employed Romeikes, a news cutting agency, and was said at times to have commanded as many column inches as a cabinet minister.

The majority of Weldon's public campaigning took place during the 1880s at a time when the prevailing ideology was that of the 'separate spheres'. Although the public space of the city was still regarded as very much the male domain, there was a number of significant challenges to this ethos which encouraged the emergence of middle-class women from the confines of their homes.[2] Whilst it was to be many years before women achieved the vote, the 'Woman Question' had been widely debated since the presentation of the first suffrage petition in 1866. Education for girls and women of all classes had expanded significantly during the 1870s; Girton and Newnham Colleges were founded at Cambridge in 1871 and 1879 respectively, and in 1878 London University began to admit women and award them degrees. Employment opportunities for women were also expanding, albeit in a limited way; and the Married Women's Property Act of 1882 gave married women rights over their own property, affording them a greater degree of financial independence from their husbands. In addition, the arrival of the department store enabled large numbers of women to shop unaccompanied in safety and comfort for the first time. Weldon capitalized on this changing environment, and through her continued public presence she provided an example to women and a warning to men.

When examining Weldon's campaigns it is important to have an understanding of both her social background and the circumstances of her marriage. She was a member of the upper middle class, whose social circle included the aristocracy and members of the royal family. She was born in 1837, the daughter of Morgan Thomas (later Morgan Treherne), a Welsh landed gentleman, and had little formal education, spending much of her childhood on the continent, where she developed her musical and linguistic skills. By the time she was introduced to London society, Weldon was noted for her exquisite voice and was much in demand as an amateur singer. In addition to performing in concerts, she took part in amateur theatricals and mixed with the pre-Raphaelite circle of Little Holland House. In 1860, against the wishes of her parents, she married Henry Weldon, an officer in the 18th Hussars. Weldon took advantage of Henry's comparatively low economic standing to engage in some pre-marital bargaining, and made him promise that after their marriage he would allow her to earn her living as a stage performer. After the marriage, Henry reneged on this agreement and Weldon was forced to content herself with amateur performances.

Having discovered that she was unable to have children, after nine years of marriage, she founded an orphanage.[3] She recruited orphans from the streets, gave them a home and taught them to sing. Her intention was eventually to found a musical academy where the orphans would be taught using what she describes as her 'naturalistic' method (*The Spiritualist*, 21 September 1877: 143). Henry clearly did not share his wife's enthusiasms for philanthropy, and in 1875 they agreed to separate. Weldon was given the lease to Tavistock House, their London home, and £1000 a year. She continued her work with the orphanage, promoting it in a horse-drawn advertising van with 'Mrs Weldon's Orphanage' and 'Mrs Weldon's Sociable Evenings' painted on the sides. In addition to the orphanage, she had become involved with a number of causes such as spiritualism, vegetarianism and anti-vivisection, and also undertook singing engagements at venues around London. In 1873, Weldon provided a home for the French composer Charles Gounod, an arrangement which was the subject of continual gossip. By 1878, Henry Weldon had tired of his wife's eccentric ventures and made arrangements with Forbes Winslow to have her locked in his private asylum. Weldon, fortunately, managed to evade their attempts to capture her, but the ordeal that she suffered at the hands of the 'mad doctors' signalled the beginning of her calls for the reform of both the lunacy and marriage laws, and her determination that she would achieve retribution come what may.[4]

When she died, Weldon left 65 packing cases of books and papers. These included her 28 volumes of journals; hundreds of packets of letters and telegrams; Statements of Claim and shorthand notes from her law suits; as well as numerous press cuttings. Although many of these documents, including the journals, have now been lost, our knowledge of Weldon's careful preservation of them indicates the importance with which she regarded these life records. I began my research into her life believing that her true story was that contained in the missing volumes of private diaries. I felt their absence very keenly, and believed that only after I had located the 28 missing volumes would I be in a position to fully understand her. Several years later I am still looking for the missing volumes, but now believe that, to an extent, they were a red herring. Weldon was an extraordinary woman who lived her life in the glare of publicity. She constantly acted and re-enacted the dramatic events of her life for an audience, and wrote in 1884 that 'nothing is attained except by sensation' (*Social Salvation*, July–October, 1884: 6). She authored her life through public documents, and it is these public stagings which perhaps provide most insight into the characters she adopted and the story she told.

It was during the late 1870s, in an attempt to finance her orphanage, that Weldon first began to deliver her autobiographical public lectures. Once a week at Tavistock House, one of Mrs Weldon's sociable evenings would take place. In common with the fashion for parlour performance, these consisted of a variety of theatrical recitations and music performed by Weldon and the orphans. The highlights of the evening were a dramatic monologue called 'The Spider of the Period'[5] performed by Sapho-Katie aged three, and Weldon's lecture on the history of her orphanage (see Grierson,

1959: 149). In 1882, the lecture was published in an attempt to raise money for Weldon's campaigns for lunacy reform. It was by now called *The History of My Orphanage or the Outpourings of an Alleged Lunatic*. She wrote in the preface: 'I publish this lecture, which I used to read at my *Sociable Evenings*, because it has been reported to me that the existence of it was one of the reasons for trying to get me into a Lunatic Asylum' (1882: 1; emphasis original).

Although Weldon goes to great lengths at the beginning of the lecture to establish herself as a genteel and retiring lady, this representation is at once belied by her physical presence in front of an audience – a woman who has consented to be hired for the amusement of the paying public. The text of her lecture consists of an account of the early years of her marriage and her experiences as a singing teacher, but the majority of it is concerned with Weldon's frequently acrimonious relationships with the musical establishment, and her belief that she was a neglected genius. As her story unfolds, Weldon constructs herself as the wronged woman and provides justifications for her actions, attempting to gain the sympathy and approval of her audience who would also undoubtedly have some knowledge of the attempts by Harry to confine her in an asylum.

The History of My Orphanage (1882) was published in the same year as Weldon's other public lecture, *How I Escaped The Mad Doctors* (1882), in which she graphically recounts the tale of her escape. The tone of her narrative is reminiscent of a sensational novel, with Weldon performing the role of the heroine in peril. On the cover it is described as:

> A thrilling narrative of Personal Experience, showing by what means large numbers of perfectly sane and intellectually endowed individuals of both sexes are immured in Madhouses for life, at the instigation of relatives; in carrying out whose behests a class of men drive a lucrative trade. An appeal to every noble-hearted Englishman and Englishwoman cry aloud for the Reform of the LUNACY LAWS.

Although, on the whole, differing in style from her other lecture, Weldon again goes to some lengths to establish herself as an innocent philanthropist with simple tastes. She writes:

> [I] never cared for admiration or society. It did not feel true and I could not feel natural in an atmosphere reeking with every

kind of luxury – I thought of the poor, I thought of the Gospel and how that a rich man could not enter the Kingdom of God – I was not of a preaching disposition. . . . I had simple tastes. (1882: 4)

In both these lectures, Weldon constructs and performs specific autobiographical personae. She adopts the role of the wronged woman whose enemies conspire to suppress her talents. However, whilst *How I Escaped The Mad Doctors* allowed her to perform the part of a sensational heroine, *The History of My Orphanage*, although purporting to provide a record of the orphanage and give advice to other women singers, merely seemed to function as a forum from which she could reply in an outraged tone to her critics.

From May 1883 until October 1884, Weldon edited a monthly journal called *Social Salvation*, in which she discussed issues of the day and promoted a number of radical causes. In it she not only serialized an account of her extraordinary life, 'The History of Mrs Weldon (written by herself)', but she also published detailed accounts of her legal actions including the sworn testimony of many of her witnesses. It is therefore not surprising that the radical causes supported by the journal were also those supported by Weldon; there were frequent appeals for the reform of the lunacy laws, the repeal of the Contagious Diseases Act and the release of the Tichbourne claimant.[6] The editor, who objected to vivisection and compulsory vaccination, also suggested that the readership adopt a policy of 'no fish, no flesh, no fowl and no intoxicants' and declared that 'every cause must have its organ' (*Pall Mall Gazette*, 20 March 1884: 11).

The emphasis of the journal on the promotion of Mrs Weldon was not limited to the written text. In January 1884, an allegorical image, in which she is depicted against a background of the sea and the setting sun, began to appear on its cover. Weldon is depicted in the engraving with her characteristic short hair; she is wearing a high-waisted classical-style dress and is standing on a rock holding a mirror in one hand and a scroll representing the lunacy laws in the other.[7] Although it is obviously an allegorical representation, the picture does not refer directly to a specific myth; rather, there are mythical symbols within its layers of meaning. The mirror, for example, can be seen as a representation of truth – Weldon's desire to reflect the truth to her readers perhaps. In classical mythology Patience, one of the four cardinal virtues, was depicted holding a mirror and a snake. She signified wise conduct, and the mirror represented the wise man's ability to see himself as he really was. In the engraving, Weldon is standing alone on a rock, which echoes Prometheus, and like many of the heroes of classical mythology she is battling alone for the salvation of humanity. Her depiction with the mirror of truth and the lunacy laws in her hands is interesting as it refers to the mediaeval iconography in which saints were represented holding their attributes.

The composition and mood of the picture owes much to the work of the German Romantic painter Caspar David Friedrich, whose *Woman in Front of the Setting Sun* (c.1818) similarly depicts a woman standing in the foreground with the rays of the setting sun behind her. Weldon had travelled widely around Europe and was likely to have been familiar with Friedrich's work. It is possible also that she felt an affinity with the ideals of the Romantic Movement, specifically its emphasis on individual genius and nonconformity. The engraving therefore provides us with a clear representation of the crusading persona adopted by Weldon in her role as social reformer, and permits us to see the ways in which she consciously constructed and manipulated her image for an audience.

In October 1885, Weldon performed in *Not Alone* (1886),[8] a play that she had written in collaboration with George Lander while serving a six-month sentence in Holloway for libelling the conductor Jules Riviere. Described as 'an original modern drama' (Weldon, 1885), the play was a further attempt by Weldon to publicize the issue of wrongful confinement, but this time in a fictionalized dramatic form. It is a domestic melodrama which draws heavily on the sensational narratives made popular by novelists such as Charles Reade and Wilkie Collins. It opens at Ivy Lodge, the home of Hester Stanhope, a philanthropist, who lives there with her husband Raymond and Rachel Levierge, a woman whom Hester has rescued from the streets and made her companion. Also sharing the house are a number of orphan children whom Hester is teaching to sing – presumably employing Weldon's naturalistic methods. Rachel Levierge has become Raymond's mistress, and the plot of the play is concerned with their attempts to dispose of Hester in an asylum.

In her choice of melodrama Weldon was possibly governed by the literary capabilities of her co-author, George Lander. Lander does not appear to have written original dramatic pieces, but rather made his living adapting popular novels for the stage. The melodramatic structure, with its stock characters and plot heavily reliant on coincidence, is likely to have presented the possibility of commercial success and, presented in this popular form, Weldon's protests against the lunacy laws would have reached a far wider public. The play seems to have had a mixed reception; during the best weeks of the tour Weldon's share of the house was £150, but at times she does not appear to have made enough money to pay the company. In May 1886, after a disastrous tour of Scotland, the company agreed to struggle down to Manchester on half-salaries. In letters written during this period to her companion Angele Menier, she complains of draughty boarding houses and blames the poor audiences on the fact that all the men in the company were 'well known fossils' (see Grierson, 1959: 252). Nevertheless, Weldon's celebrity status ensured that on arrival in town she was frequently greeted by cheering crowds, and on occasions demonstrations were organized in her honour.

The play, which stages a discussion of the discourses of madness and femininity, also provides a critique of the lunacy laws through its sensational plot. As such, it contributes substantially to Weldon's campaign, although at times this seems to be at the expense of its dramatic cohesion. The autobiographical content of the play is particularly interesting: the events of the plot do not directly parallel Weldon's story, but rather provide a sensationalized version of what might have happened had she been unable to escape from the clutches of the mad doctors. The two main female characters both bear a striking resemblance to Weldon herself. Hester Stanhope can be seen as a version of her domestic self, with the more openly radical views of her friend, Angela Pyefinch, indicating the social reformer.

Like Weldon, both Hester and Angela are advocates of Rational Dress, and this unwillingness to be constrained either literally or metaphorically is used by Raymond in Act II when finalizing the arrangements for Hester's incarceration. He explains to Dr Benjamin Feese, the madhouse keeper, that Hester's mother 'never could get her to wear stays, or high heeled shoes or crinolines, and she never could persuade her to have the slightest respect or liking for Dukes or Duchesses, or even Prime Ministers' (Lander and Weldon, 1885: 19). These lines, and a number of others throughout the play, are virtually identical to those written by Weldon either in *Social Salvation* or her public lectures. For example, in Act I scene i, when Angela Pyefinch criticizes the marriage service and declares that the words ' "with my body I thee worship, and with all my worldly goods

I thee endow" are a crying satire on the legal status of woman –
a blasphemous false oath – a disgrace to a civilized nation' (1885: 4),
she is merely voicing what Weldon had already written in May
1883 in the first issue of *Social Salvation* (May 1883: 1). A review of
Not Alone in *The Era* said of the play: 'It is easy to detect in it
references to the painful phase in Mrs Weldon's own life which for
such a long period taxed the patience of our law courts' (24 October 1885). It is clear from this comment that the audience read
much of the play as autobiographical, particularly as Weldon herself played the heroine, Hester. Although the plot does not follow
precisely the events of the conspiracy against Weldon, it is nevertheless another attempt to present an autobiographical story to a
paying audience.

During the 1880s, Weldon earned herself a reputation as an expert
on the lunacy laws and, having successfully sued both her husband and the doctors involved in her attempted incarceration, began
to represent clients and advise other legal professionals. She had
no faith in the abilities of the male lawyers, and so represented
herself in court. Although law was an exclusively male preserve,
her forays into it were tolerated and she was generally regarded
with affection for the humorous repartee and plain speaking which
she introduced to the proceedings. Weldon, who wore her own version
of the legal costume, a black gown and cap, was frequently the
object of satire, and was dubbed 'Portia of the Law Courts' and
'the lunacy lawyer in petticoats' by the press (see *Pall Mall Gazette*,
20 March 1884: 11). During this period she also began to appear in
the London music halls as Serjeant Buzfuz, a leading barrister from
The Pickwick Papers in the sketch 'Bardell vs Pickwick'. Buzfuz is a
prosecuting barrister and is acting on behalf of Mrs Bardell, who is
suing Mr Pickwick for breach of promise following his failure to
marry her. The music hall performance, which involved her dress-
ing in wig and gown, was both self-referential and parodic, as not
only was Weldon assuming the role of a barrister, but also prosecuting the reprobate male. The success of these stage performances
lay in their combination of humour and Weldon's willingness to
make a spectacle of herself.

Although the performances that Weldon gave were almost entirely concerned with the presentation of fictions of herself, the
constant fashioning and re-fashioning of her life-story leaves one
struggling to discover who she really was. During my search for
her lost diaries, I received a letter from an elderly man who

remembered, as a child, being shown a number of Weldon's possessions. He did not know the whereabouts of the diaries, but described a series of boxes, originally belonging to her, which are now held at the Birmingham City Art Gallery. These boxes are based on the principle of a Russian doll, and slot inside the other. The image of an empty box, within a box, within a box, provides the perfect metaphor for my search: at the end of the process of uncovering the endless autobiographical conceits, I have come to the conclusion that there was no single self to discover.

Notes

1 I am indebted to Anne Monroe, the daughter of Edward Grierson, for her generous loan of Weldon's remaining papers and her father's research notes.
2 See Perkin (1993) and Adburgham (1979) for their discussion of shopping.
3 Georgina Weldon had a miscarriage in autumn 1860, and was subsequently unable to have children. Since Henry was reputed to have had numerous mistresses while serving in the Hussars, the most likely cause of her infertility was venereal disease contracted from her husband.
4 For details of Weldon's early life and marriage, see Treherne (1923) and Grierson (1959).
5 I have been unable to trace a copy of this work, but it was probably a parody of Eliza Lynn Linton's 1868 article, 'Girl of the Period', published in the *Saturday Review*.
6 The case of the Tichbourne claimant was one of the most extraordinary *cause célèbre* of the Victorian period. Sir Roger Tichbourne was an aristocrat who went missing in 1854 whilst touring South America. Refusing to believe him dead, his mother placed advertisements in the press, and in 1863 a butcher from Wagga Wagga, Australia, came forward. The family, with the exception of the Dowager Lady Tichbourne, believed him to be an imposter, and determined to settle the matter in court. After nearly a year of civil proceedings, the judge declared that the claimant was guilty of perjury and in 1873 a criminal trial began. The claimant was bankrupt and could not pay for his defence, so a defence fund was established. There was enormous popular support for him, and over time the Tichbourne movement grew to encompass wider political issues such as the abolition of income tax, the exclusion of lawyers from Parliament and votes for women (Roe, 1974).
7 Weldon is depicted with a broken chain on the arm that is grasping a scroll representing the Lunacy Laws. This may be a reference to Philippe Pinel, the French doctor who freed the lunatics from their chains.
8 Lander and Weldon (1886). The première was held at the Grand Theatre, Birmingham, 12 October 1885.

References

Adburgham, A. *Shopping in Style: London from the Restoration to Edwardian Elegance* (London: Thames & Hudson, 1979)

Dresen-Coenders, L. *Saints and She-Devils: Images of Women in the Fifteenth and Sixteenth Centuries* (London: Rubican, 1987)

Grierson, E. *Storm Bird: The Strange Life of Georgina Weldon* (London: Chatto & Windus, 1959)

Lander, G. & Weldon, G. *Not Alone* (London: C. W. Mayo, 1886)

Perkin, J. *Victorian Women* (London: John Murray, 1993)

Roe, M. *Kenealy and the Tichborne Cause: A Study in Mid-Victorian Populism* (Melbourne: Melbourne University Press, 1974)

Treherne, P. *A Plaintiff in Person* (London: William Heineman, 1923)

Weldon, G. *The History of my Orphanage, or the Outpourings of an Alleged Lunatic* (London: Tavistock House, 1882)

—— *How I Escaped the Mad Doctors* (London: Tavistock, 1882)

18

Emmeline Pankhurst (1858–1928): Suffragette, Militant Feminist and Champion of Womanhood

June Purvis

When Emmeline Pankhurst died on 14 June 1928, many tributes were paid to her suffragette days when, as leader of the militant Women's Social and Political Union (WSPU), she had campaigned for the right of women in Edwardian Britain to vote in parliamentary elections on equal terms with men. Some of the obituaries referred to her autobiography, *My Own Story*, published in 1914 when she was 56 years old. Believing herself to be incompetent with a pen, she had eventually agreed, after much persuasion, to dictate her story to an American journalist, Rheta Childe Dorr. Although *My Own Story* has been described by Holton as perhaps the 'most moving apologia for militancy produced during the campaign' (1990: 11), many historians have dismissed it. Rosen, for example, claims that it is 'so replete with errors and glossings-over as to be virtually useless to the historian' (1974: 167). Similarly, Pugh asserts that the militants' own accounts, including Emmeline Pankhurst's 'bogus autobiography', are 'largely fantasy; the motive for writing them was usually to establish their own claims against other sections of or individuals in the women's movement; or simply to perpetuate the image of martydom' (1980: 40).

Such comments are somewhat puzzling to the present-day reader; indeed, the marked discrepancy between the contemporary tributes to Emmeline Pankhurst and her largely unfavourable representation by historians is a theme I wish to explore in this chapter. Of course, all biographical interpretations are selective and mine is no exception; my own life-story is written into this account in complex ways (for further discussion of these issues see, for example,

Steedman, 1990; and Stanley, 1992). In particular, I write as a white, heterosexual, middle-class feminist who admires the leader of the WSPU and who shares aspects of her world-view. I also write as a professional historian whose main concern is to research the lives of feminists in the past, in all their complexity.

Born in 1858 into a politically radical, middle-class Manchester family, the young Emmeline Goulden heard many tales about struggles for constitutional reform, including women's suffrage. However, it was not until her marriage in 1879 to a radical lawyer, Dr Richard Pankhurst, 20 years her senior, that she began to take part in political life. The birth of five children – Christabel Harriette in 1880, Estelle Sylvia in 1882, Henry Francis Robert ('Frank') in 1884 (who died in infancy), Adela Constantia in 1885 and Henry Francis ('Harry') in 1889 – somewhat restricted, but did not stop, her reforming zeal. The unexpected death of her husband, in 1898, was a devastating blow. Since he had not accumulated a great deal of money, Emmeline had to take part-time employment as a registrar of Births and Deaths for the Manchester District of Chorlton. The dreadful stories she heard from the working-class women who came to register the births of their babies, some of them girls of 13 years old who had been seduced by a father or male relative, incensed her passionate nature. Her conviction grew that if society was to progress it must be through the help of women, 'women freed of their political shackles', women with full power to work their will in society (Pankhurst, 1914: 33). At this time, the parliamentary franchise had both a gender and class bias in that it was restricted not only to the male sex but also to those men, estimated to be about 59 per cent of all adult males, who owned or occupied property (Blewett, 1965). While most socialists favoured 'adult' suffrage, for Emmeline Pankhurst the sex disqualification against women was the critical aspect of franchise reform. Indeed, like many feminists in the Independent Labour Party (ILP) who were disillusioned with the lukewarm support of their comrades on the Woman Question, she feared that 'adult' suffrage could mean manhood suffrage (for further discussion of this point see Holton, 1996, Chapter 3; and Hunt, 1996, Chapter 6).

Always a dynamic and practical person who got things done, Emmeline Pankhurst decided that women themselves must make their enfranchisement a reality. Thus, on 10 October 1903, she called to her home at 62 Nelson Street, Manchester, some wives of ILP men and, with her eldest daughter Christabel, formed the WSPU, a political organization that was to campaign for votes for women on the same terms as they may be granted to men. Membership was to be limited to women only, although men could and did help the work of the organization. Furthermore, the Union was to be free from allegiance to any particular class and from allegiance with any of the male-centred political parties of the day. 'We resolved', recollected Emmeline Pankhurst, 'to be satisfied with nothing but action on our question. Deeds, not words, was to be our permanent motto' (Pankhurst, 1914: 38).

From 1903 until August 1914 when, on the eve of the outbreak of the First World War, she called an end to militancy, Emmeline Pankhurst was the much loved leader of the WSPU. While Christabel, its Organizing Secretary, was the key strategist and main policymaker (see Purvis, 1998), Emmeline was the spiritual figurehead. She saw the Union as an army and military metaphors pervade suffragette rhetoric. 'We are soldiers engaged in a holy war', she told her followers in 1913 when guerrilla activists were engaging in widespread window smashing, arson, vandalizing letter boxes and other acts of disorder, 'and we mean to go on until victory is won' (*The Suffragette*, 30 May 1913: 541). This more violent action which involved destruction to property but not human life had been introduced in 1912 when the 'mild' militancy of peaceful demonstrations, heckling politicians and general civil disobedience had been played out. A determined woman who believed passionately in the right of women to full citizenship, Emmeline Pankhurst could be uncompromising to those who objected to WSPU policy. Consequently, there were two well-publicized splits in the WSPU, one in 1907 and another in 1912. For purposes of illustration, I shall focus here only on the former split.

At the ILP Conference in January 1907, an amendment was adopted which opposed the extension of the franchise on a property qualification to a section only of the population, a move that was contrary to WSPU policy (Rosen, 1974: 85). Disillusioned with such a response, both Emmeline and Christabel Pankhurst resigned from the ILP, although its links with the WSPU were never completely severed (see Holton, 1996). During the summer, the tensions between the pro-ILP Union members and those who favoured a separatist stance deepened. In particular, it would appear that Teresa Billington Greig argued for greater autonomy and democracy for the new provincial branches that she was frequently involved in founding and for a limit to the number of paid organizers who sat on the central committee, now based in London and not Manchester. It was rumoured that she and others 'intended a coup' against the WSPU leadership (Pankhurst, 1931: 70). Emmeline Pankhurst, who had been touring the provinces, returned to headquarters, and at the request of the Union's treasurer, Emmeline Pethick-Lawrence, and her husband, Frederick (who brought legal and business knowledge to the WSPU as well as financial backing), she declared the democratic constitution of the Union abolished, the annual conference cancelled and invited members who were still ready to follow her to do so (Pankhurst, 1931: 264–5; 1935: 70; 1959: 82). While Christabel and the majority of members supported such a decision, a small group of dissenters (including Teresa Billington Greig, Charlotte Despard and Edith How Martyn) left to form an alternative organization, later called the Women's Franchise League. Emmeline Pankhurst, who expected the vote to be won at any time, offered no apology for her action. Indeed, she later asserted that the WSPU is 'not hampered by a complexity of rules. We have no constitution and by-laws; nothing to be amended or tinkered with or quarrelled over at an annual meeting. In fact, we have no annual meeting, no business sessions, no elections of officers' (Pankhurst, 1914: 59). As Rebecca West commented in a insightful essay published in the 1930s, in the midst of her battle for democracy, Emmeline Pankhurst was obliged, lest that battle should be lost, 'to become a dictator' (West, 1933: 500). So why was she tolerated and indeed loved by her followers?

Emmeline Pankhurst was a charismatic person, a leader 'of power and magnetism' (Smyth, 1934: 278). Time and time again, Union members make reference to those personal qualities that drew people to her. Emmeline Pankhurst had 'the most magnetic charm: a dainty person with small hands, small feet, an intelligent face with a firm chin', recollected Mary Richardson (1953: 32), a one-time WSPU guerrilla activist. In a society where women were ideally expected to be full-time wives and mothers, subservient to their menfolk, Emmeline Pankhurst's message to women, as a unified category, to challenge the power of men in a male-defined world held a particular resonance. 'Our power as women in invincible', she emphasized in a circular letter dated 27 October 1910 to WSPU members, 'if we are united and determined' (Pankhurst, 1910). It was this emphasis upon the sisterhood and agency of women that empowered her followers and made her a powerful leader.

Emmeline Pankhurst's view of history, claims Holton (1990: 11–14) was one based on 'romantic feminism', largely derived from the writings of the influential historian Thomas Carlyle, who stressed the role of heroic individuals in bringing about radical change through social and political action. Seeing herself in an historic role, she shared with her followers the excitement and dangers that could result from militancy. Always in the thick of the action, she led deputations to Parliament, was roughly treated by the police and went to prison 13 times; 11 times she was released on hunger strikes and, although never forcibly fed, she intensified her resistance to the prison authorities in 1913 by not just refusing food but also going on thirst and sleep strikes. Such wreckage to her body gave her an 'otherworldly voice', whose power increased as her physical strength failed (Green, 1998: 141). Such courage also kept many women loyal to the WSPU and its leaders when they might have left (see Morley with Stanley, 1988: 176–8).

A great publicist, an actress with a flair for the dramatic (see Harrison, 1987), she could sway an audience with the power of her oratory; she spoke from the heart and from experience, without notes and with few gestures. When conducting her own defence in court, she could be defiant as well as courteous, pleading the cause of women and explaining her impatience with a man-made and man-ruled world. In October 1908, for example, Emmeline and Christabel Pankhurst and Flora Drummond went on trial for circulating handbills which called upon and incited the public 'to do a certain wrongful and illegal act, namely to rush the House of Commons' (Rosen, 1974: 111). In her defence from the dock, Emmeline Pankhurst told her life-story, stressing how she and WSPU members had tried to be patient and 'womanly', using constitutional methods, all to no avail. She explained:

We have taken this action, because as women – and I want you to understand it is as women we have taken this action – it is because we realize that the condition of our sex is so deplorable that it is our duty even to break the law in order to call attention to the reasons why we do so.... We are here not because we are law-breakers; we are here in our efforts to become law-makers. (*Votes for Women*, 29 October 1908: 81)

Her listeners, including burly policemen, newspaper reporters and spectators were moved to tears (Pankhurst, 1914: 129). Although the magistrate showed no mercy but sentenced all three defendants to imprisonment, the trial, which attracted widespread media coverage, was like a 'suffrage meeting attended by millions' (Pethick-Lawrence, 1938: 205).

Characteristically, at this trial Emmeline Pankhurst accepted full responsibility for the present agitation, a theme she frequently stressed during the campaign. On 18 February 1913, for example, a bomb planted by WSPU member Emily Wilding Davison exploded, wrecking five rooms of a partly completed house being built for government minister, Lloyd George. Although Emmeline Pankhurst did not know about this act beforehand, nevertheless she emphasized that she accepted full responsibility for what had happened. By now the 'born rebel' as Frederick Pethick-Lawrence (n.d.: 99) called her, was being watched by plain-clothed policemen, who attended her meetings and transcribed her speeches. On 24 February 1913, she was arrested for procuring and inciting women to commit offences contrary to the Malicious Injuries to Property Act of 1861 (Rosen, 1974: 189–90). On trial at the Old Bailey in April, she was found guilty with a strong recommendation to mercy. In her speech to the judge, she was again defiant, determined and courageous as she stressed that she felt no guilt since she had done her duty as a leader in sharing with her followers the dangers of militancy:

To the women I have represented, to the women who, in response to my incitement, have faced these terrible consequences, have broken laws, to them I want to say I am not going to fail them but to face it as they face it, to go through with it, and I know that they will go on with the fight whether I live or whether I die. (Pankhurst, 1914: 299; emphasis original)

The judge, however, showed no mercy and sentenced her to three years' penal servitude.

Emmeline Pankhurst, however, served less than six weeks of her sentence between the time of her conviction and August 1914 when militancy ended. Using the tactics of the 'Cat and Mouse' Act, passed in April 1913, which allowed prisoners who had damaged their health to be released on a licence in order to recover so that they would then be fit enough to be readmitted, she was repeatedly in and out of prison. On many occasions she was released in a state of collapse and, after being nursed back to health, risked re-arrest as she defied government orders not to attend WSPU meetings. On 14 July 1913, for example, she and Annie Kenney, another 'mouse' on a licence, attended one such meeting where the cheered leader announced: 'I would rather be a rebel than a slave. I would rather die than submit' (*The Suffragette*, 18 July 1913: 677). Managing to evade the police, she was re-arrested on 21 July. On 10 August a new form of protest was introduced as a number of suffragettes prayed aloud for their beloved leader at Westminster Abbey, a practice that became increasingly common. However, on 12 August 1914, on the eve of the outbreak of the First World War, she sent a letter to all WSPU members announcing a 'temporary suspension of activities' (copy in Suffragette Fellowship, Museum of London). The militant campaign had ended.

My interpretation of Emmeline Pankhurst's life contrasts sharply with the largely unfavourable representations of her presented by other writers, with the notable exceptions of Rover (1967), Spender (1982) and Holton (1990). Just as my individual biography is woven into my account of Emmeline Pankhurst's life, so it would appear that similar factors have influenced the interpretations of others. As I have argued elsewhere (Purvis, 1996), there are two key texts on the women's suffrage movement that have helped to establish dominant narratives about Emmeline and Christabel Pankhurst namely, Ray Strachey's *'The Cause': A Short History of the Women's Movement in Great Britain* and Sylvia Pankhurst's *The Suffragette Movement: An Intimate Account of Persons and Ideals*. First published in 1928 and 1931, respectively, both were republished in paperback in the 1970s and 1980s and have been widely read and widely cited.

'The Cause' is written from what may be termed a liberal feminist perspective. Strachey, a keen supporter of Millicent Garrett Fawcett, leader of the non-militant National Union of Women's Suffrage Societies (NUWSS), was critical of the Union leaders. As Dodd (1990: 127–37) persuasively argues, Strachey uses a political vocabulary drawn from liberalism to position Millicent Fawcett and the NUWSS as the constitutional, rational, progressive, civilized and democratic wing of the women's movement which was responsible for the partial enfranchisement of women in 1918 and their full enfranchisement, on equal terms with men, in 1928. Emmeline and Christabel Pankhurst and the WSPU, on the other hand, are 'cast out of the making of women's history because of their reckless activity, their passion for change, their angry propaganda and their autocratic organization' (1990: 134). Strachey's analysis helped to establish a framework within which future accounts about the

Edwardian women's movement, especially by influential liberal male historians such as Dangerfield (1935), Mitchell (1977), Fulford (1957) and Harrison (1987), were placed. For these historians the 'good' feminists are those women who have faith in the British parliamentary system and are non-militant, reasonable, patient and controlled, and prepared to work with men.

A similar role for the establishment of a dominant socialist narrative about Emmeline and Christabel Pankhurst must be allocated to Sylvia Pankhurst's *The Suffragette Movement*. Sylvia's socialist feminist outlook was often at odds with the women-centred views of her mother and her elder sister. Furthermore, the political differences between the women were exacerbated by the fact that Christabel had always been her mother's favourite child, the 'apple of her eye' (Pankhurst, 1931: 267). Such lenses coloured how Sylvia represented her mother and sister, as well as herself. Thus the WSPU policy of independence from any political party of the day, including the ILP, is condemned. Furthermore, Emmeline Pankhurst is represented not as the powerful leader of a women's movement but as a mother who neglects her less favoured children – Adela, Sylvia and Harry. When Sylvia describes the strong influence of Christabel upon her mother, claims Kean (1994: 73–4), she writes not just as an angry socialist, but as 'a rejected daughter'. Similarly, Marcus (1987: 5–6) observes that in Sylvia's account of the women's suffrage movement she is 'the heroine' who keeps the socialist faith, the Cinderella liberated by a fairy godmother in the form of the socialist giant Keir Hardie, while her mother and sister are the 'wicked' people, the 'separatist feminists', 'isolated man-haters' and celibate 'unsexed viragoes' who caused split after split within the movement.

Variations on these themes about Emmeline Pankhurst have been persistently presented by subsequent male socialist historians, such as Garner (1984) and Pugh (1990), as well as second wave socialist feminist historians, such as Rowbotham (1973) and Liddington and Norris (1978). Liddington and Norris, for example, are critical of Emmeline and Christabel Pankhurst's resignation from the ILP since it meant that the WSPU no longer 'accommodated' the demands of 'broader organizations like the ILP' and cut the Union's last remaining links with 'its roots in northern socialism' (1978: 208). Instead of mobilizing the working class into a mass movement, the Pankhurst-led WSPU becomes 'an underground organization of "guerilla" fighters . . . reduced down to an elite corps' (1978: 210).

My view is that Emmeline Pankhurst was a women-identified woman, forerunner of some of the radical feminist ideas articulated in second wave feminism. As such, she needs to be reclaimed from the denigration of so many historians and represented as she was seen in her time, as a 'champion of womanhood' (Hill and Shafer, 1909: 19).

References

Blewett, N. 'The Franchise in the UK, 1885–1918', *Past and Present* 32 (1965)

Dangerfield, G. *The Strange Death of Liberal England* (London: MacGibbon & Kee, [1935] 1966)

Dodd, C. 'Cultural Politics and Women's Historical Writing: the Case of Ray Strachey's *The Cause*', *Women's Studies International Forum* 13 1–2 (1990)

Fulford, R. *Votes for Women, The Story of a Struggle* (London: Faber and Faber, 1957)

Garner, L. *Stepping Stones to Women's Liberty* (London: Heinemann Educational, 1984)

Harrison, B. *Prudent Revolutionaries Portraits of British Feminists Between the Wars* (Oxford: Clarendon Press, 1987)

Hill, E. and Schafer, O. F. (eds) *Great Suffragists and Why* (London: Henry J. Drane, 1909)

Holton, S. S. 'In Sorrowful Wrath: Suffrage Militancy and the Romantic Feminism of Emmeline Pankhurst', in H. L. Smith (ed.) *British Feminism in the Twentieth Century* (Aldershot: Edward Elgar, 1990)

—— *Suffrage Days, Stories From the Women's Suffrage Movement* (London and New York: Routledge, 1996)

Hunt, K. *Equivocal Feminists, the Social Democratic Federation and the Woman Question 1884–1911* (Cambridge: Cambridge University Press, 1996)

Kean, H. 'Searching for the Past in Present Defeat: The Construction of Historical and Political Identity in British Feminism in the 1920s and 1930s', *Women's History Review*, 3: 1 (1994)

Liddington, J. and Norris, J. *One Hand Tied Behind Us: The Rise of the Women's Suffrage Movement* (London: Virago, 1978)

Marcus, J. (ed.) *Suffrage and the Pankhursts* (London: Routledge & Kegan Paul, 1987)

Mitchell, D. *Queen Christabel, a Biography of Christabel Pankhurst* (London: MacDonald & Jane's, 1977)

Morley, A. and Stanley, L. *The Life and Death of Emily Wilding Davison* (London: The Women's Press, 1988)

Pankhurst, C. *Unshackled, The Story of how we won the Vote* (London: Hutchinson, 1959)

Pankhurst, E. *My Own Story* (London: Eveleigh Nash, 1914)

Pankhurst, E. S. *The Suffragette Movement: An Intimate Account of Persons and Ideals* (London: Longmans, Green & Co., 1931)

—— *The Life of Emmeline Pankhurst, The Suffragette Struggle for Women's Citizenship* (London: T. Werner Laurie Ltd, 1935)

Pethick-Lawrence, E. *My Part in a Changing World* (London: Victor Gollancz, 1938)

Pethick-Lawrence, F. W. *Fate Has Been Kind* (London and New York: Hutchinson, n.d.)

Pugh, M. *Women's Suffrage in Britain* (London: The Historical Association, 1980)

Purvis, J. 'Christabel Pankhurst and the Women's Social and Political Union', in M. Joannou and J. Purvis (eds) *The Women's Suffrage Movement: New Feminist Perspectives* (Manchester: Manchester University Press, 1998)

Raeburn, A. *The Militant Suffragettes* (London: Michael Joseph, 1973)

Rosen, A. *Rise up Women! The Militant Campaign of the Women's Social and Political Union 1903–14* (London: Routledge & Kegan Paul, 1974)

Rover, C. *Women's Suffrage and Party Politics in Britain 1866–1914* (London: Routledge & Kegan Paul, 1967)

Rowbotham, S. *Hidden from History: 300 Years of Women's Oppression and the Fight Against It* (London: Pluto Press, 1973)

Spender, D. *Women of Ideas and What Men Have Done to Them, from Aphra Behn to Adrienne Rich* (London, Boston, Melbourne & Henley: Routledge & Kegan Paul, 1982)

Smyth, E. *Female Pipings in Eden* (London: Peter Davies, 1934)

Stanley, L. *The Auto/biographical I: The Theory and Practice of Feminist Auto/biography* (Manchester: Manchester University Press, 1992)

Steedman, C. *Childhood, Culture and Class in Britain, Margaret McMillan 1860–1931* (London: Virago, 1990)

West, R. Mrs Pankhurst in the *'Post-Victorians'* (London: Nicholson, 1933)

19

'The Narrow Margin of Long Days of Toil': Class and Education in the Writings of Ruth Slate

T. G. Ashplant

Ruth Slate and Eva Slawson are in many respects representative women of their class and generation.[1] Born in the 1880s into lower-middle-class families in East London, both benefited from the great expansion of white-blouse work in the period 1890–1914, which opened up new opportunities for the daughters of lower-middle- and working-class families. Each was an office worker for more than a decade, before in their early thirties gaining the opportunity for further education and career change. They were brought up in the earnest world of chapel-going nonconformity: predominantly a mixture of skilled workers and the lower-middle class, linked politically to the Liberals, but now facing profound challenges. They are, however, *untypical* in so far as a substantial body of their writings survives: Slate's diary for $10^1/_2$ of the 19 years from 1897 to 1916; Slawson's diary for the three years 1913 to 1916; and many of the letters they exchanged between themselves.[2]

Slate's and Slawson's initial identities were powerfully shaped by their gender, class location, economic opportunities, educational achievements, and religious and political inheritance. Their letters and diaries were written at most for an audience of two and with no view to publication; they were also written without the need to conceal ambivalences for the sake of a public stance, and without the tidying up which takes place in retrospective accounts. Slate and Slawson's writings provide a valuable insight into the processes of personal change which underlie what appear in the historical record as individual conversion or generational shift of allegiance. Moreover, it is precisely the overlay of social structure and longitudinal (generational and individual) change in the quotidian detail and texture of these writings that makes them a valuable source for

Class and Education in the Writings of Ruth Slate 229

women's history. The writings reveal the interaction of several structural elements – class, work, family setting, life-cycle trajectory, religion, education – with individual aspirations and struggles, and the contribution these make to public political stances. They also disclose the ambivalences, hesitancies and fluctuations integral to the development of each woman.

This chapter will concentrate on tracing just one thread in this complex web, namely, Ruth Slate's long search for further education as a means of both self-development and career advancement. Her strivings were both fuelled by and strengthening to her other struggles for personal growth. The chapter will focus especially on the years 1905–8 and 1914–16, and will use comparisons with Slawson both to contextualize and to individuate Slate's history. I will pay attention to some passages of heightened language in which Slate expressed her developing perceptions of society and of her/their place within it: writing which helped to shape her emergent identity.

Both women were third-generation lower-middle-class. Slate was born in 1884 in Manor Park, eldest child of a commercial clerk. Her grandfather had his own small business. Slawson, born illegitimate in 1882, was adopted by her maternal grandparents, who ran a small bakery, while her mother's sister Edie later took over a general shop (Thompson, 1987: 49, 93). Their social location gave the two a crucial margin of comfort over most working-class girls. Yet, like the upper-working class to whom they were socially and geographically so close, their families lived always on the margins of poverty into which they might fall. This was apparent on all sides: within their own families, among close friends, among neighbours and in the local community.

Their circumstances differed in certain ways. Slate lived with her parents until she was 25. During her late teens and early twenties, she was frequently locked in struggles with her mother, who thought her daughter unhelpful and selfish, and tried to suppress her ambitions. Slawson, by contrast, lived in a more supportive household. Just before she turned 20, when her grandparents gave up their business, she went to live with her aunt Edie, sometimes helping in her shop. In 1907, they were joined by her half-sister Gertie. The three shared many interests and commitments, and consistently gave one another support (see 49, 104, 200–1, 263).

Both were part of the rapid growth in women's clerical work during the late nineteenth and early twentieth centuries, rising from 19 000 in 1891 to 125 000 in 1911 (see Anderson, 1977: 113; Holcombe,

230   T. G. Ashplant

1973; Zimmeck, 1986; Davy, 1986). Slate left her local Board School at 14, and in 1902 became a principal clerk in a City grocers where she remained until 1914. Slawson was first briefly in service as a housemaid; she then learned shorthand and typing, and subsequently worked as a secretary in a solicitor's office in Walthamstow until 1915. Both women had occasion to complain of their poor working conditions, though these did not compare with those of many women manual workers (see Davy, 1986: 129; Holcombe, 1973: 149–50; Zimmeck, 1986: 165). Throughout Slate's employment, she remained determined to leave and did so without regret, later looking back on her time there with bitterness (Thompson, 1987: 196, 241). Slawson's conditions of work were somewhat easier, though later her complaints about work pressure and pay levels grew.

Slate and Slawson were brought up in the nonconformist chapel-going culture, and met at Manor Park Chapel in 1902 (see McLeod, 1974, chapters 5 and 6). It would be hard to overstate the continuing importance of their religious inheritance, in both its language and ethical creed, and its networks of friendships and contacts. These persisted despite the questioning of their faith which both women, like many of their own and the previous generation, embarked on in early adulthood, and which was to take them away from the earnest avowals of late adolescence to individual, more eclectic, spiritual stances. Nonconformity was now in its final flowering; the last traditional religious revival occurred in 1904–5. Yet it was also being radically transformed by theological and intellectual questioning. One response to this was what may be termed ultra-liberal nonconformity, concerned especially with social progress. This development was brought into national focus by Rev. R. J. Campbell, a Congregational minister, who launched his New Theology movement in 1907, and founded the Progressive Thought League (PTL) (see Robbins, 1993; McLeod, 1974: 183–4). Nonconformity was responsive also to what contemporaries called 'the social question'. Nonconformists, especially Methodists, had traditionally been concerned with drink and temperance, and Manor Park Chapel took up that question again when the 1905 revival reached London.

Through her diary entries, we can view Slate already starting to consider the emphasis on drink problematic, as she begins to see the extent of local poverty. The chapel held a mission, culminating in a procession to local pubs, accompanied by the Salvation Army band. When Slate begged bystanders to come to a chapel meeting, one replied: 'It's no use you talking to me Sally, talk to our employers, them as overworks and underpays us, mate, talk to them.' Though many drinkers did take the pledge, she ends on a questioning note: 'I am not sure what is the attitude of my mind towards missions' (Thompson, 1987: 62–5). Subsequent examples of domestic violence exacerbated by drink in the neighbourhood led her to reflect on 'the unhappiness and misery going on under our very eyes, which has been going on for years, while the Chapel and Churches are blindly concerned with their own petty bickerings. It is terrible!' (66; 68–70). Neither woman underwent a dramatic rejection of Christianity, nor did they embrace an alternative faith; but a combination of such disillusionment as Slate felt after the revival, at the contrast between social need and sectarian bickering, and their growing acquaintance with other faiths and anti-religious writings, led to a modification of their beliefs.

Both women yearned for greater education, despite encountering considerable problems in their efforts; they returned to this longing, and the tensions it generated, repeatedly in their writings. When still only 16, Slate had written in her diary:

> I have, and always have had, a craving to be clever and to learn. Therefore I read these books. My ambitions may never be satisfied, thwarted by circumstances, but they remain in me. Naturally reticent, I seldom shew these feelings and am thought very discontented. I must read while I can. (27)

Slate was drawn both to widening her general education and to acquiring commercial skills to secure a better job. Yet she found it a considerable strain studying alongside her work and in the face of demands that she help at home. She was forever joining evening classes then leaving again, a situation which eventually engendered some bitterness. Slawson, by contrast, living in a rather freer atmosphere outside the confines of a patriarchal family, had a little more scope to pursue her educational ambitions. Both women avidly attended sermons and lectures; Slate's diary regularly comments on the quality of the preaching she has heard; and they read widely both fiction, and religious, historical and political writing. They questioned and discussed the texts they read both by themselves (as in Slate's diary) and with each other through letters and during study evenings together. Slate's comments on her own reading, between 1906 and 1908 in particular, are concerned with the major questions she was exploring at that time. She read Renan and

Blatchford on religion, remarking on the latter's statement that a certain Buddhist's character seemed nobler than Christ's: 'I could never have dared such a thought, and yet I often wonder how much is just the unconscious clinging to systematic and thoroughly taught childish beliefs' (Thompson, 1987: 86; see also McLeod, 1974: 138–9; and Smith, 1992: 266–7).

Their early religious questionings, the constant search to extend their education, and the engagement with politics that was soon to follow, have to be put in the context of their chafing against constraints on them as women, and of their aspirations for independence. The fragmentary nature of the surviving writing makes it difficult to reconstruct a full picture even of Slate's personal development. Nevertheless, it is possible to identify certain phases of personal growth during her mid-twenties. What the texts reveal is the interaction of these different elements in her life. Forays into wider intellectual and social circles have to be set against growing unhappiness at home and at work, and her increasingly difficult relationship with her fiancé, a young fellow clerk, Walter Randall (Wal). She had met him through chapel in 1904, and they had become engaged two years later; but as Slate's questioning and self-confidence grew, so did tension between them.

1907–8 saw an accelerating involvement in the public sphere, as both women began to approach the world of politics. This did not result solely from the rhythms of their individual development; 1908, like 1904 and 1905, was a high point of unemployment and accompanying political agitation (see Brown, 1971, chapters 2 and 4). As for many in the previous generation who had founded the socialist movement around 1890, religious interests and connections acted as a bridge into political involvement. Slate's first contacts with both socialist and suffragist movements came via Christian contexts (Thompson, 1987: 30, 100–1). In January 1907, she had been powerfully enthused by R. J. Campbell and the debate he provoked. Her diary records that:

> To the amazement of Dad and Mother, and also to myself, for it seemed that some foreign voice spoke through me, I declared with vehemence that what the revival people had been praying for had come, though not in the way they expected. (97)

Politically, Slate and Slawson were drawn to the Independent Labour Party (ILP) and the Women's Labour League (WLL). The ILP expanded rapidly in London between 1905 and 1910; its stronger branches tended to be precisely in districts of 'black-coated proletarians', and among its London leadership were members of the ethical movement (including Campbell). It supported women's franchise, held a range of positions on the relation between class and gender oppression, and gave space for women's political activity (see P. Thompson, 1967: 221–35; Hannam, 1992; Thane, 1990: 124–5). Slawson was the more committed socialist, joining both organizations in 1908/9, while Slate was much more tentative. Early in 1909, both women attended a WLL meeting on behalf of unemployed women. A passage in her diary foreshadowed what was soon to follow:

> Wal, of course, was not so enthusiastic as myself, and spoke of Socialism as stirring up class and sex strife. Again I could not agree with him and said so, and this time I seemed able to let myself go and spoke with a fluency and fervour which surprised myself. I felt conscious of power, where it came from I know not. Perhaps out of this long chaos form is slowly shaping. (Thompson, 1987: 137)

This process of personal change and public exploration came to a head in 1909, a crucial year in Slate's development, during which time her circumstances changed dramatically. In March, she broke off her engagement; and her sister Daisy died, severing the last ties binding her to home. By now she was bitter at her lack of educational and career opportunities, and in her diary account of a day spent with Elizabeth Brown (an older Quaker woman who had been her mentor for the previous three years) and Edward Grubb (Brown's employer, and editor of a Quaker paper), she gave vent in rare form to her feelings.

> Part of the conversation was between Mr Grubb and Elizabeth only, as when they spoke of Syriac writings. . . . As I listened, the feelings of progress which have recently encouraged me seemed to leave me – I realized what a difference there is between the 'little knowledge' and broad culture. In my own circle lately, I have been conscious of a certain power – here I was dumb. . . . I could only think with a certain bitterness of that enormous difference and of the unfairness of unequal opportunity. 'I have the brains', I thought, 'and the willingness to use them, but I have never had the chance.' Even now every little effort at

234 T. G. Ashplant

self-improvement has to be made at the expense of recreation.
Why should it be so? (141–2)

The last three quotations from Slate reveal a continuous struggle
over two years to articulate her own views. The first two display an
awareness of a new power, though they do not claim this as individual agency, but rather displace it outside the self, perhaps a legacy
of her religious upbringing. The third picks up the theme of the
second ('conscious of /a certain/ power'), only to undercut its value
in the context of the wider world, in which she recognized herself
as 'dumb'.

In November 1909, Slate finally left home and took lodgings.
She kept in touch with her family and continued to worry on their
behalf, but was no longer prepared to sacrifice all her own ambitions in being a dutiful daughter (147). She continued to attend
socialist meetings and to read socialist literature; but it is not clear
if she ever joined the ILP, which Slawson was to leave, disillusioned, in 1912.

What influences brought these women to ethical socialism? First,
their experiences of the workplace. It is clear from later comments
that Slate, in particular, harboured some bitterness about her treatment over the years (see 124, 149). The major problems (apart from
pay) concerned the systematic overwork ('sweating') for which her
employers were famous, and the bullying of staff that accompanied
it. Second, questioning their Christian faith led them not only to
reconsider specifically religious doctrines, but also to think again
about how the world might be made better – an aspect of nonconformist praxis neither woman ever renounced. Third, the powerful
but repeatedly thwarted struggle to extend their education, which
led to Slate's angry outburst about 'unequal opportunity'. Fourth,
as can be traced very clearly in Slate's case, striving to make a life
for herself, against the pressures of both family and fiancé, drove
her to an increasingly clear articulation of her own viewpoint. The
passages just quoted record the emergence of an individual voice –
and one that need not be confined to the privacy of the diary but
could on occasion be articulated aloud.

Living independently, Slate now had more time and energy to
further her intellectual and personal development. In 1914, she
secured a scholarship to the Quaker-run Woodbrooke Settlement;
and the 18 months Slate spent there, besides enabling her to study
full-time and secure the education she had longed for, also further

widened her horizons. She undertook a mixture of academic study (in economics, philosophy, social studies, education and comparative religions) with industrial visits and work placements in areas of social work. Her confidence grew steadily, in step with her achievements. She wrote to Slawson: 'I am glad, dear, not so much for my own sake, but because I feel such little triumphs as mine may do much towards vindicating the intelligence of those who have not had many opportunities' (276). In June 1915, she received a Diploma in Social Studies from the University of Birmingham. After a few months of temporary work, she accepted a post as a Welfare Worker at Rowntree's in York, moving there in January 1916.

While at Woodbrooke, Slate had agitated on her friend's behalf, and Slawson was offered a scholarship in October 1915. Able to discuss their shared experience of full-time study, both women became more critical of their past lives, in ways which rearticulate some of the themes which initially led them towards ethical socialism. Just when it seemed that for Slawson new opportunities were opening, she suddenly and shockingly died of undetected diabetes in March 1916 (295). Slate was devastated by the loss of her closest friend for 14 years, with whom she had shared so much change and so many hopes for a fuller life. Her diary, in which Slawson had been such a vivid presence, now became a site for mourning. Slate's new confidence in placing herself within the world, as well as the shock of her profound loss, is represented when she looks back:

> I was pondering yesterday on the stress everyone at Woodbrooke seemed to lay on Eva's 'humility'. How little they understood either of us! Much of that humility was the lack of self-confidence which both Eva and I have felt to be the curse of our lives, and which has been unduly and unhealthily fostered in us by mistaken religious training and hard circumstances. I never before *quite* realized what a very different world Eva and I represented there – yet I should find it very difficult to explain myself to an ordinary Woodbrooker! (300; emphasis original)

Slate's analysis, in this penultimate diary entry, of the nature and roots of their 'humility' – with its emphasis on 'mistaken religious training and hard circumstances' – displays a new trenchancy. In her memorial notice for Eva in the *Woodbrooke Chronicle*, Ruth *did* find words to express subtly her sense of their difference (301–2). To a sketch of the typical Woodbrooke student, who 'may look back upon a life which, in regard to its circumstances, has been comparatively easy', she contrasts a rarer type:

> A soul which has striven and suffered much – a Student whose life has been handicapped by meagre opportunities and worn by the effort to fulfil itself in the narrow margin of long days of toil. To these Woodbrooke is as an oasis in a desert, reviving health and energy, and above all the capacity to dream dreams and see visions of things that are to be.

In these final pages of her writing, Slate situates the construction of her own and Slawson's personalities in the material and ideological contexts of their past and present lives as white-blouse proletarians striving for a richer life. She expressed her understanding both privately and publicly in language marked simultaneously by a continuing religious legacy and a new hard-won clarity of perception.

Notes

1 This paper originated in interdisciplinary courses on women and writing in Britain, 1850–1940, which I have co-taught for several years at Liverpool John Moores University. I am grateful to my colleague Dr Glenda Norquay, who through this initiative introduced me to the issues involved in women's writing, and who commented helpfully on an earlier draft; and to several cohorts of students from whose enthusiastic and perceptive engagement with women's lives and texts I have learned much. I owe the impetus for this particular essay to Connie Hancock and Morag Reid.
2 Thompson (1987). All otherwise unattributed page references are to this source.

References

Anderson, G. L. 'The Social Economy of Late-Victorian Clerks', in G. Crossick (ed.) *The Lower Middle Class in Britain 1870–1914* (London: Croom Helm, 1977)

Brown, K. D. *Labour and Unemployment 1900–1914* (Newton Abbot: David & Charles, 1971)

Davy, T. '"A Cissy Job for Men; a Nice Job for Girls": Women Shorthand Typists in London, 1900–39', in L. Davidoff and B. Westover (eds) *Our Work, Our Lives, Our Words: Women's History and Women's Work* (Basingstoke: Macmillan, 1986)

Hannam, J. 'Women and the ILP, 1890–1914', in D. James et al. (eds) *The Centennial History of the Independent Labour Party* (Halifax: Ryburn, 1992)

Holcombe, L. *Victorian Ladies at Work. Middle-class Working Women in England and Wales 1850–1914* (Newton Abbot: David & Charles, 1973)

McLeod, H. *Class and Religion in the Late Victorian City* (London: Croom Helm, 1974)

Robbins, K. 'The Spiritual Pilgrimage of the Rev. R. J. Campbell', in *Religion and Identity in Modern Britain* (London: Hambledon, 1993)

Smith, L. 'Religion and the ILP', in D. James et al. (eds) *The Centennial History of the Independent Labour Party* (Halifax: Ryburn, 1992)

Thane, P. 'The Women of the British Labour Party and Feminism, 1906–45', in H. L. Smith (ed.) *British Feminism in the Twentieth Century* (Aldershot: Elgar, 1990)

Thompson, P. *Socialists, Liberals and Labour: The Struggle for London, 1885–1914* (London: Routledge, 1967)

Thompson, T. (ed.) *Dear Girl: the Diaries and Letters of Two Working Women 1897–1917* (London: The Women's Press, 1987)

Zimmeck, M. 'Jobs for the Girls: the Expansion of Clerical Work for Women, 1850–1914', in A. V. John (ed.) *Unequal Opportunities: Women's Employment in England 1800–1918* (Oxford: Blackwell, 1986)

Part VI
Matrilineality

20
One, Two, Three: Sylvia Plath's Verse Dramas

Nicola Shaughnessy

Most readers of Sylvia Plath, if asked to identify the most obviously 'autobiographical' area of her writing, would probably first point to her poetry, alongside (although perhaps with more qualifications) prose works such as *The Bell Jar* and *Johnny Panic and the Bible of Dreams*. Whilst a number of critics have made determined efforts in recent years to disentangle the literary effects of Plath's poetry from the biographical facts and myths that continue to circulate around her work (see Rose, 1991), many readers and critics persist not only in hearing in it the raw, immediate and compelling voice of its author, but also consider this 'confessional' element to count as an index of spontaneous authenticity. But for Plath herself, the relationship between personal experience and writing was both more considered and more complex:

> I think my poems immediately come out of the sensuous and emotional experiences that I have . . . I believe that one should be able to control and manipulate experiences . . . with an informed and an intelligent mind. I think that personal experience is very important, but certainly it shouldn't be a kind of shutbox and mirror-looking, narcissistic experience. (Orr, 1966: 169)

The autobiographical impulse was a vital element in her work, but Plath negotiated the dangers of narcissism by playing with the conventions of autobiography. Paradoxically, not only does she inhabit and interrogate the 'confessional' mode in her poetry, she also proffers and withholds identifications between the author and the subjects of her fictions. In this chapter I want to focus on Plath's two verse dramas, 'Dialogue over a Ouija Board' and *Three Women*,

241

as experiments in this vein, and, in the case of the latter, as an exploratory mode of autobiographical writing that uses the play of voices to give free rein to memory, fantasy, dreams and the imaginary. Raymond Williams writes that the 1950s radio and verse plays of Christopher Fry, T. S. Eliot, Louis MacNeice and Dylan Thomas aimed at 'a drama in which, essentially, states of consciousness would be an action' (Williams, 1987: 175). Plath's verse dramas offered a gendered intervention into this form, which operates critically upon poetic, dramatic and autobiographical mediums.

In his comment on the origin of 'Dialogue over Ouija Board', Ted Hughes points to its biographical context:

> SP occasionally amused herself . . . by holding her finger on an upturned glass, in a ring of letters laid out on a smooth table, and questioning the 'spirits' . . . 'Dialogue over a Ouija Board' . . . used the actual 'spirit' text of one of the ouija sessions. (Plath, 1981: 276)

The dialogue examines the appeal of dabbling in the occult as a kind of game. Game-playing is central to the conception of the 'Dialogue' in more ways than one; it is an instance of what Steven Gould Axelrod calls Plath's 'cryptograms' as her need for duplicity is transposed into dramatic game-playing. Drama thus provided a form in which the desire to 'tell the truth' and simultaneously to 'camouflage' through disguise could be realized (Axelrod, 1990: 143–4). This is, amongst other things, a text that contains a thinly veiled dramatization of the relationship between Plath and Hughes, particularly as writers. In a journal entry dated 9 August 1957, Plath talks about the progression of her verse drama: 'a clear blue-white morning about 9.30, and me coldly and gingerly writing about 14 lines on my long lumbering dialogue verse poem with two people arguing over a Ouija board' (Plath, 1982: 170). During this period Plath and Hughes were having a seven-week 'writing vacation' on Cape Cod. Hughes was enjoying considerable literary success with several publications and prizes: his *The Hawk in the Rain* had been selected by the Poetry Book Society as its Autumn choice and his poems had also appeared in numerous periodicals. Plath, however, remained relatively unpublished. In the journal entry in which she discusses 'Dialogue over a Ouija Board' she refers to 'Ted's success, which I must cope with this fall with my job, loving it, and him to have it, but feeling so wishfully that I could make both of us feel better by having it with him' (172).

Given this context, the argumentative form of the 'Dialogue' becomes significant as the text dramatizes the tensions and conflicts between the two writers, each competing for supremacy. Throughout the dialogue the two players, Leroy and Sibyl, are engaged in a gendered power struggle, conducted on the grounds of language. The aptly named Leroy, 'the King', masters the scene, endeavouring to control and to direct the proceedings. Sibyl, the antique virgin of classical mythology, is initially more passive and cautious. The Ouija board becomes a battleground as Sibyl and Leroy each try to appropriate Pan, and the power over language that the spirit represents:

> *Do you know how my father is?*
> LEROY: He's left
> For Yes, dragging our fingers after.
> SIBYL: *How*
> *Is he, then?* He spells. I-N. He'll lift
> The glass yet as he glides. P-L-U-
> M-A-G-E. In plumage. I'd never have thought
> To say that. That must be his: his word. (278)

To Leroy's mounting irritation, Sibyl races to put words together, experimenting with different combinations of letters as she endeavours to decipher the unusual combinations and syntax:

> O-F-R. He'll
> Jog off in jabberwocky now and lose us
> ... A-W-W. He's gone off: what English
> Word wears two w's? O-R. Or what?
> M-S. Manuscript? He stops. (279)

She responds to the patterns of letters as a riddle to be solved and, for the most part, appears to enjoy the game of word-play and association.

The Carrollian reference is an apt one: in *Through the Looking-Glass*, the nonsense poem 'Jabberwocky' features in the philosophical debate about language between Alice and Humpty Dumpty, who tells her that 'when *I* use a word ... it means just what I choose it to mean – neither more nor less'; and that, moreover, he can 'explain all the poems that ever were invented – and a good many that haven't been invented yet' (Carroll, 1992: 163–4). Whereas Alice's response to nonsense is sensuous ('It seems very pretty . . . but it's *rather* hard to understand!) Humpty Dumpty's interventions are authoritative and interpretative, directed towards definition, the fixing of meaning, arresting the play of the signifier. Plath's text, where Sibyl plays Alice to Leroy's Humpty Dumpty, echoes Carroll's interest in the hermeneutic flexibility of language ('the question is . . . whether you *can* make words mean so many different things'), as well as his concern with questions of linguistic ownership and authority: 'The question is . . . which is to be master – that's all' (Carroll, 1992: 163). Leroy's interventions, like Humpty Dumpty's, are, in short, patriarchal. He becomes exasperated with Sibyl and corrects her, appropriating and codifying the letters of the Ouija board text:

> You persist in spelling half hints
> Out of a wholeness. Worms, not wings is what
> Pan said. A plumage of raw worms. (279)

There is something distinctly Hughesian about the language Leroy employs, both in terms of the nature references and in the violence of his images. Indeed, the dialogue as it develops between Leroy and Sibyl explores the role of the author and stages debates between the masculine and feminine in language. Leroy is the kind of writer Roland Barthes identifies as the *écrivant* and Sybil is Barthes' *écrivain*. As Susan Sellers summarizes, the difference is between the writer 'who believes they have something to say and uses language to say this as unequivocally as possible' and the writer 'who explores the potential of language to generate (multiple) meanings' (1991: 7). The text that Leroy produces is *lisible*, or 'readable', as the meaning is clearly spelt out and 'the role of the reader is reduced to passively following the words on the page' (l. 284). Sibyl, however, produces a *scriptable* or 'writable' text, 'since the participation of its reader is actively sought to co-produce meanings' (1991: 7).

The conventional equation of masculinity with logic, rationality and order (i.e. mind and intellect) and femininity with illogicality, intuition, chaos and hysteria (i.e. the body or physicality) informs the text and is debated within it. It is language, ultimately, which constructs and controls Leroy and Sibyl as subjects. Both are writers for whom words are tools, yet both are also 'written', entangled in the gendered vocabularies they perpetuate. If anyone has the upper hand in this drama, it is neither Leroy nor Sibyl, but Pan. The spirit medium brings Leroy and Sibyl to blows in his refusal to

be controlled by either of them. Although it is possible to read
'Dialogue over a Ouija Board' as a dramatization of the fraught
relations between Plath and Hughes as competing writers, the text
uses the dramatic medium to escape from the conventional parameters
of autobiography as well as from the formal restrictions of poetry.

Underpinning all this, I believe, is an experience which challenged
any notion of unitary subjectivity. At the time of the composition
of the 'Dialogue', Plath feared that she was pregnant. As she saw
it, this represented a threat to her autonomy as a writer. Her description of the experience is in the same journal entry as the reference
to 'Dialogue', dated 9 August 1957:

> I have never in my life, except that deadly summer of 1953, &
> fall, gone through such a black lethal two weeks. I couldn't write
> a word about it, although I did in my head. The horror, day by
> day more sure, of being pregnant ... the idea of 20 years of
> misery and a child being unloved, as it inadvertently, through
> our fault, killed our spiritual and psychic selves by freezing them
> into a stasis out of the necessity of sacrificing everything to earning
> money. (Plath, 1982: 171)

'Dialogue over a Ouija Board' was produced immediately afterwards:
a text in which we see a couple divided by Pan, 'A sort of psychic
bastard / Sprung to being on our wedding night / Nine months
too soon for comfort' (280). The 'Dialogue' reads as a staging of
the unresolved conflict between the mind and body, with Pan, the
threatening muse – also a foetus – at its centre. Leroy's paternal
simile is thus particularly telling (284):

> Do we have to battle
> Like rival parents over a precocious
> Child to see which one of us can call
> Pan's prowess our own creation, and not the other's
> Work at all.

When Sibyl smashes the glass shortly afterwards, in a symbolic self-
administered abortion, she destroys the divisive third party and
the two speakers achieve a modicum of union. Yet this involves
the destruction of Pan, in a dramatic and violent gesture. Plath
feared that pregnancy would 'end me, probably Ted, and our possible impregnable togetherness' (171).

'Dialogue over a Ouija Board' can be seen as a rehearsal for *Three Women*, Plath's only other verse drama which was written after her experience of two births and a miscarriage. However, the first thing I wish to note about *Three Women* is that it was a piece written for radio, a factor influencing both its poetic and its dramatic form. Its writing marked a transition for Plath, in that, according to Hughes, it was at this point that 'she began to compose her poems to be read aloud' (Plath, 1971: 7). Her involvement in radio broadcasting through the BBC's Third Programme encouraged and sustained this attention to the oral dimension of her poetry. But the practice of using the author as reader also tended to foster identifications between the poet and the poem, equating the voice of one with that of the other. If *Three Women* is placed in the context of this kind of broadcast poetry, then the fact that it was written for, and delivered by, three voices other than that of the author herself differentiates it as a poem from the confessional mode of her other work. Although there is a significant autobiographical element to the text, its conditions of production mean that it is refracted through the voices of its performers rather than being identified with the 'voice' of its author. However, the initial impact of the play is effected through another characteristic of the medium: its erasure of the visible bodies of speakers and performers even as it insists upon the immediacy and tangibility of the speaking voice. Here, the three characters are literally 'talking heads 'as the medium of radio removes the women's bodies and pregnancies from sight.

This strategy needs to be read in its historical context. *Three Women* presents the woman's testimony of her own experience of pregnancy in opposition to developments in antenatal care and medical practice at the time of writing. In the background are the radical changes to American and British maternity care in the 1950s, as childbirth became increasingly medicalized and institutionalized, and antenatal technology became increasingly sophisticated. These developments accelerated the transformation of the pregnant body into an object of scrutiny and surveillance. As Ann Oakley observes, women became the 'objects of mechanical surveillance rather than the recipients of antenatal care': hence, 'the mother vanishes and the focus is on the child/fœtus' (Oakley, 1986: 194, 214). Paradoxically, by rendering invisible the pregnant body which is the subject of a medical scrutiny that erases the identity of the mother, *Three Women* seeks to recover the voice of the mother herself.

In her choice of a home birth and community midwife care, Plath differed from her subjects in *Three Women*, all of whom have hospital births. Although the three voices draw on Plath's own varied experiences of childbirth and miscarriage, echoing her autobiographical accounts, the hospital setting is also a distancing device. The mother exists as a predetermined role which each of the women is forced to inhabit so that the mother, as an identity, is a critical part of the 'other' which the subject will be to others. The institutional, socially constructed mother role which each of the three women feels compelled to perform is passive, nurturing and self-abnegating. For the First Voice, the adoption of the role is involuntary. She sees herself as subject to, rather than in control of, nature and emphasizes her passivity and inactivity: 'I am ready' and 'I am used. I am drummed into use' indicate her acquiescence in a predetermined role (Plath, 1981: 180). In lines which echo the effect of disembodiment produced by the radio medium, she describes her body as if she stood outside it: 'Swabbed and lurid with disinfectants, sacrificial' (179). An autobiographical element is evident. The First Voice's description of the birth directly echoes Plath's letter to her mother describing the birth of her son:

Who is he, this blue, furious boy,
Shiny and strange, as if he has hurled from a star? (181)

Then, in her letter she writes, 'at 5 minutes to 12 . . . this great bluish, glistening boy shot out onto the bed in a tidal wave of water' (Plath, 1975: 443).

However, whereas Plath's letters are largely celebratory, clearly written for her mother, the tone here is ambivalent. Towards the end of the play, for example, the First Voice describes her responses to her child as she looks through the hospital window at the rows of cots. Although there is a degree of awe in her voice as she surveys 'these miraculous ones, / These pure, small images', a sense of detachment persists as she automatically responds to her baby's demands:

He is turning to me like a little, blind, bright plant.
One cry. It is the hook I hang on.
And I am a river of milk.
I am a warm hill. (183)

This is typical of the shifts of register which characterize the verbal text: moving between personalized utterance and a kind of choric commentary, the 'I' of the text is dispersed across a non-linear succession of shifting and contradictory metaphors. Even as the verbal text circulates around the invisible maternal body, the body itself exceeds and evades linguistic and poetic definition. The repetitive approximations of metaphor dramatize the relation of the female subject to her body in terms of the dialectic of embodiment and disembodiment that is central to the play:

> There is no miracle more cruel than this
> I am dragged by the horses, the iron hooves . . .
> I am the center of an atrocity.
> What pains, what sorrows must I be mothering?
>
> Can such innocence kill and kill? It milks my life.
> The trees wither in the street. the rain is corrosive . . .
> I shall be a sky and a hill of good: O let me be! (180)

The Second Voice is unable to fulfil the mother role, as she describes the trauma of miscarriage. As the play develops the Second Voice is constantly shifting from self-recrimination ('Is this the one sin then, this old dead love of death?') to anger at the figure of Mother Nature who is conceived as a witch-like, monster mother:

> Old winter-face, old barren one, old time bomb.
> Men have used her meanly. She will eat them.
> Eat them, eat them, eat them in the end. (181)

Note the shift whereby the Second Voice implicates herself as the monster: 'I am accused . . . / I am a garden of black and red agonies. I drink them' (182) and then conjures the figure of the 'other' in the form of the 'dark earth', mother nature. Her horror and guilt is displaced into the third person as she distances herself from the evil mother representation: 'she is the vampire of us all' (181).

Throughout the dialogue, motherly virtue is associated with passivity and conformity; badness is associated with deformity and infertility. For the Third Voice, pregnancy unplanned; she is resistant to the institutional mother role, but is particularly conscious of the split between self and other which pregnancy creates. 'I wasn't ready', she states, but 'the face / went on shaping itself with love,

as if I was ready' (178). After the birth of her daughter, she distances herself from the 'red, terrible girl' (182). But the institutional
mother role is one that the speaker cannot easily abandon. As she
leaves the hospital, the Third Voice mourns her loss of identity:

> There is very little to go into my suitcase.
> There are the clothes of a fat woman I do not know. (184)

Throughout the play, then, the three voices describe motherhood
in terms of trauma and crisis. The dialogue is not a straightforward
celebration of pregnancy or childbirth, but voices the conflicts and
ambivalence which, for Plath, constitute maternal discourse. In an
analysis which is particularly pertinent here, Ann Kaplan identifies
'three main kinds of discursive mothers':

> The mother in her socially constructed, institutional role (the
> mother that girls are socialised to become, and that historical or
> real mothers strive to embody); Second, the mother in the un-
> conscious – the mother through whom the subject is constituted . . .
> and third, the mother in fictional representations who combines
> the institutionally positioned mother and the unconscious mother.
> (Kaplan, 1992: 6–7)

This tripartite model is integral to a text which itself gives voice to
a female trinity, as its speakers adopt and discard shifting maternal
roles. If the female trio is an archetypal dramatic structure (one
immediately thinks of Chekhov's three sisters and Shakespeare's weird
ones, Lear's daughters, Beckett's *Come and Go*), it provides Plath
with a means of splitting, redefining and reinventing the 'autobiographical I'. But perhaps the three-part structure also offers a way
of reading *Three Women* as an autobiographical text. Staging three
voices which further divide and multiply the more one reads or
listens, *Three Women* reshapes the raw material of maternal experience as an (at least) triple-tongued discourse, ranging between Self,
Other and somewhere in between, evading the autobiographical binary
of truth versus fiction while remaining true to that experience. In
both of her forays into the dramatic medium, Plath reinvented her
marital and maternal experience by substituting the mask for the
mirror, but also took the opportunity to rehearse, to play with, the
textual production of subjectivity.

References

Axelrod, S. G. *Sylvia Plath: The Wound and the Cure of Words* (Baltimore: Johns Hopkins University Press, 1990)

Carroll, L. *Through the Looking Glass*, in D. Gray (ed.) *Alice in Wonderland*, 2nd edn (New York: W. W. Norton, [1871] 1992)

Kaplan, A. *Motherhood and Representation: The Mother in Popular Culture* (London: Routledge, 1992)

Oakley, A. *The Captured Womb: A History of the Medical Care of Pregnant Women* (Oxford: Blackwell, 1986)

Orr, P. (ed.) *The Poet Speaks* (London: Routledge & Kegan Paul, 1966)

Plath, S. *Winter Trees* (London: Faber and Faber, 1971)

—— *Letters Home* (ed.) A. Schrober Plath (London: Faber and Faber, 1975)

—— *Collected Poems* (ed.) T. Hughes (London: Faber and Faber, 1981)

—— *The Journals of Sylvia Plath* (eds) T. Hughes and F. McCullough (New York: Valentine Books, 1982)

Rose, J. *The Haunting of Sylvia Plath* (London: Virago, 1991)

Sellers, S. *Language and Sexual Difference: Feminist Writing in France* (Basingstoke: Macmillan, 1991)

Williams, R. *Drama from Ibsen to Brecht*, rev. edn (London: The Hogarth Press, 1987)

21

Double Vision: Mother(s) in Simone de Beauvoir's *Memoirs of a Dutiful Daughter* and *A Very Easy Death*

Alison Fell

Motherhood, maternity and the mother–daughter relationship haunt much of Simone de Beauvoir's writing – fictional, philosophical and autobiographical. This is true not only in terms of the institution of motherhood which Beauvoir demystifies, but also in relation to her own mother, Françoise de Beauvoir. In Beauvoir's fiction, the female characters are often involved in painful and oppressive mother–daughter relationships which repeat a pattern of conflict marked by jealous rivalry, claustrophobic possessiveness and lack of real exchange or communication. This pattern follows that of Beauvoir's own problematic mother–daughter relationship as it is delineated in her autobiographical writing. Even in *The Second Sex* (1949), which, as a philosophical text, claims to base its conclusions about mothers and motherhood on sociological research and objective reasoning rather than on subjective experience, it can be argued that Beauvoir's discussion of mothers and daughters feeds not only on her existentially grounded beliefs about the socially constructed nature of maternity and femininity, but also on her understanding of her own experiences as a daughter.

The mothers who appear in various guises in Beauvoir's fictional and non-fictional texts are characterized by a complex intermeshing of her philosophical beliefs and personal experiences, via what can be termed public and private maternal narratives. This blurring of public and private in relation to the mother not only marks the ways in which Beauvoir represents 'Françoise de Beauvoir' in her writing, it also marks the ways in which she represents herself as a daughter. Consequently, it is possible to distinguish an underlying tension in the texts between, on the one hand, the 'Mother' in her socially constructed, institutional role and, on the other hand, Beauvoir's painful and problematic personal relationship to her 'mother'. Beauvoir's autobiographical representations of her mother are not singular or stable visions, but shifting representations that blur the boundaries between public and private, between 'Mother' and mother. A comparison of Beauvoir's first volume of her autobiography, *Memoirs of a Dutiful Daughter* (1958), with *A Very Easy Death* (1964) (a short narrative recounting her mother's death from cancer), reveals the highly complex and inherently fragile nature of Beauvoir's maternal constructions. This chapter will argue that if the *Memoirs* recount the story of the birth of an intellectual through a singular vision of the mother, *A Very Easy Death* traces the unbecoming of that self through a blurred, double vision of the mother.

In many ways, the 'Françoise de Beauvoir' of the *Memoirs* resembles the numerous 'case-studies' of mothers used to justify Beauvoir's arguments in *The Second Sex* The biographical passages detailing Françoise de Beauvoir's childhood and adolescence, for example, provide the reader with a quasi-sociological and seemingly objective account of a middle-class French woman's psychological development. Here, Françoise's past life is used, at least partly, to explain her present character. Her unquestioning religious beliefs, it is suggested, stem from her convent education where the nuns' warm and maternal care provided her with the love and security she did not find with her own family. Similarly, her snobbish obsession with social conventions is related to her inexperience and insecurity as a young married woman who had to cope with her husband's unfamiliar social sphere. From this perspective, 'Françoise de Beauvoir' is examined and constructed in the text as a subject-in-history. The description of her neck as 'squeezed into whalebone collars' (Beauvoir, 1958: 51; 1959: 37) seems to be emblematic of her similarity to the other women in *The Second Sex*. In existential terms, she is a willing victim of society's relegation of women to the place of the Other. Split by her 'bad faith' into a contradictory and divided subjectivity where she must deny her authentic self in order to conform to the demands of an ideologically constructed femininity, Françoise shows all the signs of the obsessive and smothering love towards her daughter that are denounced in the section on motherhood in *The Second Sex*:

[The mother] tries obstinately to checkmate the girl's will to escape; she cannot bear to have her double become an other. . . .

> She is doubly jealous; of the world, which takes her daughter
> from her, and of her daughter, who in conquering part of the
> world robs her of it. (1949: 381; 1972: 534)

In her narrative of a daughter's escape from an over-possessive and
jealous mother, the mother–daughter relationship Beauvoir inscribes
in the *Memoirs* fits smoothly into the theoretical paradigms set up
in *The Second Sex*.

However, despite passages resembling the detached, existential
analysis of *The Second Sex*, from a narrative point of view the character
of Françoise de Beauvoir in the *Memoirs* is principally established
in terms of negative juxtaposition with her daughter or with her
husband, rather than in terms of an individual female subject in
her own right. As Laurie Corbin points out in her study *The Mother
Mirror* (1996), by locating the character 'Françoise de Beauvoir' as
her daughter's negative other, the identity of the character 'Simone
de Beauvoir' is established as that which her mother is not: non-
bourgeois, non-religious, non-feminine and non-maternal. The
biographical description of Françoise at the beginning of the *Memoirs*
functions more as a means of distancing the narrator from, and
therefore ironizing, the young Simone's initially enthusiastic adoption
of her mother's femininity than as a means of exploring her mother's
individual subjectivity.

Françoise de Beauvoir is evoked throughout the *Memoirs* as a woman
who has uncritically embraced patriarchal constructions of femininity
and maternity and oppressively attempts to impose them on her
daughter:

> And that is how we lived, the two of us, in a kind of symbiosis.
> Without striving to imitate her, I was conditioned by her. She
> inculcated in me a sense of duty as well as teaching me un-
> selfishness and austerity. My father was not averse to the limelight,
> but I learnt from Mama to keep in the background, to control
> my tongue, to moderate my desires, to say and do exactly what
> ought to be said and done. (1958: 56; 1959: 41)

The reader, guided by the voice of the present narrator, thus ap-
plauds Simone's rebellions against the claustrophobically stifling and
carefully regulated mother–daughter relationship and shares the young
Simone's growing horror of the 'revolting fate' her mother comes
to represent (1958: 512; 1959: 360). The figure of the mother in

the *Memoirs* acts, therefore, as a kind of touchstone for the reader to identify the different stages of Simone's journey of liberation from her bourgeois past. Beauvoir's representation of Françoise de Beauvoir may masquerade as objective, sociological description, but in the text it serves mainly to give substance and definition to the birth of Simone de Beauvoir as a writer and intellectual.

If the *Memoirs* place Françoise de Beauvoir in a socio-historical context, this context is limited to her maternal role. Ironically, Beauvoir can be seen to fall into the same ideological trap she was attempting to demystify in *The Second Sex*: that of allowing women no identity other than that of mother. It is this subsuming of female identity into maternity that Julia Kristeva attacks in her essay 'Stabat Mater' (1977). In its place, Kristeva calls for a discourse of motherhood that is not based upon the enforcement of women's repudiation of the 'other woman' – of, in other words, her mother. Such a discourse would allow for relation to our mothers as singular subjects, located in their specificity and their difference from the absolute woman.

In the *Memoirs*, Beauvoir's representation of Françoise de Beauvoir seems far from answering Kristeva's plea to locate women in their specificity rather than exclusively as mothers. Françoise becomes, in effect, not *a* or *my* mother, but *the* Mother – the mother of *The Second Sex* who seems to symbolize, for Beauvoir, the oppressive bourgeois Catholic femininity she so detested. Beauvoir's transformation of her mother into an inflexible signifier in this way sacrifices her mother's individual subjectivity, and instead functions to give voice to her own difference, to her own identity. This, then, can be categorized as a 'public' maternal narrative which succeeds in merging public and private mother(s) into a seamless and unified whole.

In *A Very Easy Death*, however, the singular vision of the mother begins to fall apart. This is partly, perhaps, a result of the differing foci of the two texts, and Beauvoir's differing motivations for writing them. If *Memoirs of a Dutiful Daughter* follows, to a large extent, the familiar autobiographical tradition of spiritual quest, *A Very Easy Death* is more difficult to categorize. Although unquestionably autobiographical, it bears little resemblance to the more 'public' autobiographical narratives with their long descriptions of foreign visits and political activism of the successful Beauvoir–Sartre couple produced during the 1960s. In *All Said and Done* (1972), her final volume of autobiography, Beauvoir evokes the therapeutic and cathartic value that the act of writing *A Very Easy Death* held for her:

Before actually setting down to it I had never thought of writing *A Very Easy Death*. At those times when my life has been
hard for me, jotting words down on paper – even if no one is to
read what I have written – has given me the same comfort that
prayer gives to the believer: by means of language I transcend
my particular case and enter into communication with the whole
of mankind. (1972: 136; 1977: 134–5)

While *Memoirs of a Dutiful Daughter* was written from a stable, controlling and already ordered perspective, *A Very Easy Death* was a
desperate attempt to create and impose order, through writing, on
the disorder that characterizes the author's reaction to her mother's
death. In *All Said and Done*, Beauvoir admits that her narrative did
not, in fact, provide the stabilising and ordering influence she desired, but rather left her with a sense of the limitations of language
as a means of imposing order and meaning:

I went through phases when the idea of holding a pen sickened
me. After I had finished *A Very Easy Death* I felt utterly inca-
pable of writing; I had felt an irresistible urge to write this account
but when I had finished it literature seemed to me pointless.
(1972: 151; 1977: 150)

One of the reasons *A Very Easy Death* leaves Beauvoir with this
sense of futility is the fact that her attempt to re-write her mother
as the 'Françoise de Beauvoir' of the *Memoirs* fails.

To some extent, the two narratives echo each other in their representations of the mother. The second section of *A Very Easy Death*,
for example, consists of a mini-biography of her mother, similar in
style to the biographical section in the *Memoirs*. Again, there is an
attempt to explain the mother's present character in terms of her
past. The picture the narrator paints of her mother is a more detailed,
sympathetic and positive one than that of the *Memoirs*, but is similarly structured according to Beauvoir's existential assumptions about
the nature of female identity:

Thinking against oneself often bears fruit; but with my mother
it was another question again – she lived against herself. She
had appetites in plenty; she spent all her strength in repressing
them and she underwent this denial in anger. In her childhood
her body, her heart and her mind had been squeezed into an

armour of principles and prohibitions. She had been taught to pull the laces hard and tight herself. A full-blooded, spirited woman lived on inside her, but a stranger to herself, deformed and mutilated. (1964: 61; 1969: 38)

Here, although her mother is portrayed as a victim rather than a perpetrator of patriarchally constructed femininity, we can still recognize a state of 'bad faith' emanating from her participation in the socially constructed gender norms.

However, the other sections of *A Very Easy Death*, which in many ways dominate the narrative, consist of detailed descriptions of the progression of her mother's illness. With a detached and strangely fascinated eye, the narrator describes the deterioration of her mother's body:

On the left there was an intravenous drip, connected with Maman's arm. From her nose there emerged a tube of transparent plastic that passed through some complicated apparatus and ended in a jar. Her nose was pinched and her face had shrunk even more: it had the saddest air of submission . . . the nurse put a thin tube to her mouth with the other end in a glass of water. I was fascinated by the sucking motion, at once avid and restrained, of her lip, with its faint downy shadow, that rounded just as it had rounded in my childhood whenever Maman was cross or embarrassed. (1964: 38–9; 1969: 25)

The fascination partly stems, it would seem, from the change from the maternal body of the past, immediately associated with the oppressive maternal presence of her childhood, and the deteriorating maternal body of the present. At times, Beauvoir cries out in horror at the ways in which her mother's body is objectified by what Michel Foucault (1989) has termed the 'medical gaze', rendering her mother powerless and robbing her of any agency. Beauvoir writes:

This body, suddenly reduced by her capitulation to being a body and nothing more, hardly differed at all from a corpse – a poor defenceless carcass turned and manipulated by professional hands. (Beauvoir, 1964: 26; 1969: 18)

As *A Very Easy Death* progresses, and the narrator obsessively focuses on the body of her dying mother, Françoise de Beauvoir seems to increasingly become 'the patient' rather than 'the Mother'. In the different context of the clinic, class issues cease to have the same value, and the mother–daughter relationship undergoes profound changes. Her mother's religious beliefs and social prejudices have less and less significance as the illness develops:

> Her illness had quite broken the shell of her prejudices and her pretensions; perhaps because she no longer needed these defences. (1964: 85; 1969: 53)

Roles are exchanged as Françoise comes to depend upon her daughter like a child depends upon its mother: for food, love and knowledge. It is now the daughter who must decide whether or not to censor the truth in order to protect her mother's psychological well-being. The differences between, in Foucauldian terms, the discursive context of the clinic and that of the *Memoirs*, where Françoise is represented in terms of a bourgeois wife and mother, produce conflicting and unstable representations of Françoise de Beauvoir in *A Very Easy Death*. In the biographical section, and to some extent in the final analytical sections describing the aftermath of the mother's death, there is an attempt to construct the mother as a stable signifier as in the *Memoirs*, but this clashes in the text with the long and painful descriptions of Françoise as a patient suffering at the hands of the doctors.

The changes in the representation of the mother in *A Very Easy Death* are mirrored by a corresponding change in the representation of the daughter-narrator. Beauvoir describes, for example, an uncontrollable outburst of grief that surprises her by its intensity:

> Suddenly, at eleven, an outburst of tears that almost degenerated into hysteria. Amazement. When father died I did not cry at all. I had said to my sister: 'It will be the same for Maman'. I had understood all my sorrows until that night: even when they flowed over my head I recognized myself in them. This time my despair escaped from my control: someone other than myself was weeping in me. (1964: 43; 1969: 29)

Beauvoir's detached, philosophical understanding of her mother and their relationship – her singular, public vision – breaks down, and as a result she no longer recognizes herself. The stability of the 'writing-self' is challenged as the mother fails to fit comfortably into the discursive paradigms set up in the *Memoirs*. As a result, Beauvoir's own identity is no longer clearly defined in terms of opposition with the mother; rather, she seems to experience a merging of their subjectivities. The basis of her own subjectivity, it seems, is intimately related to her understanding of that of her mother:

> I talked to Sartre about my mother's mouth as I had seen it that morning. And he told me that my own mouth was not obeying me any more: I had put Maman's mouth on my own face and in spite of myself, I copied its movements. Her whole person, her whole being, was concentrated there, and compassion wrung my heart. (1964: 43–4; 1969: 28)

Once the representation of Françoise de Beauvoir becomes that of a patient, of a desexed suffering individual, she can no longer be confined to the role of the 'Mother', and this rocks the very core of her daughter's understanding of her own identity.

In *All Said and Done*, Beauvoir narrates a number of dreams she has after her mother has died. In one dream, her mother appears as 'a young and beautiful figure without a face' (1972: 118; 1977: 117) who is at the edge of a large lake, which Beauvoir recognizes as the lake at the house of her lover, Nelson Algren. She is unable to cross the lake in order to reach her mother, although it is essential that she does reach her in order to warn her of an impending danger. A second dream is described in more detail:

> I found myself with Sartre and many others on an enormous platform set up in the middle of a square. A kind of meeting or a ceremony of a political nature was being held. Suddenly I realized that I was on the very edge a hundred feet above the ground . . . I felt that I was going to fall: I tried to cling to one of the widely-spaced pillars and to creep back, but the slightest movement was dangerous. At that moment, a woman dressed in white – perhaps a wedding dress – did fall, turning over and over and hitting the ground with terrible force. 'It is my mother', I said to myself. (1972: 126; 1977: 125)

In the dreams, Françoise de Beauvoir appears as a faceless young woman, either before, or at the time of, her marriage, rather than the older more familiar maternal figure of the autobiographical writing. Beauvoir is always separated from her, despite sensing that this younger version of her mother is in danger. While Beauvoir is freely acting as a sexually emancipated woman, in the case of the first dream at her lover's house, or as a political activist, in the case of the political rally in the second dream, her mother is unable to join her, already condemned, it would seem, to an anonymous life as a wife and mother. It can be argued that these dreams mirror Beauvoir's awareness, albeit unconscious, of her inability in her autobiographical texts to represent her mother fully within the confines of her own narrative strategy.

Françoise de Beauvoir's identity as a singular subject, who is not simply the negative other of her daughter's own identity as a liberated intellectual, only makes a vague, shadowy appearance in her dreams and rarely appears in her autobiographical writing. In other words, whilst the public, maternal narrative tends to dominate the private one, Beauvoir's partial awareness of the limitations of the singular vision of her mother is also responsible for the blurred, double vision of the mother in *A Very Easy Death*. Françoise de Beauvoir may remain, for the most part, restricted to the maternal role, but it is the cracks in this representation which give *A Very Easy Death* much of its power. Faced with her mother's body in a differing discursive context, the public Mother and private mother ceases to merge into a unified, controllable whole, and as a result the daughter-narrator loses control over the representation of Françoise de Beauvoir's life.

References

Beauvoir, S. *Memoirs of a Dutiful Daughter (Mémoires d'une Jeune Fille Rangée)*, trans. J. Kirkup (Harmondsworth: Penguin, [1958] 1959)
—— *A Very Easy Death (Une Mort Très Douce)*, trans. P. O'Brian (London: Penguin, [1964] 1969)
—— *The Second Sex*, trans. H. M. Parshley (Harmondsworth: Penguin, [1949] 1972)
—— *All Said and Done*, trans. P. O'Brian (Harmondsworth: Penguin, [1972] 1977)
Corbin, L. *The Mother Mirror: Self-Representation and the Mother-Daughter in Colette, Simone de Beauvoir and Marguerite Duras* (New York: Peter Lang, 1996)
Foucault, M. *The Birth of the Clinic* (London: Routledge, 1989)
Kristeva, J. 'Stabat Mater', in *Histoires d'amour* (Paris: Denoël, [1977] 1992)

22
The Autobiographical Voice in Lily Braun's Fiction

Nicola Brice

Lily Braun's unshakeable belief in the supreme importance of the experience of motherhood is central to her fictional and autobiographical writing. The theme of motherhood thus provides an interconnection between the two literary forms. This study will compare Braun's treatment of the concept and experience of motherhood in her autobiographical journals, *Memoiren einer Sozialistin I / II* (*Memoirs of a Socialist I / II*, 1908, 1911), with her portrayal of a literary mother in her fictional novel *Die Liebesbriefe der Marquise* (*The Marquise's Love Letters*, 1912). By examining the interplay between Braun's autobiographical and fictional work, new dimensions within her fiction emerge.

The exploration of blurred boundaries between autobiography and fiction and the deconstruction of autobiographies as objective accounts of (male) histories are recurrent themes within recent studies of autobiography. Barbara Kosta succinctly summarizes the emergent critical consensus:

> Despite their different approaches, contemporary critics agree that autobiography has abdicated its function as the storehouse of truth. Instead, autobiography is widely regarded as the site of self-invention and self-enactment. (1994: 187)

My reading of Braun's journals both endorses and is informed by the acceptance of the autobiographical document as a place of self-creation and the fallibility of autobiographical truth. I read Braun's journals as autobiography in the sense that they function as an act of self-representation, enabling Braun to restructure retrospectively her political beliefs and selectively relate details of her practical campaigns.

My comparison, however, is concerned less with the fictional element of Braun's journals than with the presence of an autobiographical voice in her fictional novel. The recent rediscovery of Braun as a prominent feminist socialist of the *fin-de-siècle* has foregrounded her autobiographical writing.[1] Her fiction has been dismissed as mere *Trivialliteratur*.[2] By juxtaposing the relationship between the autobiographical journals and the fictional novel, this chapter will highlight the significance of Braun's fiction within the wider context of her work and her philosophy of motherhood. The chapter is divided into three sections. In the first, I discuss Braun's concept of motherhood in her journals; the second section addresses her fictional portrayal of a mother in the novel; and in the final section, the presence of an autobiographical voice in the novel is explored.

*　　*　　*

Informed by her own experience as a mother, in the journals Braun attempts to clarify her political position, above all with regard to her understanding of motherhood. The main features of Braun's concept of motherhood in the journals concern her belief in motherhood as a superior experience, the conflict between the mother and the working woman, and her sympathy and admiration for unmarried mothers.

It is the experience of motherhood that forms the core of Braun's political ideology. Alfred Meyer rightly points to the quintessential importance of Braun's concept of motherhood within her political vision: 'Underlying all her ideological positions was her belief in the uniqueness of the feminine experience, especially the close bond between mother and child' (1985: xiv).[3] In her journals, Braun passionately asserts: 'Maternal love is the strongest feeling in the world, stronger than sexual passion, stronger than hunger' (Braun, 1911: 421, trans. Meyer, 1985: 127).[4] Her bold comparison with sexual passion suggests not only that motherhood brings fulfilment, but implies that by forfeiting this fundamental experience a woman will be unfulfilled. Her attitude could be read within the context of the time as reactionary. The affirmation of motherhood endorses the ruling nineteenth-century ideology of a biologically determined calling providing the most worthy, virtuous occupation to which a woman could devote herself. However, Braun's picture of motherhood broke with the capitalist family structure with the mother at its centre. She emphatically encouraged women to enter the work-ing world, if they so desired, but without abandoning their identity as mothers. She believed that the qualities inherent in mothering, such as altruism, tolerance and compassion, would enrich the public sphere.

In her journals, Braun debated how the two roles of mother and working woman could effectively be combined. Dual participation by women in production and in reproduction was to be achieved by the destruction of the monogamous family. Braun blamed the family unit, a product of capitalist opportunism, for its oppression of women, arguing that marriage deromanticized love and repressed women who were tied to domestic duties and had no legal rights in the marriage contract:

> Marriage seemed to me like a moralistic old spinster who con-stantly spoils the fun of young unbridled passion with her preaching. Love needs a holiday mood, marriage needs the every-day. Love is an intoxication, marriage is sober. Love demands freedom, marriage dependency. One partner has to subordinate him/herself to the other, if the peace of the house is to be pre-served. Wherever subordination enters a loving relationship, love itself disappears. (Braun, 1911: 222–3, trans. N. Brice)[5]

Marriage is presented as an outdated institution that fails to satisfy either partner. As a solution, Braun advocated the idea of a com-munal household with a pooling of chores and a more active male involvement in childrearing. By placing children in progressive day-centres, staffed by trained carers of both sexes, mothers *and* fathers would be liberated to work. In her antipathy towards marriage, Braun sympathized with unmarried mothers and refused to see illegiti-macy as a sign of a corrupt society, even admitting to an envy of unmarried mothers. Illegitimate children for Braun were the product of true love and a union of passion, since they were not the result of economic convenience, they represented the élite of humanity.

In her evaluation of her political position on motherhood, Braun destroys the public/private dichotomy that dominated political think-ing in the early twentieth century. The private and political spheres are unified on two levels. First, her journals reveal how Braun's life is dominated both by her commitment to the public sphere of party politics and to the private sphere of motherhood, and show how the one informs the other to produce a political ideology of motherhood. Second, they reflect how this ideology is strongly influenced by essentially private experiences. Meyer accurately characterizes this dynamic tension between Braun's life experiences and her philosophy of motherhood:

> To separate life from ideology is an altogether artificial separation, particularly in the case of Lily Braun, who very self-consciously sought to live out her philosophic and political convictions, which, in turn, she very self-consciously derived from her own personal experiences. (1985: ix)

Braun's call for children's liberation exemplifies the way in which personal thinking dictated her political thinking. Reacting against her own repressed childhood and adolescence, Braun regarded conventional upbringings with the focus on obedience as soul-destroying. The ideal mother would act as both comforter and comrade whose unselfish love would allow the creativity of her children to develop. Similarly, Braun's altruistic love for her son influenced her belief in the close mother–child bond. Her maternal devotion is accentuated by the fact that her son is the first subject mentioned in her journals:

> This is the most beautiful night of the year, the night when forest and field are a-whisper and a-murmur with old fairy tales, the night, my son, which presented you to me: a mid-summer-night's child, a Sunday child. Eleven years ago it is today. And yet to me it is as if it were only yesterday that you lay at my breast, that you babbled the first words, put your little feet one before the other for the first time. And now you are a big boy! Your childhood is preparing to bid you farewell. (Braun, 1908: 1, trans. Meyer, 1985: 165)[6]

Braun tenderly reflects that her son is no longer solely dependent on her. Thus she reveals her intention to live by her philosophy which required a mother to relinquish control of her child and let him/her make his/her own mistakes in the world.

However, Braun's radical philosophy is undermined by two problematic aspects: one, her ardent desire for a son, rather than a daughter, and two, her essentialist perspective. One could argue that in her preference for a son, Braun was being a realist. As society privileged men, perhaps she felt a son would have to endure less suffering in the pursuit of his personal and political goals. Nevertheless, her overwhelming wish for a son does undermine her liberating arguments for the equality of women. Equally, Braun's essentialism conflicts with her insistence on freedom of choice for women. Since maternal love, in Braun's view, brought out women's innate social instincts, Braun viewed motherhood as a duty not an option. While she did express sympathy for single or infertile women, she maintained that to choose not to have children was a violation of one's femininity. At one point she even stated that a childless woman was a second-class woman. Despite her idealization of the role of the mother, Braun believed that every woman should have the right over her own body. Her fight for abortion to be legalized represents a pragmatic side to her nature, which is easily ignored. As a legislator she achieved little, but as a thinker, she was radically ahead of her time.

*   *   *

The novel *Die Liebesbriefe der Marquise* touches on negative and positive aspects of Braun's philosophy as it is revealed in the journals. It comprises a fictional collection of letters, received by the Marquise of Montjoie, which are predominantly from their addressee's male admirers in France in the second half of the eighteenth century. The letters expose the personal affairs of the Marquise and her associates. The reader is thus confronted with a depiction of motherhood within a specific social dimension, far removed from Braun's own. Important aspects of the maternal question, on which Braun focused in her journals, are nevertheless raised in the novel. Although neither Braun's concern with the conflict between the mother versus the working woman nor her call for children's liberation are of relevance in the context of the novel, the text reflects her belief in the superiority of the mother–child bond and her abhorrence of the institution of marriage, as well as society's hypocritical attitude towards illegitimacy.

According to the letters, the Marquise undergoes a dramatic change in her attitude towards motherhood. Unhappily married to an older man, she had no desire to have children, preferring a frivolous Parisian lifestyle to the domestic sphere. It is the Marquise's husband who reveals her reaction to her first pregnancy: 'I want – I want no child of yours! I am ashamed of this child!' (Braun, 1912: 79, trans. N. Brice).[7] The Marquise's anger does suggest that it is not the idea of a child in itself that revolts her, but the idea of giving birth to her *husband's* child. Here we have a fictional echo of Braun's conviction that motherhood was only a positive experience when the child had been produced out of a genuine love between its parents. Indeed, as the Marquise does not love her husband, she initially abandons her care of their young son until a sense of guilt and duty prompts her to return to him. She claims that the fulfilment of her duty as a mother will shape the content and create the purpose of her life, yet sadly reflects that the task fails to uplift her: 'I don't find the task edifying, it depresses me' (Braun, 1912: 196, trans. N. Brice).[8] Her attitude could not be further removed from Braun's own experience of motherhood. The Marquise's relationship with her son is driven by *Pflicht* (duty) and not *Mutterliebe* (maternal love).

Nevertheless, when she becomes pregnant for the second time, by her lover Friedrich, the Marquise instantly professes to love the child in her womb. Braun's desire for children to be born as products of a love outside of marriage is reflected in the Marquise's happiness. Friedrich himself wishes her to abort this child, and subsequently to leave the Marquis: 'If you bravely sacrifice the first fruit of our love, then we'll still have the sweet present and the hope of a liberating future, in which you will be able to bear happy children' (Braun, 1912: 373, trans. N. Brice).[9] The Marquise's unhappiness about the prospect of becoming a mother for the first time was evidently a result of her unhappy marriage. Ironically echoing Braun's condemnation of the economic foundation of marriage, the Marquis himself sums up the dominant view on marriage commenting that were it a union of love, it would not last. In the novel, illegitimacy is presented as a scandal, yet the Marquise feels no shame at her illegitimate pregnancy and is delighted at the prospect of mothering the child of her one true love. One cannot claim that, in common with Braun, the Marquise admires the concept of illegitimacy, but the birth of an illegitimate child provides her with great happiness. On several occasions, the Marquise shows her contempt for the hypocritical attitude of male-dominated society: she exposes the fact that adultery was acceptable in private, not in public, and that were there to be an illegitimate child, it would be both the mother's responsibility and her shame. Her sympathy towards her husband's illegitimate nephew proves her scorn for society's conventional attitude.

*   *   *

The thematic overlap between the fictional novel and the autobiographical journals indicates an autobiographical basis for Braun's fiction, in which the mutual preoccupation with motherhood is firmly rooted in Braun's personal experience of pregnancy and caring for her child. Both fictional and autobiographical writing reveal the same tensions. In the journals, the integrity of the bold first-person narrator with her radical proposals for a re-evaluation of motherhood is undermined by essentialist beliefs and the desire for a son. Similar paradoxes emerge in the novel. The radicality of the views on motherhood is undermined by the fact that we only ever see motherly affection expressed towards sons and we are presented with male characters who are clearly denied by virtue of their sex, any understanding of the mysteries of pregnancy, childbirth and the role of the mother.

However, the autobiographical voice of the journals is not directly transferred to the character of the Marquise. There are certain similarities: in common with Braun, the fictional Marquise was of aristocratic descent and develops a strong social conscience – but such parallels are insufficient to classify the Marquise as a thinly veiled version of Braun. Moreover, any attempt to identify Braun with the Marquise is simplistic because it neglects the role of the other characters and the structure of the novel. In *The Marquise's Love Letters*, the Marquise herself has no voices; our picture of her is pieced together from the information contained in the letters of her correspondents. Thus Braun's concept of motherhood is refracted through a multiplicity of voices and while her autobiographical voice is undoubtedly present, it cannot be tangibly attached to any one character.

The author's choice of form accounts for significant differences between the exploration of motherhood in the two works. In the journals, a female first-person narrator daringly explores her politics of motherhood; and in the novel, the main female protagonist, the eponymous heroine, does not even speak. The reader's image of the Marquise is constructed entirely by writings of her correspondents, all of whom are men. The Marquise is thus objectified and can only ever be perceived by the reader from a male vantage-point. By silencing the Marquise, Braun silences the female voice in the novel, the female voice that speaks with such power in the journals. However, the deliberate silencing of the Marquise enables the epistolary novel to be read as a critical variation on autobiographical writing by men who imitated the female voice. Just as male novelists appropriated the female voice for their own purpose, so Braun takes on the male voice to expound her radical views. The denial of narrative authority to any one male voice has the advantage of allowing for a more complex image of the Marquise to be constructed. One could also argue that by silencing the Marquise, Braun has chosen to show how history has silenced women. If this is the case, the fiction compliments the autobiography, the one shows how women have been silenced, the other reveals that it is possible for them to speak.

Yet this reading of the novel is problematic as it ignores Braun's awareness of her readers. The novel and the journals were designed to appeal to two different social groups: the journals would have been read primarily by SPD members, whereas the novel was targeted at bourgeois women. It is doubtful whether the bourgeois reader of romantic fiction would have interpreted the novel in such a sophisticated fashion. For early twentieth-century readers, the silencing of the Marquise would not be read as a radical comment on male oppression of women but as an accurate reflection of the inevitable position of women in contemporary society. In another way, Braun's awareness of her reading public could account for her silencing of the Marquise. As the novel would reach a wider audience, Braun perhaps felt compelled to protect herself from condemnation for views which she believed the more enlightened readers of the journals would accept. Had the Marquise spoken for herself, parallels might have been drawn between the fictional character and Braun, which might have prevented publication of the novel. The expression of Braun's radical ideas by male characters would have rendered them less subversive within a male-dominated society and permitted wider dissemination than otherwise possible. For example, the account of the taboo subject of childbirth in the novel, similar in its tone and sentimentality to Braun's account of childbirth in her journals, is voiced by Friedrich. In the mouth of a man it becomes more acceptable to a wider audience. In this way, Braun reframes her autobiographical voice, she does not exclude it.

To conclude, I would argue that Braun's fiction moves beyond its function as a source of income and transgresses the expectations of the narrowly defined category *Trivialliteratur*. Her autobiographical voice manifests itself evidently in the thematic overlap between the journals and the novel. Both fiction and non-fiction reveal the utopian aspects of Braun's personality and politics. The journals are perhaps of more direct relevance to the real lives of her readers, as Braun's utopian ideals are played out against details of her practical campaigns. Ironically, the silencing of the Marquise gives rise to a more radical expression of Braun's ideas. As it operates in a fictional context which bears little relation to the lives of contemporary women, in the novel Braun is able to explore more freely the utopian dimensions of her concept of motherhood, although by doing so she isolates her readers from twentieth-century politics. Nevertheless, Braun's passion, the freeing of women via the reappraisal of motherhood, is as alive in her fiction as it is in her political autobiographical writing.

Notes

1   Born into an aristocratic Prussian family in 1865, Braun came to despise the pretensions of her class and the restricted role it offered women. She gained autonomy working as a Goethe scholar, but declined the offer of a permanent academic career in view of her growing interest in social issues. In 1895, alienated from her family, she joined the German Socialist Party, the SPD. After the death of her first husband, she was married again in 1896 to the socialist Heinrich Braun and gave birth to her only son, Otto, in 1897. The party never fully accepted Braun, due in part to her aristocratic background, but also on account of her conflict of loyalty between her commitment to mainstream party politics in the SPD and her emphasis on the improvement of women's lives outside of the political sphere. Often in defiance of the official party line, Braun campaigned vigorously for women's right to abortion and for the decriminalization of prostitution. She officially resigned from the party in 1915, only a year before her untimely death from a suspected heart attack.
2   Weigel (1984) describes the German category of *Trivialliteratur* which classified women's sentimental popular novels in the nineteenth century as 'fiction that is insignificant and cheap as well as, or because it is, "popular"' (1984: 53).
3   Meyer's approach to Braun is not a literary one. In his excellent biographical study of Braun, Meyer (1985) addresses her political position towards socialism and feminism. He makes reference to her autobiographical journals and her non-fictional writing such as pamphlets, letters, and speeches.
4   'Mutterliebe ist das stärkste Gefühl in der Welt, stärker als die Leidenschaft der Geschlechter, stärker als der Hunger' (Braun, 1911: 421).
5   'Die Ehe kam mir vor wie eine moralische alte Jungfer, die der jungen unbändigen Liebesleidenschaft durch ihre Predigten das Leben ständig vergällt. Die Liebe braucht Festtagsstimmung, die Ehe braucht den Alltag. – Die Liebe ist ein Rausch, die Ehe ist nüchtern. Die Liebe fordert Freiheit,

die Ehe Abhängigkeit. Einer muß sich dem anderen unterordnen, wenn der Frieden des Hauses gewahrt sein soll, wo aber in der Liebe Unterordnung anfängt, flieht sie selbst' (Braun, 1911: 222–3).

6 'Das ist die schönste Nacht des Jahres, die Nacht, in der's in Wald und Feld von alten Märchen rannt und flüsteret, die Nacht, mein Sohn, die dich mir geschenkt: ein Sonnwendkind, ein Sonntagskind. Elf Jahre sind es heute. Ist es mir doch, als wäre es erst gestern gewesen, daß du an meiner Brust gelegen, daß du die ersten Worte lallest, zum erstenmal die Füßchen setztest. Und nun bist du ein großer Junge! Die Kindheit bereitet sich aufs Abschiednehmen vor' (Braun, 1908: 1).

7 'Ich will – ich will kein Kind von Ihnen! Ich schäme mich dieses Kindes!' (Braun, 1912: 79).

8 'Aber die Aufgabe erhebt mich nicht, sie drückt mich nieder' (Braun, 1912: 196).

9 'Opferst Du mutig die erste Frucht unserer Liebe, so bleibt uns die süße Gegenwart und die Hoffnung auf eine befreiende Zukunft, in der Du glückliche Kinder gebären kannst' (Braun, 1912: 373).

References

Braun, L. *Memoiren einer Sozialistin I / II* (*Memoirs of a Socialist I / II*) (Munich: Albert Langen, 1908, 1911)

—— *Die Liebesbriefe der Marquise* (*The Marquise's Love Letters*) (Munich: Albert Langen, 1912)

Meyer, A. G. *The Feminism and Socialism of Lily Braun* (Bloomington: Indiana University Press, 1985)

Kosta, B. *Recasting Autobiography: Women's Counterfictions in Contemporary German Literature and Film* (Cornell: Cornell University Press, 1994)

Weigel, S. '"Woman Begins Relating to Herself": Contemporary German Women's Literature (Part One)', *New German Critique*, 31 (1984) 53–94

23
Autobiography/Auto-mythology: Mina Loy's *Anglo-Mongrels and the Rose*

Alex Goody

The work of Mina Loy, a well-known contemporary of H. D., Gertrude Stein, T. S. Eliot and Ezra Pound (who commended her contribution to modernism), has since fallen into relative obscurity. Perhaps one of the reasons for her fall from prominence, aside from the linguistic, semantic and typographical experimentalism of her writing, is Loy's heterogeneous textual employment of her own life. There is, indeed, an autobiographical aspect in much of Loy's work, in the *Love Songs to Joannes* or the novel *Insel*, for example, but she never offers a straightforward transposition of personal experience nor an assured assumption of an ironically biographical persona.

Loy's depiction and interpretation of her own life can be described as *auto-mythological*, that is, an individualized (and personally applicable) adaptation and conglomeration of an eclectic range of mythical structures and stories which fundamentally refutes the transparent process of personal realisation celebrated in the Romantic artist-hero. This is especially true of her longest poetic work, *Anglo-Mongrels and the Rose* (1923–5), in which Loy recounts the development of a child, Ova, within the context of her mixed genealogical heritage, and cultural and personal experiences. This narrative, in turn, enables an exploration of the evolution of a female artistic consciousness and aesthetic awareness and is crucially structured around a series of key autobiographical incidents reiterated elsewhere in Loy's prose writings, especially the unpublished novels *Islands in the Air* and *The Child and the Parent*.

In the auto-mythological *Anglo-Mongrels*, Loy conflates the self-revelatory aspects of autobiography with the fiction and universal applicability, of myth, embedding the account in a wider socio-historical context. However, there is no absolute, pre-existing structure that Loy has recourse to; she does not attempt to reproduce a specific mythic or narrative form, or to represent her own life with confessional accuracy. Thereby Loy not only avoids the simplistic self-aggrandisement of autobiography (or indeed the prurient speculation of autobiography's audience), but also complicates the ironical detachment of high modernist narratives and undermines the truth-value of mythical forms. In using myth, personal experience and history, *Anglo-Mongrels* functions as a form of analysis at multiple levels, producing both a psychic analysis of self and artistic consciousness and a socio-cultural analysis of the ideological conditions of personal realisation and artistic expression.

Anglo-Mongrels consists of 20 individual pieces; the first two longer poems introduce Exodus and English Rose (Ova's parents), and are followed by 18 shorter poems. Although the whole sequence is written in the third person, the character of Ova, who is central to the shorter poems, can be seen as the 'auto-mythological' representation of Loy herself. The major figures in Loy's life are characterized as follows: 'Exodus', the Jewish immigrant tailor or 'wondering jew' (Loy, 1923: 15) represents Loy's father, Sigmund Loy, while 'English Rose' – also called 'Alice' and/or 'Ada' – a 'Rose of arrested impulses' (Loy, 1923–24: 41) represents her petit-bourgeois mother, Julia Bryan. Ova's parents come to represent metonymically the wider social, political and historical context of which she can have no experience. With these two key figures, therefore, Loy portrays the different ideologies that produce the various forces of dispossession and repression that Ova experiences, based on class, gender and race. Esau Penfold and Colossus (presented as Ova's peers in the sequence) represent respectively Loy's first and second husbands, Stephen Haweis and Arthur Cravan. The names of each of these figures points to their role in the poems and foregrounds Loy's unruly use of myth and history. The implications of the name, Ova, are various, most pointedly suggesting a nascent feminine selfhood (Ova as ovum), and also recalling the name of Loy's first daughter, Oda Janet, who died on her first birthday.

With her auto-mythological narrative, Loy weaves a complex web of personal experience, individual mythology and contemporary history, none of which appears distinct from one another. She draws, for example, on a broad range of cultural sources for her characters' names and conflates various historical events in the depiction of these characters. A clear instance of Loy's intertwining of personal, historical and mythic strands occurs in the opening lines of 'English Rose' (poem 2):

> Early English everlasting
> quadrate Rose
> paradox – Imperial
> trimmed with some travestied flesh
> tinted with bloodless duties dewed
> with Lipton's teas
> and grimed with crack-packed
> herd-housing
> petalling
> the prim gilt
> penetralia
> of a lustre scioned
> core-crown;
>
> Rose of arrested impulses
> self pruned
> of the primordial attributes . . .
>
> A World-blush
> glowing from
> a never-setting-sun
> Conservative Rose
> storage
> of British Empire-made pot-pourri
> of dry dead men making a sweetened smell
> among a shrivelled collectivity
>
> Which august dust
> stirred by
> the trouser-striped prongs of statesmanship
> (whenever politic)
> rises upon the puff of press alarum
> and whirling itself
> deliriously around the unseen
> Bolshevik subsides
> in ashy circularity
> 'a wreath' upon the unknown
> soldier's grave (1923–4: 41–2)

The identity and role of Ada, the English Rose, is defined through images of English Imperialistic power, and notions of England as the Motherland. Such historically grounded symbolization typifies English womanhood as the preserver of traditional values: chastity or the denial of the body; conformity to class division and oppression; and the unquestioning acceptance of authority. Alongside her critique of Victorian ideology, Loy explores recent historical events (the Great War, the rise of Bolshevism). These divergent strands are united by Loy's basic analysis of the reactionary manipulation of popular consciousness and its repressive and paralysing effects.

The cultural construction of identity and prejudice is central to Loy's depiction of the father, Exodus. As a Jewish immigrant he is forced to deny his unique heritage of scientific and artistic curiosity and accept a predefined role in English society with its institutionalized ideology – the 'wondering jew' must become one of the 'wandering jews' aspiring to acceptance into an intolerant Western culture: 'Crushed by the Occident ox / they scraped / the gold gold golden / muck from off its hoofs –' ('Exodus', 1923: 11). Ova, as the offspring of 'traditional / Israel and of Albion' ('Ada Gives Birth To Ova', 1923–4: 50), inherits her selfhood through the historically constructed identity of her parents. So she is, like them, denied the right to self-definition and self-realization and defined as the opposite of, or the object of, Western culture. However, this 'composite / Anglo-Israelite' ('Ada Gives Birth To Ova': 50), the female-mongrel Ova, transgresses the boundaries of cultural and ideological hegemony therewith demonstrating the rigidity and instability of the authority it invests.

In the succinctly titled sixth poem of the sequence, 'Opposed Aesthetics', Loy portrays the position of Ova as potential artist, in comparison to the privileged position of Esau Penfold:

> As the arrested artists
> of the masses
> whose child faces
> turned upon Beauty
> the puny light
> of their immobile recognition
>
> made moon – flowers out of muck
> and things desired
> out of their tenuous soul – stuff

Until the Ruling Bluff
demanded a hell – full
of labour
for half a belly – full

So did the mongrel – girl
of Noman's land
coerce the shy
Spirit of Beauty
from excrements and physic –

While Esau of Ridover Square
absorbs the erudite idea
that Beauty IS nowhere
except posthumously to itself
in the antique

And trains
the common manifestations
of creation
to flatten
before his eyes
to one vast monopattern. (1925: 149–51)

Esau embodies the leisured upper class, the shallow adult world, British culture and Imperialism, and tradition, in opposition to Ova, who represents working and aspirant classes, the world of the child, the displaced or dispossessed, and 'popular' culture. In this poem it becomes clear that these conflicting positions, and the aesthetics that follow from them, are predicated upon their respective relationships to tradition: Esau is the historical heir of culture, Ova and the mass of humanity are the fodder of history and the Other of culture. Esau's aesthetic – that of the powerful, Imperialist England – is manifestly the regulative ideal, functioning as the hegemonic artistic order against which Loy's female modernist aesthetic is pitched in the sequence as a whole.

Ova is not really the opposite of Esau Penfold though, since her role is occupied by the figure of Colossus of poem 10, 'Enter Colossus'. The title of the poem, recalling the title of 'Enter Esau Penfold', indicates the diametric opposition between Esau and Colossus, and Colossus does reject all those aspects that confirm Esau's identity;

he rejects tradition, privilege, polite company, even the verity of words themselves, and represents strength, vigour and self-creation, in contrast to the pseudo-vigour and emulation of Esau. Colossus is perhaps the Dadaist Icon, to Esau's Decadent dilettante, or the masculine to Esau's impotence. But, both Esau and Colossus have opportunity and privilege (whether they reject it or not) which is based simultaneously on their class, race and gender identities – Colossus, like Esau, is the heir to a defined racial and social identity ('The male fruit / of a Celtic couple', 'a little gentleman / like his ancestors', 'Enter Colossus', Loy 1925: 160–1). It is this status, alongside the inherent privilege Colossus' gender bestows upon him to be an active individual, which enables him to be an original artistic self. Ova does not personify a third or mid-point between these two figures; rather, she occupies an ambiguous discursive space, dispossessed of an authorized artistic selfhood.

Anglo-Mongrels is fundamentally concerned with the development of aesthetic consciousness, and thus offers an investigation of Loy's aesthetic as a response to the literary-cultural context of modernism, locating the sources of this aesthetic in her own experiences as a displaced individual. With the complex/compound identity of the figure of Ova, Loy gestures towards her own ethnic heritage and, more importantly, emphasizes the discontinuity and alien nature that she 'inherits' as the result of her own mismatched parentage. Significantly, Anglo-Mongrels does not offer an epiphanic self-realization, or even allow the personal utterance of the protagonist: there is no final climax (the closest thing to it occurs in the middle of the sequence with the fifteenth poem, 'Illumination'). Loy merely concludes with a restatement of Ova's Otherness as middle-class, mixed-race and female. In the final poem, 'The Social Status of Exodus', she offers a refiguring of Ova's externality to history and cultural expression through the denial and ostracism that her father undergoes.

Loy employs autobiography not to provide a linear sequence leading up to an epiphanic culmination, but to enable her to both explore and express, through her own consciousness and experience, a certain conception of the self-in-the-world. This analytical process recalls the Freudian psychoanalytical method, and Loy uses Anglo-Mongrels, in part, to specifically critique the normative assumptions of the 'Father of psychoanalysis'.[1]

In 'Ova Begins To Take Notice' (poem 5), Loy depicts an incident in which the process of attaining selfhood and language through loss is enacted:

> She must
> make her a rose
> out of red thread
> but red
> ness is inadequate
> to the becoming of a rose
> – The – red – reel – rolls – (1925: 141)

In an intertextual allusion to Freud, this cotton reel game can be seen as an evocation of just that moment of language acquisition, where language-as-desire is predicated on a subject/object dichotomy. Language becomes an (always doomed to fail) attempt at regaining an original unity with the maternal. Through her attempt to symbolize her (always lost) mother, 'a rose', Ova recognizes the inadequacy of the linguistic sign: language fails to function as anything other than a futile, static attempt to capture the kinetic process of existence.

The ultimate loss of '– The – red – reel –' demonstrates that the control that language attempts to enact (the words '*fort*' and '*da*' controlling the frustration and fulfilment of desire) is impossible for Ova to maintain within her world. Thus, Loy portrays Ova's response to the strangeness of language in contrast to the original union of subject with object, and in doing so suggests an alternate view of signification based on the conception of language as the individual physical manifestation of the signified.

Loy suggests that each linguistic articulation should be a creative act of embodiment, a 'materialization' ('Ova Begins To Take Notice': 145). The example she gives of this process presents it as the necessary phenomenology of an infant consciousness such as Ova's – it is an unmediated artistic response, a mode of perception which resonates strongly with the aesthetic examined in poem 6, 'Opposed Aesthetics'. Ova hears the ' half inaudible', 'iridescent hush' of the word 'iarrhea' ('Ova Begins To take Notice': 146). The strangeness and resonance of this 'new word' inspires a simultaneous association of visual sensations – a lost red ball, the colour green, the brooch – which 'embodies the word' (147):

> A
> lucent
> iris
> shifts
> its

irradiate
interstice

glooms and relumes
on an orb of verdigris (148)

Loy is not merely evoking the association of ideas that produces poetry; she exceeds the notion of poetry as a condensation of ideas. Beginning with the implications and resonances of language itself, Loy offers a definition of poetry as the oral, aural and visual manifestations of an insight; in these lines each word is set apart, the patterned typography emphasizing the fact that these individual units together form an artistic whole. The visual and verbal repetition of 'i' invokes an eye/I homonym, indicating the process of self-realisation underlying Ova's perceptive acts.

Because the instigation to this process is '[d]iarrhea' it can be linked to the 'excrement and physic' of 'Opposed Aesthetics' and Loy's wider exploration of the beauty of the commonplace. She demonstrates that, within the abject of culture and the individual, lies a potential for great poetic insight.[2] Her aesthetic view, based upon the unstable foundations of the personal, is not static or objective – Ova experiences only a temporary manifestation which '– – evaporates / into the Increate' ('Ova Begins To Take Notice: 148). What Loy presents, therefore, is a vibrant and active apperception of the world through language: language acquisition, rather than simply instating the subject/object split and offering the male subject mastery and control of objects, can, through its very instability, enable a transgressive recognition of the interpenetration of sign and significance, of image and sound, of the spiritual and the physical.

In 'Ova Begins To Take Notice', Ova's experience of language stands as a response to the masculine entry into the Symbolic, and ultimately into the role of *he who names* within the logocentric order. The process whereby selfhood is achieved by expulsion of the Other (abjection) and the Symbolic order is attained, within which Woman only exists as symbol, is an impossibility for the infant Ova. Ova's emergence into the world, and the emergence of her self-consciousness, leads to great dilemmas and contradictions and she is intellectually and physically restrained by her circumstances. She can neither reject the old order and its traditions, as Colossus does, or accede to it as Exodus does, because her social position, as 'mongrel', middle-class and female, denies her access to the sanctioned power of self-definition. It is through her identification with the 'masses' (which is already implicit in Loy's representation of the position of women/her mother), and acceptance of her heritage of dispossession, that Ova comes to an individual aesthetic understanding which might enable a transvaluation of the norms of her situation: her estrangement from language, her body, and active selfhood, becomes fundamental to her aesthetic and sense of self.

Ova is not in the (gendered) position to control and manipulate the significance of language and the body, and achieve an easy transcendence (of the immanent, of the mundane). From her ambiguous situation, Loy suggests how the power of the Symbolic can be subverted; a transgression of cultural authority which constitutes a fundamental aspect of her poetic. For Loy, language and/or poetry is lacking in vitality and spontaneity (life in the Nietzschean sense) because of the very power of signification, which reduces an object to an abstract idea. The rediscovery of the resonances of language, as sound, visual image, and metonymic reference, is, in a sense, a reclaiming of that very body that bears the weight of signification. Further, it offers a way to undermine the dualities of the Symbolic, just as the use of auto-mythology blurs the distinctions between subjective and objective, personal and impersonal. What the aesthetic of *Anglo-Mongrels* fundamentally suggests is an interpenetration of the mundane and the transcendent, the corporeal and the supernal, represented through Loy's poetry as the reclamation of the female body.

Notes

1 Loy came into contact with Freud prior to the completion of *Anglo-Mongrels*, she met him and sketched his portrait in Vienna, 1921 (see Loy, 1985: lxxi).
2 Within psychoanalytical terminology, the abject is that which is expelled from the self and so marks the boundaries of the self; it can include human waste, food, filth, blood, a corpse, even the maternal body. The process of abjection plays a similar role as the fort–da game in the representation and control of the absence/presence of the mother, and the boundaries of the self. Kristeva describes the abject as 'the jettisoned object' (Kristeva 1982: 2), and writes:

> What is abject is not my correlative, which, providing me with someone or something else as support would allow me to be more or less detached and autonomous. The abject has only one quality of the object – that of being opposed to I. (1)

Therefore:

> It is not lack of cleanliness or health that causes abjection but what
> disturbs identity, system, order. What does not respect borders, posi-
> tions, rules. The in-between, the ambiguous, the composite.(4)

References

Freud, S. *Beyond The Pleasure Principle*, trans. J. Strachey, no. 4 of The International Psycho-analytical Library (London: Hogarth Press, 1971)

Kristeva, J. *Powers of Horror: An Essay on Abjection*, trans. L. S. Roudiez (New
York: Columbia University Press, 1982)

Loy, M. *The Last Lunar Baedeker* ed. and intro. R. L. Conover (Manchester:
Carcanet, 1985)

—— 'Notes on Religion', ed. K. Tuma, *Sulfur*, 27 (Fall 1990) 13–16

—— 'Exodus', *The Little Review*, 9 (Spring 1923) 10–18

—— 'English Rose' and 'Ada Gives Birth to Ova', *The Little Review*, 9 (Autumn
and Winter 1923–4) 41–51

—— 'Anglo-Mongrel and the Rose', *Contact Collection of Contemporary Writers*
(Paris: Three Mountains Press, 1925) 137–94

Mitchell, J. and Rose, J. (eds) *Jacques Lacan and the Ecole freudienne*, trans.
J. Rose (New York & London: W. W. Norton and Pantheon Books, 1985)

Index

Abraham, Nicolas, 206
Abrams, Philip, 11
academic, xxi, xxii, xxvii–xxviii,
    4–5, 28, 119, 121, 127, 129, 138,
    141–2, 175, 177, 235; female,
    xxvii, 138–51; feminist, 4, 133;
    intellectual orthodoxy, xxiii;
    interdisciplinarity, xx, 120, 141,
    228 n.1; self-inscription, xxviii,
    165–73 *passim*
Africa, 16, 59; African
    womanhood, 21, 58–9, 61–2;
    missionaries, 174–86 *passim*;
    Mozambique, 177–8, 184–5
    passim; *see also* West Africa;
    South Africa
African-American, 65–76 *passim*,
    129–37 *passim*
African National Congress (ANC),
    175, 184
Afrikaner, 17 n.7
age, 70, 166
agency, 234, 256
St Agnes, Industrial School, 176,
    179
alienation, 53, 120–1; alienated
    identity, 44, 47, 49
America, nineteenth-century, 65–76
    passim; *see also* United States
Amstrad, 140–2, 147
Anderson, Elizabeth Garrett, xxiv,
    35–6 *passim*, 39
Anderson, Louisa Garrett, 35
Anglican Society for the
    Propagation of the Gospel
    (SPG), 174, 176–7; Training
    Home (Wandsworth), 176
anthropology, 54, 56, 58, 60, 131,
    177, 178
Antoinette, Marie, 200–1 *passim*
Apollinaire, *The Breasts of Tiresias*,
    143

archaeology, 10
archive, 6, 9–10, 108, 203; official
    documents, 6, 46–50 *passim*,
    108, 110
Aristotle, 120, 142
Artaud, 143
artistic consciousness, xxxii, 270–9
    passim; *see also* identity; self
Ashcroft, Bill, 109
Ashplant, T.G., xv, xxx, 228–37
Aston, Elaine, xv, xxi, xxvi,
    119–28
audience, 3, 9, 119–51 *passim*, 210,
    213, 215, 271; *see also* drama;
    performance; theatre
Augustine, St, 109
aural, 277
Austin, Gayle, 119
authenticity, 34, 36, 39–40 n.4, 58,
    68–9, 188, 190, 241, 252
authorial presence/absence, 54–5,
    87, 105, 113, 138, 203, 241–50
    passim
authority, xxiii, 12, 33–42 *passim*,
    43, 47, 51, 54–8 *passim*, 60–1,
    74, 188, 244, 267, 273, 278
autobiography, xxi–xxxii *passim*,
    3–30 *passim*, 33–42 *passim*, 53,
    65–87 *passim*, 91, 93, 96–116
    passim, 121–2, 127, 130, 133,
    136, 138, 140–2, 155–95
    passim, 199–218, passim,
    241–79 *passim*;
    autobiographical 'I', xxiii, 37,
    39–40, 75, 78, 249, 270–9;
    autobiographical act, 36;
    autobiographical discourse, 36,
    200; autobiographical subject,
    xxvii, 35, 39, 155–95;
    autobiographical narrative, 35,
    65–76 *passim*, 113, 188, 190,
    193; autobiographical subject,

Musée de l'homme, 132
myth, xxxii, 108–9, 136, 156, 161,
    199, 212–13, 241, 243, 270–9
    passim

Nabokov, Vladimir, 107, 108;
    Speak, Memory, 107
Napoleon, Bonaparte III, 111
name/ing, 11, 60, 73, 77, 91,
    114
narrative, xxii, xxiv, xxvii–xxviii,
    xxx, xxxii, 33–53 *passim*, 55,
    59, 61, 65–77 *passim*, 87–104
    passim, 106, 108, 110–11, 113,
    115, 119–30, *passim*, 165–73,
    176, *passim*, 187–95 *passim*,
    203–4, 211, 251, 253–7, 259,
    266–7, 270–1; closure, 168;
    conversion, 74; grand, xxxii;
    male, 120; modernist, xxv,
    87–95 *passim*, 96–104 *passim*;
    narratological landscape, xxii;
    narrated, xxviii, 165–73, 187,
    193; narrator, xxviii, 53, 97–8,
    100, 113, 115, 165–73, 187,
    253, 255–7, 266; national,
    33–52 *passim*; personal, xxii,
    xxiv, xxviii, xxx, xxxii, 43–52
    passim, 187–95 *passim*, 121,
    123, 176; private, 102, 254,
    259; public, 254–5, 259;
    romance, 123; self-conscious,
    xxiv, 43–52 *passim*; slave,
    65–76 *passim*; strategies, xxiv,
    43, 53, 65–76 *passim*; style, 55,
    61; voice, 68, 90, 253; *see also*
    autobiography; auto/biography;
    (auto)biography;
    autoethnography, auto/
    mythology; biography; female;
    history; life-histories; life-
    stories; life-writing; memoirs;
    memories; Personal Narratives
    Group; self
National Association of Colored
    Women, 134
National Coal Board, 37
National Council of African
    Women, 183

National English Literary Museum
    (NELM) Grahamstown, 3 n.1
National Union of Mineworkers
    (NUM), 36–7; miners' strike
    (1984–5), 37–8
National Union of Women's
    Suffrage Societies (NUWSS), 224
nation-state, 17, 89, 93
nationalist symbols, 49, 50, 273;
    /woman, 48
Nava, Mica, 157
Netscape Navigator, 140
New Labour, 121
Newnham College, Cambridge, 40
    n.4, 208
New Theology movement, 230
New York American, 89
New Yorker, 88
Nicholson, Helen, xvii, xxix, xxx,
    208–17
Niedecker, Lorine, xi, xxv, 77–85;
    'Club 26', 82; Corman, Cid,
    83; 'The Graves', 78 n.2; Hein,
    Harold, 78 and n.2, 81–3; 'I
    knew a clean man', 78 n.2,
    82–3; 'I married', 78 n.2, 83–4;
    'In the great snowfall before
    the bomb', 78 n.2; Millen, Al,
    78 and n.2, 82–4 *passim*;
    mother, 78–9; *My Friend Tree*,
    83; Niedecker, Daisy (mother),
    78 and nn.2 and 4, 79–80;
    Niedecker, Henry (father), 78
    and n.2, 79; 'Old Mother turns
    blue and from us', 78 n.2, 80;
    'Paean to Place', 78 n.2; 'Poet's
    Work', 78–9; 'The men leave
    the car', 78 n.2, 82; 'You are
    my friend', 78 n.2, 81–2;
    Zukofsky, Louis, 78 and n.4,
    79–82, 84; Zukofsky, Celia, 81
Nietzsch, Friedrich Wilhelm, 278
non-verbal communication, 171
Norburn, Canon Dick, 182
Norcliffe, Isabella 'Tib', 202
Norquay, Dr Glenda, 228 n.1
Norris, J., 225
Nottingham Trent University, 3
    n.2, 140 n.1

Saatchi and Saatchi, 39
Salvation Army, 230
Sammlung, Hugo Ball (Parmasens), 190 n.1
Sanders, A., 89
Sappho, 'sapphism', 200
Sartre, Jean-Paul, 258
Saturday Review, 210 n.5
Scanlon, Joan, 127; *Surviving the Blues*, 127
Scargill, Arthur, 36–7
Schönfeld, Christiane, xviii, xxviii, 187–95
Schreiner, Olive, xi, xxiii, 3, 5–10 *passim*, 13, 17–25 *passim*, 27–88; *An English South African's View of the Situation*, 18; *From Man to Man*, 21; *Thoughts on South Africa*, 17–19 *passim*; *The Story of An African Farm*, 21–2, 24; *Women and Labour*, 21–2; *Undine*, 21; *see also* Cronwright-Schreiner
Schreiner, Will, 24
Schumaker, Wayne, 187
science, 4, 18, 35, 54–7 *passim*, 59, 61–2, 106, 177–8 *see also*, writing
Scott, Ann, 18, 20; *Olive Schreiner*, 18, 20
SCUDD (Standing Conference of University Departments) Scarborough 1996 Identities and Realities: Issues in Research and Practice, 140, 142–3, 149
self, xxii–xxv, xxvii–xxx, xxxii, 4, 24, 33–62 *passim*, 66–8, 70, 84, 87, 91, 96, 109, 111, 121, 123–37 *passim*, 138, 140–2, 150, 160, 165–73 *passim*, 187, 190, 192–3, 202–3, 205–6, 212, 229, 234–5, 247–9, 251–9 *passim*, 260, 270, 271, 273, 275, 277–8; alienated, 54; autobiographical, 187; authenticating, xxiv, 53–62, *passim*, 190, 252; British, xxiii, 33–42 *passim*; -censorship, 70;

coherent, 172; competing, 141; consciousness, 43–52 *passim*, 67, 96, 129–37 *passim*, 202, 277; constructed, 187, 206; -creation, 260, 275; -declaration, 55; -definition, 55, 192, 273, 278; development, 229; diminished, 54; -discovery, 68; dissembling the, xxvii, 129–37 *passim*; -evaluation, 171; experiencing, 53–4; fabric, 124–7; fashioning, 135; as hero, 39; -identity, 68, 130; inscription, xxii, xxiii, xxviii, xxx, xxxii; male, 35; masking the, 54; -modification, 54; multiple, 136; narrating, 53–4, 165–73 *passim*, 193, 203, 205; obscured, 54; and other, xxiii, 4, 40, 130, 165, 247–9, 252–3; parodied, 54; performative, 124, 130, 141–2, 150, 212; personal, 121, 123; political, 121; -presentation, 202; -realization, 271, 273, 275, 277; reassembling the, xxvii, 129–37 *passim*; -recognition, 91; -recrimination, 248; -referential, 66, 68; -reflexive, 170; -representation, 54–5, 119–28 *passim*, 124, 165–73 *passim*, 193, 260; reinventing the, xxvi, 119–28 *passim*; -revelation, 270; self-ish, 127–8; sexual, 121; social, 121, 124; and state, 49; unified, 193; writing-, 257; writing a, xxiv, 33–62 *passim*, 257; *see also*, identity; gender; representation; sexuality
selfhood, xxxii, 34, 167–8, 273, 275, 277–8; artistic, 275; male, 34; *see also* feminine
Self-ish, xxvi, 120–8 *passim*
Sellers, Susan, 244
Serbia, 88
sex, xxi, xxix, xxxi, 24, 56–8, 61, 70, 82, 97, 99–100, 102, 119–21, 135, 166, 169, 172–3,

universality, 57, 67, 151, 270
University of Auckland, Faculty of Arts, 3 n.1
University of Birmingham, 235
University of Cape Town, J. W. Jagger Library, xi, 3 n.1, 7
University of California at Berkeley, 43
University of Hull, 129; Drama Department, 129; Popular African American Theatre, 129, 131
University of Kent, 142
USSR, 44; *see also*, Russia

veil/unveiling, 187–8, 194, 199, 228, 242
Vicinus, Martha, 199
Virago, 127
visual texts, 4
voice, xxx, xxxii, 6, 16, 23, 25, 33, 44, 68, 70–2, 87, 90, 103, 108, 120, 124, 134, 170–1, 41–50 *passim*, 253, 260, 266–7; female, xxxii, 44, 120, 260, 266, 267; gagging, 70, 71; male, 44, 267; 'talking heads', 246; tongue, 71, 72, 103, 134; *see also* silence
Vuoluoki, 93

WSPU, xxx, 218–27 *passim*
Walby, Sylvia, 169
Walker, Anne, xxix, 206–7
Walkerdine, Valerie, 155
Ward, Mrs Humphry, 103
Waterstone's Bookshop (Canterbury), 140 n.1, 149
Weir, Jane, xii
Weldon, Georgina, xxix, 208–17; Feese, Benjamin, 214; *How I Escaped The Mad Doctors*, 211–12; Levierge, Rachel, 213; *Not Alone*, 213–15; 'Portia of the Law Courts', 215; Sapho-Katie, 210; Stanhope, Hester, 213–15; Stanhope, Raymond, 213–14; 'The History of Mrs Weldon', 212; *The History of*

My Orphanage or the Outpourings of an Alleged Lunatic, 211–12; Thomas, Morgan (father), 209; Weldon, Henry, 208, 209, 210, 211, 215
Wells, H. G., 89–90
Weston, Denise, xi, xx
West Africa, 55–7; Ikun, 57–8; Fan, 59–61; secret societies, 56–7, 59
West, Rebecca, xxv, xxvi, 87–95, 221; Andrews, Henry, 92; *Black Lamb and Grey Falcon*, xxv, 87–95; *The Birds Fall Down*, 89; *The Meaning of Treason*, 89
West Yorkshire Archive Service, Calderdale, xi
Whitbread, Helena, xi, xxix, 200–4
White, Hayden, 106, 112, 129–30; *Tropics of Discourse*, 130
White, Barbara, 65
Whitman, *Leaves of Grass*, 83
Whitley, David, 41 n.6
Wilde, Oscar, 34 n.1
Williams, William Carlos, 'The Last Words of my English Grandmother', 80
Williams, Patrick, xi
Williamson, J., 160
Williams, Raymond, 242
Wilson, Harriet, 157
Wilson, Harriet, xxiv, xxv, 65–76; Allida, 65, 68, 69; ante-Bellum North, 69, 72; the Bellmonts, 65–6, 68, 70; Mr. Bellmont, 71; Mrs. Bellmont, 67, 71, 72, 73; C. D. S., 68, 69; Fido, 65; Frado, 65–72; Frado/Fido, 65; Henry, 73; Jane, 73; Lewis, 73; Mary, 71, 72; 'our nig', 68; *Our Nig*, xxiv, xxv, 65–76; Thorn, Margaretta, 68, 69; Wilson/Frado, xxv
Winslow, Dr Lyttleton Forbes, 208, 210
The Woman Question, 208, 219
Woodbrooke Chronicle, 235
Woodbrooke Settlement, 234–6 *passim*